Total quality training

The quality culture and quality trainer

Brian Thomas

McGRAW-HILL BOOK COMPANY

London · New York · St Louis · San Francisco · Auckland
Bogotá · Caracas · Hamburg · Lisbon · Madrid · Mexico · Milan
Montreal · New Delhi · Panama · Paris · San Juan · São Paulo
Singapore · Sydney · Tokyo · Toronto

Published by
McGRAW-HILL Book Company Europe
Shoppenhangers Road, Maidenhead, Berkshire, SL6 2QL, England.
Telephone: 0628 23432
Fax: 0628 770224

British Library Cataloguing in Publication Data
Thomas, Brian
Total quality training: the quality culture
and quality trainer.
I. Title
658.312404
ISBN 0-07-707472-6

Library of Congress Cataloging-in-Publication Data
Thomas, Brian (Brian Alun)
Total quality training: the quality culture and quality trainer/
Brian Thomas.
p. cm. — (The McGraw-Hill training series)
Includes bibliographical references and index.
ISBN 0-07-707472-6
1. Employees—Training of. 2. Total quality management.
I. Title. II. Series.
HF5549.5.T7T46 1992
658.3'124—dc20 91-39994

2345 CL 95432

Typeset by Book Ens Limited, Baldock, Herts
Printed and bound in Great Britain by Clays Ltd, St Ives plc

For Charmian, and to the memory of my father

Contents

Acknowledgements

Many people have contributed a great deal to this book. Some formally and many more informally. I would like to thank a number of friends: first Mike Davis, who operates in the sobering reality of running a business in a highly competitive and rapidly changing environment. His comments and suggestions over the past 18 years or so have always checked whatever tendencies I have to confuse the theoretical with the realistic.

I would also like to thank my friends Hugh and Gloria Foster who have spent very many years working in what is euphemistically termed, 'front-line assembly operations'. Every manager, trainer and motivational guru would benefit from sharing the wisdom such experience generates.

My colleague Dawn Charles has formally contributed a great deal to the book and has been an invaluable source of information and critical comment. I appreciate this very much.

I would also wish to thank all those trainers, managers and learners who have patiently completed my research questionnaires and inventories and given (often painfully) honest answers to my questions concerning the effectiveness of training and development. Very many thanks to you all.

My thanks also go to Vicky Spanovangelis who compensated for my total inability to draw illustrations.

Lastly, the book would not have been possible without the encouragement, support and illuminating insights of my wife, Charmian, who is the best problem solver I have ever met. To her must go the biggest thanks of all.

Series preface

Training and development are now firmly centre stage in most organizations, if not all. Nothing unusual in that—for some organizations. They have always seen training and development as part of the heart of their businesses—but more and more must see it that same way.

The demographic trends through the nineties will inject into the marketplace severe competition for good people who will need good training. Young people without conventional qualifications, skilled workers in redundant crafts, people out of work, women wishing to return to work—all will require excellent training to fit them to meet the job demands of the 1990s and beyond.

But excellent training does not spring from what we have done well in the past. T&D specialists are in a new ball game. 'Maintenance' training—training to keep up skill levels to do what we have always done—will be less in demand. Rather, organization, work and market change training are now much more important and will remain so for some time. Changing organizations and people is no easy task, requiring special skills and expertise which, sadly, many T&D specialists do not possess.

To work as a 'change' specialist requires us to get to centre stage—to the heart of the company's business. This means we have to ask about future goals and strategies and even be involved in their development, at least as far as T&D policies are concerned.

This demands excellent communication skills, political expertise, negotiating ability, diagnostic skills—indeed, all the skills a good internal consultant requires.

The implications for T&D specialists are considerable. It is not enough merely to be skilled in the basics of training, we must also begin to act like business people and to think in business terms and talk the language of business. We must be able to resource training not just from within but by using the vast array of external resources. We must be able to manage our activities as well as any other manager. We must share in the creation and communication of the company's vision. We must never let the goals of the company out of our sight.

In short, we may have to grow and change with the business. It will be hard. We shall not only have to demonstrate relevance but also value for money and achievement of results. We shall be our own boss, as accountable for results as any other line manager, and we shall have to deal with fewer internal resources.

The challenge is on, as many T&D specialists have demonstrated to me over the past few years. We need to be capable of meeting that challenge. This is why McGraw-Hill Book Company Europe have planned and launched this major new training series—to help us meet that challenge.

The series covers all aspects of T&D and provides the knowledge base from which we can develop plans to meet the challenge. They are practical books for the professional person. They are a starting point for planning our journey into the twenty-first century.

Use them well. Don't just read them. Highlight key ideas, thoughts, action pointers or whatever, and have a go at doing something with them. Through experimentation we evolve; through stagnation we die.

I know that all the authors in the McGraw-Hill Training Series would want me to wish you good luck. Have a great journey into the twenty-first century.

ROGER BENNETT
Series Editor

About the series editor

Roger Bennett has over 20 years' experience in training, management education, research and consulting. He has long been involved with trainer training and trainer effectiveness. He has carried out research into trainer effectiveness and conducted workshops, seminars and conferences on the subject around the world. He has written extensively on the subject including the book *Improving Trainer Effectiveness*, Gower. His work has taken him all over the world and has involved directors of companies as well as managers and trainers.

Dr Bennett has worked in engineering, several business schools (including the International Management Centre, where he launched the UK's first masters degree in T&D) and has been a board director of two companies. He is the editor of the *Journal of European Industrial Training* and was series editor of the ITD's *Get In There* workbook and video package for the managers of training departments. He now runs his own business called The Management Development Consultancy.

Introduction

This book is concerned with the application of *total quality management* (TQM) principles to training and development. It is aimed primarily at people who have, as part of their professional responsibilities, the task of attempting to develop the effectiveness of organizations by developing the effectiveness of the people who work within those organizations.

It is also aimed at those who wish to understand the TQ philosophy and consider its application to learning environments. The people who will find the material in this book of interest and use, therefore, include trainers and training managers within organizations, freelance trainers and consultants, lecturers in further and higher education, managers at all levels within organizations, front-line supervisors and team leaders.

The relative amounts of time that are officially recognized as being appropriately devoted to the development of others will of course vary depending on particular organizational roles. The full-time trainer within organizations will be charged almost exclusively with that responsibility. Managers are increasingly perceived as having an important and legitimate role in this area and supervisors and team leaders are also recognizing that the development of others is integral to the effectiveness of their own roles and responsibilities.

Organizations, faced with accelerating and unpredictable rates of change in such areas as technology, demography, market preference, patterns of work and legislation will only survive if the people they employ are effectively trained and fully committed to the organizations' growth and development. This commitment stems from a real sense of personal involvement, respect and value.

A central emphasis of this book is that providers of goods and services (training included) must be committed to the creation and maintenance of quality. Quality is the key to the future success of our economy so it must, if we are to survive, pervade all that we do.

The quality of training provided in this country has, historically, been extremely patchy and the situation has not improved significantly. If we can *consistently* provide quality training, then I am convinced that we will see the training profession awarded the status and importance that are necessary if we are to succeed in an increasingly competitive world.

In this book I have taken the major principles of TQM and applied them to the training and development function. In this sense the book is primarily concerned with the provision of quality training and development services. However, in writing the book I have found that it is extremely difficult to separate the concept of quality *in* training (the provision of quality training and development services) from concepts of training *for* quality (training that is aimed at the production of quality goods or services of a particular type)—I see the two as being inextricably linked. *All* training—irrespective of its subject matter—that is truly *quality training,* will inevitably exert a positive influence on individuals that extends much further than the particular training context involved. This influence will, in turn, affect the individual's contribution to the provision of quality goods and services in all operational areas.

QT is concerned with the development of a quality culture throughout training and development activities. It is not restricted merely to those areas that have an obvious potential impact on the interface between the organization and the ultimate receiver of goods or services. QT principles apply equally to training programmes that focus on topics such as customer care, statistical process control or just-in-time inventory management as those that focus on trainer development, office systems, costing, health and safety, time management, performance appraisal, staff recruitment, computer programming and first aid. The quality philosophy must permeate all organizational functions.

In this sense the approach advocated in this book may be considered as TQM in the fullest sense of the words *total, quality* and *training.*

Quality is *not* just the flavour of the month; it is not going to go away. It is also *not* a quick fix. Achieving quality will involve a lot of hard work, a lot of hard questioning, a lot of change, a lot of honest appraisal of the way things are currently done and an enormous amount of commitment. Despite this it can, and is, being achieved.

Training and development have a central—arguably *the* central—role to play in making quality a reality. Before we profess an ability to assist in the healing of others, however, we would be wise to take a long hard look at *ourselves* and the quality of service *we* provide.

There is a well-worn adage in the restaurant business that if you serve a customer a good meal he will tell four people so, but if you serve him a *bad* meal he will tell twelve. There have been a lot of 'bad meals' served in training, in both the public and private sectors.

The quality principles of customer orientation, defect prevention, 100 per cent delivery *every* time and continuous improvement apply just as forcefully to training as they do to the manufacture of electrical goods. Every trainer must become a quality expert and a quality obsessive—nothing less will do.

I hope that this book provides some inspiration and guidance for those who wish to understand the TQ message and use it to enhance their professional training effectiveness.

As to the structure of the book, the first third outlines the development, philosophy and practical consequences of the TQ approach. I firmly believe that all training professionals, whatever their particular area of expertise, must develop a thorough understanding of these basic ideas and concepts. To that end, this section of the book contains few direct references to specific training contexts other than where they serve to illustrate the point being made. I would, however, urge the reader not to skip to the more familiar training-oriented sections (primarily the latter two thirds), but to assimilate the ideas presented in the initial sections before moving on.

One final comment about the format of this book. In general, the examples I have used and the situations I have described are drawn from my experiences in attending and running training programmes and from personal research into the genuine feelings our customers have about the services we provide. Also, the majority of examples are taken from work with managers, trainers and supervisors.

I hope, however, that this will not deter those who currently do not have formal training and development responsibilities from considering the book to be of use to them. A key factor in the development of quality is that people at all levels in an organization accept their responsibilities as managers of their own resources and as decision makers, planners and change agents. In this sense, all of us who attempt to positively influence the effectiveness of others are engaged in a form of management development and so all our interactions can be considered as training events.

1 The quality revolution

In the 1950s British motor cycles were recognized as being the best in the world and our domination of world markets reflected that recognition. Also, during the 1950s, Japanese goods had a justifiable reputation for being cheap and nasty. Today, *Japanese* motor cycles are recognized as being among the best in the world and sales of Japanese motor cycles in this country accounted for 95 per cent of the market during the 1980s. Volume production of British motor cycles has long since ceased.

The Atlantic and Pacific Tea Company (A&P) enjoyed an undisputed position as the USA's leader in grocery marketing for 60 years. In 1961 A&P had over 4,500 stores with more than twice the cash volume of its nearest rival Safeway and ranked fifth among all US firms in terms of total sales.

By 1981, however, A&P had closed more than 3000 stores, sales were less than 40 per cent of Safeway and the company had incurred losses of $400 000 000 in the preceding decade. That year they occupied bottom place on the US index of profitability and growth among the top 12 major food chains.

What happened in these cases?

As a sixties motor cycle enthusiast I witnessed the beginning of the end as far as the British motor cycle industry was concerned. At first the majority of people ridiculed the tin and die-cast Japanese 'buzzboxes' that had begun to trickle into motor cycle showrooms. Some people bought them none the less and when they did, along with the manuals (and a worthwhile toolkit), there was sometimes a questionnaire with a stamped addressed envelope that asked for the owner's opinions about the bike—what was good about it, what was bad about it, what could be improved. Bike owners are an ideal group to get information like that from. Because of this, each time a new model was introduced, it was significantly better than its predecessor—and not merely with regard to cosmetic changes such as colour or exhaust pipe arrangement, it was functionally better. Eventually I tried one. I was amazed. First, it did not leak oil (all British bikes, even when brand new, invariably leaked some oil). Second, it had an electric starter, and it worked. Other surprising things came to light during my first trial ride. The brakes were effective, even in wet conditions. On British machines the brakes were widely regarded as being somewhat of a gesture in terms of road safety. Also the lights adequately illuminated the road ahead during night riding. This clinched it—I bought one. Eventually so did everyone else.

Why did I succumb? Because the Japanese bikes were *better*. They had fewer faults and more of the things I wanted from a bike. Where did they get the information from in order to meet my needs? Among other things, they asked their customers. They didn't assume that they had infallible knowledge of what we wanted and they did not adopt a 'take it or leave it' philosophy. They found out what we wanted and they supplied it.

To my other example. While A&P declined dramatically in the 20 years between 1960 and 1980, exactly the opposite occurred for the fortunes of J.C. Penney, a competing chain store in much the same business. At almost the same time that A&P were going into rapid decline, J.C. Penney began a period of accelerated growth that saw them achieve third position in terms of total sales of all major grocery and retail stores in the US by the early 1980s—more than double the volume of A&P.

What happened here? A&P had achieved its success on the formula of low price, dependability and few frills. Own brands were stacked on plain shelves in no-nonsense stores in largely urban areas. However, following World War II a number of important economic, social and demographic changes occurred in the United States.

The better off moved from urban areas to the suburbs while Americans in general became more affluent, more mobile and increasingly demanding in their expectations of goods and services. J.C. Penney reacted by expanding its lines, modernizing the surroundings of its stores, improving control through the use of automation and moving where the people were moving. A&P stayed put, with the old formula that had worked in the past.

Both of these studies share common themes, the power of the customer, the ability to respond effectively to change and the desire for continuous improvement. These three factors; customers, flexibility and continuous improvement form the conceptual bedrock of what has come to be termed the quality revolution.

What is quality?

The word quality, and the term high quality in particular, usually conjour up a number of images: expensive cars, expensive clothes, expensive video recorders . . . expensive anything. Quality is commonly associated with *cost*—'you get what you pay for'. As a freelance consultant I learned very early on that to underquote on a potential training contract is suicide. I could almost hear them think, 'If he's that cheap he can't be any good'.

Always associating quality with cost, however, is a mistake. For example, I have occasionally eaten at restaurants where the bill amounts to two or three times that which I am normally prepared to spend. I cannot honestly say that the food has tasted two or three times better or that the service and surroundings are improved in proportion to the increased charges.

Quality is not about expense, technical excellence, elegance or durability; quality is about perceptions and expectations. A hand-crafted tortoiseshell fountain pen with an engraved gold nib, costing £300, is a quality writing instrument, but a mass-produced plastic ballpoint pen that does not leak or smudge, operates until the ink is exhausted and costs 20p is also a quality writing instrument.

Quality is about expectations of functional performance. *A quality product or service is one that fully meets the expectations and requirements of those who purchase or use it.* No more and no less. We *expect* the fountain pen to be beautiful and elegant, to write well and last a lifetime; we *expect* to lose the ballpoint pen before it is even used up.

Quality can only be measured in terms of requirements and conformance to requirements. It therefore follows that the process by which requirements are decided is fundamental to the provision of quality goods and services. There are two main ways of going about this:

- **the traditional way**—develop and produce a product or service that you are geared up for and can make a profit on and persuade potential customers that this is what they need.
- **the quality way**—find out precisely what the customer requires and supply that in a cost-effective manner, if you can.

The traditional approach is endemic to the majority of products and services offered, training included. The quality approach operates the other way round so that whereas the first method is *supplier-led*, the second is *customer driven*.

The British motor cycle industry stuck with the first method to the death, literally. As long as no one else did otherwise, there was a kind of monopoly and captive market. The British motor cycle industry of the fifties and early sixties produced motor cycles that suited its own requirements in terms of design and production capability, experience, expertise and tradition and you either bought one of them or you did not have a bike. Unfortunately (for British manufacturers), Japanese manufacturers were prepared to listen to customers, to adapt, to invest in research and development, to continuously improve their product, to reduce unit costs and innovate. So were J.C. Penney in the US. A&P saw the light by 1982, changed its management structure and approach and is continuing to rebuild.

Why quality?

The lesson we must learn from the demise of the British motor cycle industry, the decimation of our consumer electronics industries and the steady onslaught of foreign motor car and service industry competitors is that quality is here to stay.

The quality paradigm is a philosophy that generates an approach and set of practical down-to-earth management tools that must pervade the complete spectrum of organizational functions and training in particular if we are to survive as a competitive nation in the markets of the twenty-first century. Customers are slowly but surely taking the reins and voting with their money. Competition on a world basis is a reality and the worst is yet to come as emerging nations apply the lessons learned by the Japanese.

The quality paradigm is a simple one and it applies as forcefully to services such as training as it does to the production of motor cycles or video recorders. The paradigm is, get it right.

The consequences of ignoring the importance of quality

What are the consequences of not getting it right? The more dramatic of them are obvious, decline and/or extinction when someone else *does* get it right. There are other less obvious factors at play, though.

British motor cycle manufacturers were, after all, 'getting it right' until the mid sixties and so were A&P in the United States, but what sort of 'right' was it?

In terms of motor cycles it was predominantly the right of the single option—take it or leave it. British motor cycles were not abysmal, they had some very good qualities as well as some very bad ones. The problem was that no one in the motor cycle industry did very much about the bad points. Triumph, for example, were recognized as being the leaders in engine design and production but the roadholding qualities of their machines left much to be desired. Norton, on the other hand, had exactly the opposite reputation. To remedy this many owners and some small-scale producers took it upon themselves to cannibalize the best of both and produce 'mongrel' machines that even evolved a name—Triton, a combination of the parent companies' trade names.

Neither Triumph nor Norton seemed to take heed of these customer developments, which were very highly publicized at the time in motor cycle magazines, but simply carried on churning out good engines in awful frames and vice versa even though their customers wanted Tritons or, to be more accurate, motor cycles that had Triton specifications. They were even prepared to pay more than the price of a brand new Triumph or Norton for a used Triton. This was a marked indication of customer dissatisfaction that the industry ignored. The reluctance to produce motor cycles that met the specifications required by their customers (quality motor cycles) meant that the industry was not maximizing its market potential, it was essentially losing business.

In addition to this somewhat specialist market omission, many potential first-time customers were put off by the poor safety reputation motor cycles had, their perceived unreliability and the general muckiness of the machines. All of these problems were essentially design problems and could (as Honda showed) be overcome.

It is therefore clear that a hidden consequence of failing to provide quality goods and services is that *business is artificially constrained*. Customers sometimes purchase a product or service because there is not much else on offer, but this does not mean that they are satisfied with it. Other potential customers may come to the conclusion that what is on offer is not worth purchasing at all. These are hidden losses that are difficult, or perhaps impossible, to accurately quantify, but they are there and they are *real* losses.

One of the assertions of this book is that hidden losses are inversely proportional to a commitment to quality, this applies to all businesses, training included.

Why don't we have quality now?

It is generally accepted that the quality revolution began in earnest in Japan during the 1950s and that its protagonist was an American statistician, Dr W. Edwards Deming.

Deming challenged the accepted wisdom that quality adds cost and that doing things cheaper always means doing things better. Deming's thesis is that in the long term quality always pays. His approach is, not surprisingly, highly statistical and he believes that the widespread understanding and use of statistical methods is essential to competitive success (we will consider the more relevant and accessible statistical approaches in Chapter 3).

Deming's ideas were enthusiastically taken on board by senior Japanese industrialists during the 1950s and significant results began to emerge during the latter portion of the sixties—the rest of course, is history.

America woke up to the quality message in the late seventies and is energetically applying quality principles across a spectrum of production and service industries. We in Britain are mainly still in bed. There are of course notable exceptions—Jaguar, in recent years, and others. However, the lack of quality provision in this country, particularly evident in many public and private service sectors, is a painful reminder that all is far from being well.

Why is this? The reasons, of course, are various and involve the history and culture of our nation, our values and aspirations, both individual and collective, our concepts of work, traditional divisions between management and workers and so on. The subject is enormous and lends itself to seemingly endless sociological, political and economic debate. I do not intend, or want, to add to this, but I would like to examine the more pragmatic and common challenges that we must tackle if we are to achieve quality.

2 Major barriers to the achievement of quality

Supplier-led approaches

There is a natural tendency, when designing and producing a product or service, preparing for a job interview or deciding to become a freelance consultant to ask, 'What are my strengths?' These strengths will include the knowledge and expertise at our disposal and may also include material resources that are available to you, such as capital, premises, traditional equipment, new technology and so on.

When we have identified our strengths it then seems logical and sensible to work from them rather than from our weaknesses and, of course, it is. At least in the short term. If you are a skilled multiprocess welder living in a manufacturing development area with access to a small but well-equipped industrial workshop, you would be ill-advised to set up in business as a childminder. To capitalize on strengths is eminently sensible, but only when these strengths are matched to opportunities and requirements. When there is some mismatch between them, our strengths may take on the role of handicaps as we doggedly continue to work from a base that is inappropriate to requirements.

Action that is based on an analysis of strengths is, by definition, an introspective process—it forces us to look inward and, in doing so, it may blind us to the realities of actual requirements in the outside world.

Most services and products are conceptualized within the constraints of available resources and expertise and many are geared to the particular strengths that an organization has. Although I do not have access to the actual information, I am sure that the British motor cycle industry, when it existed, also played to its strengths. I am sure that it produced motor cycles that maximized the use of production capability, caused the minimum of disruption to plant layout and fully utilized the skills and experience of its designers, managers and production workers. Unfortunately, however, they were not the motor cycles that people wanted to buy.

An obsession with internal strengths can lead to very peculiar decisions and practices. When I worked as an engineering designer I witnessed a remarkable instance of this phenomenon. A particular organization became momentarily obsessed with the fear that it was being left behind in terms of newly emerging developments (this was the mid sixties) in computer-controlled machinery. To alleviate their unease, a computer-aided milling machine was purchased for the works toolroom (no one ever explained the rationale behind this decision). After a few months use, the toolroom manager realized that the full capacities of the machine were not being utilized (it was capable of wonderful things) and that this should be remedied before the general manager began to ask awkward questions about costs and benefits. I, as a product designer, was therefore instructed to incorporate into a current design project at least one component that would demand heavy use of the new machine. Talk about the tail wagging the dog.

I am reliably informed that this phenomenon is alive and well in the computer industry today. A colleague working in the field of systems analysis contends that the vast majority of organizations purchase computer systems that are overcapable by a factor of up to 50 per cent. Computer manufacturers make them because they have the knowledge, expertise and capability to make them. It's challenging, technically demanding, interesting and fun and computer salespeople are good at selling them.

This is all very well until someone offers a computer system that does everything you require it to do plus a little bit more than you can understand, but, because it doesn't include a lot of other bits that provide possibilities you will never use, it's 30 per cent cheaper. Then there is a problem.

The word processor I used when writing this book has functions and capabilities I barely understand and have never used because I don't require them, yet I have paid for their development and incorporation. Conversely, it lacks certain other functions that I would like very much. The instruction manual I have received is incredibly difficult to follow and does not provide intelligible answers to many of my relatively simple queries. It has obviously been written by someone with extensive knowledge of the system and he or she probably enjoyed producing it, but I, the customer, find it very nearly useless.

Producing goods and services that are based primarily on internal strengths and expertise is a dangerous strategy and one that is all too common. Doing what we can do, even when that is excellent, is no substitute for doing what is *required*. It may work to some extent in the 'take it or leave it' environment, but that environment is vanishing rapidly.

The problem with customers

An organization exists to serve its customers; they are its rationale for being—well, at least in principle. However, it very often happens that customers come to assume the role of arch enemy in the eyes of many organizations: customers fill forms out incorrectly, ask stupid questions, jam vending machines, cannot use instruction manuals for word processors, do not articulate their training needs clearly, the list is endless.

Many organizations respond to customer difficulties through the delegation of blame—the customer is the problem. In some cases organizations take 'preventive' action, which usually exacerbates an already poor customer–provider relationship (witness the stark defence-oriented appearance of most Department of Social Security benefit offices). In some instances, the relationship of provider and customer has virtually disappeared; how good is your doctor at keeping to specified surgery appointment times?

Customers, being human, come in all shapes and forms and some will be extremely demanding, irrational and, occasionally, just plain stupid. However, customer difficulties and particularly customer complaints constitute the most powerful resource any organization has in terms of ensuring that the products and services they provide continue to improve and satisfy the ever-changing requirements of the real competitive world.

The vast majority of customers are highly appreciative of products and services that meet their needs and requirements and they display their appreciation by continuing to buy from those who supply them. A satisfied customer is, after all, the most credible advertisement any organization possesses.

Throughput orientation

Many organizations measure success in terms of throughput—numbers of washing machines produced, passengers carried, patients dealt with, forms processed, students recruited, trainees trained and so on. In many cases a department or organization's future in terms of resource allocation is directly linked to such measures. Some occupations, notably sales, bulk production of raw materials and assembly-line work also link individual earnings and bonuses to numbers.

This philosophy often generates considerable problems as far as the development of quality is concerned. If the criterion of effectiveness is numbers through the system, quality automatically becomes a secondary concern for those whose financial well-being is directly linked to throughput. Who is responsible for quality?

This difficulty is usually approached in terms of some form of inspection function being set up. Thus quality becomes a concern separate from the production of a particular product or the delivery of a particular service—somebody else's responsibility. A significant percentage of rejects is seen as inevitable (otherwise there would be no need for an inspection function) and anything that threatens to reduce throughput must be avoided like the plague.

Quality, as we have already noted, begins and ends with conformance to requirements, throughput is secondary. Only when conformance to requirements has been achieved on a reliable and predictable basis does the improvement of throughput become a development target.

It is interesting in this respect to note that when detailed information was sought concerning the major reasons why there are differences in the relative productivity levels of Japanese and British car manufacturers, it transpired that the final assembly line at a particular Nissan plant was, in fact, running *slower* than comparable lines in the UK. As productivity levels are higher at Nissan it must follow that the emphasis placed upon the production of cars that conform to specified requirements is ultimately more cost effective than the throughput—inspection—re-work strategy that operated in the UK.

Variable standards of performance

Quality is essentially about standards of acceptability, standards that are clearly and unambiguously stated and adhered to 100 per cent on all occasions. Without clearly defined standards, acceptability becomes a matter of individual perception, what seems right is right, and, as with many human endeavours, individual standards of acceptability differ widely and tend to deteriorate steadily over time.

Quality is not about perfection, it is concerned with the task of meeting clearly specified, measurable and achievable levels of performance. These levels of performance can be applied to the manufacture of products such as video recorders, motor-cycle engines or convenience foods and, equally, may be applied to the delivery of services such as health care, legal advice or the provision of training.

The absence of clearly defined standards of performance lies at the heart of many quality problems and often constitutes one of the most serious weaknesses of poor management. To achieve quality people must be absolutely clear about what is expected of them and in no doubt whatever that management throughout the organization is resolutely committed to seeing that these performance standards are maintained. The most effective method of achieving this aim does not rely on processes of inspection and control, but, rather, on a philosophy of enabling people to do what is expected of them by removing organizational and individual barriers to the achievement of quality. This philosophy must be translated into an organizational culture in which performance requirements are clearly communicated and seen as being sensible, achievable and desirable.

Managing the status quo

My own management experiences in engineering, education and training frequently led me to the conclusion that crises were fairly inevitable and that, sooner or later, something was bound to go wrong. I came to believe that one of my major responsibilities as a manager was to deal with these crises effectively and to somehow keep the show on the road. I even came to feel some sense of pride in my firefighting abilities; after all, much of what we in this country respect in a leader centres on the ability to be effective in a crisis—'If you can keep your head . . .'—I am not at all convinced of that now. Most of the crises I had to deal with were, on reflection, potentially within my control and preventable. Many of the fires I fought stemmed from a management outlook that focused on the achievement of short-term goals, a tendency to look for good news rather than bad and the philosophy that 'If it ain't broke don't mend it', taught to me early in my training as an engineer.

This 'crisis-centred' approach to management is, inevitably, reactive. It focuses attention on maintaining the status quo and intervening only when the existing system comes into difficulties. When there is no crisis, when the system is running effectively, quotas are being met and people are happy, the role of management is . . . what?

If there are no problems then what is management's role? I often ask this question during management training sessions and receive fairly predictable responses: 'Plan ahead' (to avoid future crises), 'keep the wheels oiled', 'praise people', 'deal with backlogs' and so on. Very few managers ever say, 'Look for opportunities to further improve the existing system'. No problems means that everything is working OK and, if it ain't broke . . .

A management approach that focuses attention on the task of 'keeping things going' is inevitably doomed to failure because the world is not staying put, it is moving on. Today's solutions are just that, things that work today. They may not work in a year's time and will almost certainly be obsolete in ten.

Optimizing the existing system is the beginning rather than the end of management's responsibilities. In order that we may remain competitive, we must adopt a philosophy of *continuous development and improvement*. We must be constantly aware that our methods of management and organization, the skills of our work-force, our products and services are operating in the context of an ever-changing environment, one that will become increasingly challenging in the future. They effectively have a sell-by date and if we continue to use them beyond that time they will make us ill, or perhaps even worse.

A note on attitude problems

Worker attitude

The problems identified above are of course not exhaustive and some managers may comment on the fact that the list does not include 'worker attitude' as a critical factor. Very many managers rate poor worker attitude as being one of the major problems that must be overcome if quality is to be achieved. Some years ago I, too, would have made much the same comment; now I feel differently. After all, what *is* 'worker attitude'? Is it something that exists as a fundamental characteristic of an individual or group—'the workers'—that they are born with and remains constant irrespective of external influences? I very much doubt it.

The attitudes we have are formed by our past experiences and reinforced or challenged by current and future experiences. Many organizations have shown a marked tendency to undertrain and overmanage their personnel, particularly those at the bottom of the traditional organizational pyramid. Too many people are required to leave their brains at the door when they commence their work and, consequently, channel their natural creative energies into activities that are detrimental to the organization. This is a terrible and unsustainable waste.

Attitude and the TQ approach

The move to a TQ approach requires fundamental changes to be made in the way we work and the way management manages. This transition is not an easy one, particularly for management. For many people the experience of significant organizational change in the past has been a negative one: redundancy, relocation without sufficient warning or consultation, increased responsibilities and so on. The bulk of major changes within organizations are made in response to some form of crisis; very few organizations make substantial changes with the aim of improving an already adequate state of affairs.

The transition to a TQ approach is not plain sailing and is not achieved overnight. People commonly resist change as their past experiences often tell them that this is a sensible precaution to take. However, it is a regrettable fact that the vast majority of organizations have failed to maximize the single greatest asset they possess: the people who work for them. The TQ approach aims to completely reverse this state of affairs.

TQ means total involvement, an on-going opportunity to be creative and to make things happen. TQ demands that people fully accept their responsibilities in helping the organization conform to the requirements of its customers, but this is not the whole story. TQ also demands that each individual, at any level within the organization, has the right to be heard and the right to have changed that which needs to be changed.

3 Total quality—philosophy and procedures

Clarity and accuracy

Quality can only be achieved through the collection and analysis of accurate information. In many ways this is the central theme underpinning the whole quality movement. Quality is based on *clarity* and *accuracy*:

- **clarity** in determining requirements and quantifying standards
- **accuracy** in assuring that these requirements and standards are achieved.

Market clarity

Every business must be clear about the market need it is aiming to satisfy. Confusion in market targeting leads to a confused product or service that ultimately fails to completely satisfy anyone.

In many ways it is similar to taking the decision whether to be in the business of supplying hand-crafted tortoiseshell fountain pens, mass-produced low-cost ballpoint pens or a market somewhere between these extremes. Each market niche has its own particular nuances as far as requirements are concerned.

In some cases, the functional performance of the product or service is the overriding factor and appearances are of minimal concern. Inflatable life rafts, for instance, fall into this category, as do surgeons. In other cases functional performance is not the most critical aspect influencing customer satisfaction—spectacle frames and clothing being two examples among many.

Cost may be the critical factor in some instances, when we buy petrol, for example, and be less important in others—we do not automatically purchase the cheapest theatre seats available.

The provision of quality products and services requires a clear understanding of the precise nature of the business we are in. To return to the previous example, the producer of expensive fountain pens is most probably catering for the status and luxury goods market rather than one whose prime interest is calligraphy.

Customer clarity

Achieving market clarity is the first stage in the process of analysis that leads to quality. However, 'markets' are, after all, hypothetical entities. 'Markets' do not purchase goods and services, customers do that. It therefore falls to us to be clear about the exact nature of the customer base we are working to. This is often more complex than we assume.

The complex customer

Let us imagine that we are in the business of mass-producing convenience prepared foods. Who is our customer? Most people answer that it is the paying public. This, of course, is true, after all if no one ultimately buys our products, we are done for. It is *true*, but it is not the *whole* story.

In order that our products reach the buying public, we must first convince the retail trade that they are worth stocking on their shelves. They, of course, will also be interested in the product's potential appeal to the consumer, but they will be interested in other factors, too: how reliable a supplier are we, do we consistently meet our delivery dates, are we able to be flexible in terms of delivery batch size, can we respond effectively to rush periods, can we deliver stock that is not damaged in transit, what is our policy on invoicing, will we accept a sale or return clause, are we geared up for effective merchandizing campaigns, and so on.

The paying customer is not usually concerned with these aspects of our service, but, if we are to reach them, we must be aware of the requirements of prospective retail outlets. A retailer may decide to stock a competitor's product (even when it is inferior) if internal requirements are better met by them than by us. In this sense there are two major customers: the retailer and the buying public. We must be clear about the requirements of each if we are to beat the competition.

This example highlights the complex nature of many customer bases. Effective organizations are very aware of this fact and structure their provision according to the diverse requirements involved. The McDonalds fast food chain is a good example.

Who are McDonalds' customers? One way of answering this question is to find out what type of advertising an organization concentrates on. In McDonalds' case, the majority of advertising is directed at children and the organization sees children as its central customer market. How many adults, given the option of a range of free meals, would eat at McDonalds rather than a French, Italian or Indian restaurant? Ask a six-year-old for their preference, though, and you will see why they advertise to children!

Children, however, are rarely of independent financial means and must persuade an adult to take them to McDonalds and also pick up the tab at the end of the meal. McDonalds recognizes this fact and structures its services to attract children *and* make the accompanying adult feel catered for, too. Their restaurants are extremely clean, particularly the toilets (not a vital issue for most children); the service is very fast (so adults are not required to keep children amused for long periods); the decor is a mixture of child and adult orientation; prominently displayed fact sheets tell adults that the hamburger, which most adults eat as a snack, is practically the healthiest food in existence (again not a big vote winner with six-year-olds) and so on.

McDonalds recognizes that it has a differentiated customer base with a range of needs to satisfy and responds very effectively.

Accurately recognizing customer priorities

It is clear from these examples that the provision of quality goods and services demands accurate information concerning market and customer needs, but, again, this is not the whole story.

Customers, being human, prioritize certain aspects of a product or service as being more important than others. Returning to the restaurant business, at the more expensive end of the cost spectrum, a high-class French restaurant would be ill-advised to adopt the fast service strategy that is so successful at McDonalds. Customers at this end of the market are not really dining in order to 'fuel up', so to speak. Friendliness of service, advice concerning menu selection, a good wine list, a relaxed and relaxing atmosphere are as important, if not more than, the actual standard of food being served.

Recognizing that customers have priorities in terms of certain aspects of a product or service enables providers to direct resources and plan improvements in the most effective way. For example, an expensive restaurant may be well advised to replace a noisy air-conditioning system rather than expanding its menu and employing an extra chef if there is not enough money to do all these things.

It is essential that providers recognize the difference between those aspects of a product or service that are, in many ways, taken for granted and those that motivate customers to purchase one product or service rather than another.

Herzberg's research

The psychologist Frederick Herzberg clarified the relationship between factors that cause individuals to feel good about a particular experience and those which cause them to feel bad. Herzberg recognized that there is a complex relationship between satisfaction, dissatisfaction and motivation. We are dissatisfied when our basic requirements are not met and yet we are not necessarily motivated when they are. For example, we may be adversely affected by the fact that the heating in our office is not working effectively on a cold day and our motivation to work hard may be impaired. However, few of us are motivated to put in a good day's work as a direct consequence of having an effective heating system in operation.

Herzberg recognized that factors which cause dissatisfaction are not necessarily capable of generating enthusiasm or motivation. In many ways dissatisfiers, (Herzberg termed them Hygiene factors) tend to move individuals about a baseline in terms of enthusiasm and motivation. When they are present the individual moves below his or her baseline of average motivation, when they are removed, the individual returns to the baseline level.

In order that an individual's motivation or enthusiasm may be increased, other factors (Herzberg, not surprisingly, termed these Motivators) must be present. Figure 3.1 clarifies these points.

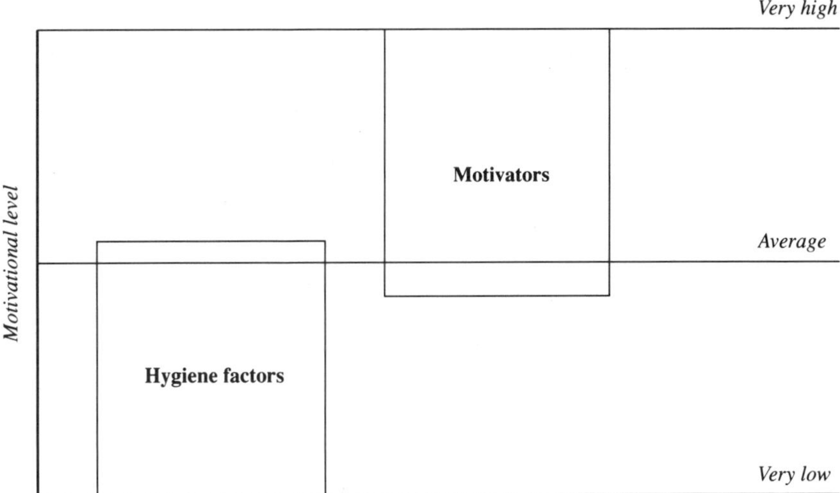

Figure 3.1 *Herzberg's factors influential on behaviour*

As can be seen from the diagram, Hygiene factors are essentially potential demotivators because, if Hygiene needs are not met, demotivation is a common consequence. However, Hygiene factors have limited potential in generating high levels of commitment and effort. In contrast, Motivators are very powerful agents for commitment and effort and the presence of one or two Motivators will often eliminate the demotivating effects of many inadequate Hygiene factors.

Herzberg's research focused on motivation at work and he identified common Motivators and Hygiene factors associated with work situations.

Hygiene factors included such things as working conditions (including the heating system), salary and job security. Motivators included factors such as a sense of individual achievement, recognition and the possibility of advancement. When powerful Motivators are present in our jobs, we may continue to work hard even if the heating system does not operate at all!

Herzberg's concept of motivation can be usefully applied to the study of customer satisfaction. Different aspects of a provider's product or service can be analysed in terms of Hygiene factors (potential dissatisfiers) and Motivators (potential enthusers). For example, we would be dissatisfied with a newly purchased car if the doors failed to close effectively, but we are not overly enthused by the fact that they invariably do. However, we are usually impressed by a car that does not develop irritating rattles and has low fuel consumption.

Such analysis helps clarify the important aspects of a service or product from the *customer's* point of view and provides vital information concerning the priority areas in which improvement should be focused. A common problem stems from the fact that Hygiene factors are usually more easily identified, have higher 'visibility', than Motivators and are easier to act upon. However, Hygiene factors are extremely vulnerable to the law of diminishing returns where customer satisfaction is concerned and the rule here is, 'good enough is enough'. It is pointless to upgrade the decor and facilities of a purpose-built prestige training centre if the customer's first contact is with a rude and unhelpful telephone receptionist. It is poor recompense to sit in a comfortable, well-equipped seminar room if the trainer has very little to offer that is relevant to the problems you wish to solve.

It is also important to recognize the fact that as products and services develop over time, Motivators have a tendency to become Hygiene factors. As a child I was enthralled by our very small, snowy screened black and white TV set; my own children are dissatisfied with their personal 17-inch portable colour TV because it lacks a remote control. Customer expectations rise continuously and so the aim of quality is to identify, anticipate, meet and sometimes even exceed those changing expectations.

Recognizing the fact that customers attach differing priorities to various aspects of a product or service is, of course, only the first step towards the provision of quality. The next step is to develop techniques that enable us to accurately identify and quantify these priorities.

The importance of accurate information

We noted at the beginning of this chapter that accurate information is the foundation upon which quality is built, this point cannot be overemphasized. The identification of key variables and the systematic analysis and monitoring of process operations constitute the basic tools of a TQ philosophy.

Dr W. Edwards Deming, the central character in the quality revolution, argues that the use of sophisticated statistical techniques lies at the heart of the quality movement. Other gurus, notably Philip Crosby, consider quality to be more dependent on management styles and organizational cultures. All views are relevant to the quality debate and much can be learned from leading thinkers in the field. All however agree that quality means conformance to specified requirements and the elimination of non-conforming products and services. All, too, agree that measurement of key variables and processes is essential if quality is to be achieved. This inevitably leads to a requirement for effective methods of quantifying the fundamental aspects of a product or service and an ability to accurately monitor the processes through which products and services come into being.

It is fair to say that the statistical techniques commonly used in *quality management* are most readily applied to the volume manufacture of products such as automobiles and consumer goods. These techniques are founded on accurate measurement and systematic sampling. It is infinitely easier to accurately measure the diameter of 1 in 500 crank-shafts than it is to accurately measure the effectiveness of a particular training course. In this sense the application of highly sophisticated statistical techniques is more challenging when directed at the improvement of services such as training than it is in the manufacture of physical products. Challenging, but not impossible. On the other hand, there are many powerful yet simple techniques that have direct relevance to service industries and are particularly useful in the context of training.

Matched pairs analysis

I have no idea where this technique originated. I was first introduced to a variation of it in the context of project planning and decision making in the engineering industry. I have since adapted it for use in training and management development.

The technique uses a grid structure to elicit a series of matched comparisons with the aim of identifying priorities for action. To offer a practical example, I use the grid with managers to help them identify the most important problems they must tackle in order to improve their effectiveness. The first stage of analysis is to ask managers to compile a list of the major day-to-day difficulties (I usually call them 'stoppers') that prevent them from being as effective as they wish to be. These problems are then transferred onto the analysis grid and a comparison in terms of importance is made between each matched pair of problems. Scores are allocated to each problem on the basis that ten points must be divided between them in relation to their relative importance. If they differ widely, eight points may be allocated to one and two to the other, while items of equal importance would score five points each and so on. When the grid has been completed, each row is totalled and a final score and ranking determined. People are often surprised by the results of this analysis.

As with most mathematical ideas, a picture is usually worth a dictionary full of words and Figure 3.2 will hopefully clarify the technique. I have used some commonly elicited management stoppers to give a flavour of actual use.

Comparisons are made, beginning at the top row, progressing across each row, then down to the next (the diagonal of the grid is obviously blocked out). Thus, in the first comparison, staff attitude is contrasted with staff shortages. In Figure 3.2, case staff attitude rates most serious (just) and is allocated a score of six points. The remaining four points are awarded to staff shortages and entered in the first slot of the staff shortages row (which pairs with staff attitudes) and so on.

When all comparisons have been made, the individual scores in each row are added up and a rank order of importance is achieved.

I have found this technique to be extremely effective in many training contexts, it can be used, as above, to aid individuals in clarifying their priorities and it can also be used effectively with problem-solving groups and in the context of team development.

The strength of the technique is that it enables people to become *quantitative* in their analysis of problems by attaching numerical values to critical dimensions in order that a decision on priority action may be made

	Staff attitude	Staff shortages	Poor equipment	Lack of support from above	Staff sickness	Interpersonal problems	Poor communications	Lack of authority	Slow decision making	Moving goal posts	Score	Rank
Staff attitude		6	5	4	6	5	3	4	5	5	43	6
Staff shortages	4		5	3	5	6	3	4	4	5	39	8
Poor equipment	5	5		4	5	6	4	5	6	6	46	4
Lack of support from above	6	7	6		7	7	5	5	6	7	56	1
Staff sickness	4	5	5	3		5	4	4	4	5	39	8
Interpersonal problems	5	4	4	3	5		4	4	4	4	37	9
Poor communications	7	7	6	5	6	6		6	6	6	55	2
Lack of authority	6	6	5	5	6	6	4		6	6	50	3
Slow decision making	5	6	4	4	6	6	4	4		5	44	5
Moving goal posts	5	5	4	3	5	6	4	4	5		41	7

Figure 3.2 *Matched pairs analysis—management 'stoppers'*

using objective data. The technique works best with 6 to 10 variables, but becomes unwieldy in excess of 14.

A common difficulty that faces organizations and individuals who decide to embark on the TQ journey is 'Where do I start?' Matched pairs analysis is a simple technique that offers a source of direction to the new traveller.

Pareto analysis

It is a well-established fact that the world is an unfair place, particularly in economic terms. Wealth and power are not distributed equally among the world's population but concentrated in the hands of minorities. The nineteenth-century Italian economist Vilfredo Pareto estimated that 80 per cent of his country's wealth was concentrated in the hands of just 20 per cent of the population. This is probably true (or perhaps even more true) of most countries today. This phenomenon of imbalance is often referred to as the 80–20 rule and it can be seen to operate in many different contexts.

In statistical terms, it is derived from cumulative percentage plottings (known as Lorenz curves) that indicate that 80 per cent of one variable commonly accounts for 20 per cent of another. Such imbalances are frequent in the retail trade where 80 per cent of a store's profit is often generated by just 20 per cent of all goods sold. Equally, 80 per cent of the faults in a complex machine are commonly caused by 20 per cent of the machine's components (compare how often cars break down as a result of electrical or cooling system faults in comparison with transmission or suspension faults). Such imbalances are further examples of statistical phenomena that have direct relevance to the pursuit of quality.

An analysis of such imbalances, often termed Pareto analysis, allows us to identify the most important factors that influence the quality of goods and services provided, the 'vital few' as opposed to the 'trivial many'.

A Pareto analysis of customer complaints can identify major areas of concern and ensure that resources are directed towards the rectification of those faults responsible for the bulk of customer dissatisfaction.

In common with all other statistical techniques, Pareto analysis requires that relevant data is available in order that an analysis may be carried out. The example in Table 3.1 is from an imaginary collection and analysis of customer complaints at a busy restaurant. We will assume that the study was undertaken over a period of six weeks.

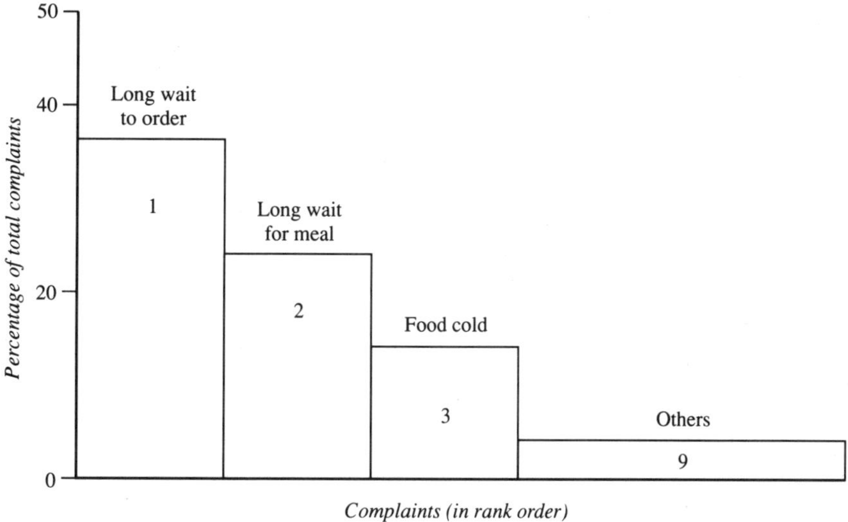

Figure 3.3 *Pareto analysis*

Pareto analysis of customer complaints: restaurant (period of study, six weeks)

1 Collection of data

Data will be collected in two ways:

1 through manager's interview of customers on completion of meal
2 through recording spontaneous customer complaints

Complaints identified through 1 receive 5 points.
Complaints identified through 2 receive 10 points.

Summary of data

Complaint	*Total no.*	*Cat 1*	*Cat 2*	*Points*
1 Food cold	13	8	5	90
2 Unfriendly service	2	2	0	10
3 Food undercooked	1	0	1	10
4 Food overcooked	4	3	1	25
5 Dirty cutlery	1	1	0	5
6 Restaurant cold	3	3	0	15
7 Long wait for meal	19	16	3	110
8 Tables too close	2	2	0	10
9 Small portions	1	1	0	5
10 Long wait to order	27	19	8	175
11 Music choice	1	1	0	5
12 Size of tables	1	1	0	5

Total no. of complaints: 75 *No. of spontaneous complaints:* 18
Total no. of complaint points: 485

Percentage analysis of complaints (in rank order)

Type of complaint	*Rank*	*No. of complaints*	*Percentage of total*	*Cumulative percentage*
Long wait to order	1	27	36	36
Long wait for meal	2	19	25	61
Food cold	3	13	17	78
Food overcooked	4	–	–	–

Table 3.1 *Example of Pareto analysis*

It emerges from Table 3.1 that the three highest ranking sources of complaint (25 per cent of sources recorded) are responsible for 78 per cent of all complaints received. Further analysis reveals that they generate 76 per cent of all complaint points and 87 per cent of spontaneous customer complaints.

Pareto analyses are commonly presented in histogram or bar chart form, which highlights the critical factors visually. A histogram of the results from Table 3.1 is shown in Figure 3.3.

The information obtained from a Pareto analysis is often useful in identifying underlying causes of problems and selecting effective solutions. If we were simply to look at the source of most complaints in our restaurant (long wait to order), the remedy may seem obvious, speed up the order-taking process or employ extra waiters. From our analysis, however, we can see that this has no obvious beneficial effect on the second most common complaint (long wait for meal) and may actually make the situation *worse*.

An obvious remedy for the second category of complaint is to speed up preparation of meals or employ more chefs. However, the third most common complaint concerns cold food, this may indicate that some meals are prepared at adequate speed but are left too long before being served.

Overall, the information suggests that management would be wise to examine the system for taking orders, passing them to the kitchen, prioritizing them, preparing them and serving them.

The statistical basis of quality

The comedian Dave Allen points out that statistics indicate that 30 per cent of road accidents are caused by drunk drivers and 70 per cent of accidents occur within a 5-mile radius of home. This, he says, means that 70 per cent of road accidents are caused by sober drivers and that outside of a 5-mile radius of home the chances of having an accident are reduced considerably. He then follows through to the conclusion that the safest way to drive therefore is to be drunk and never come within five miles of home!

Although this example is humorous, it is true that statistical information can be, and frequently is, used to say what the user *wants* it to say. Of course, as with this example, the misuse involves certain omissions such as the percentage of drunks (as a group) who are involved in road accidents compared to the percentage of sober drivers (as a group) who are involved. Although the initial statistics indicate that drunken drivers account for only 30 per cent of road accidents, this has to be set against the relative numbers of drunk versus sober drivers on the roads. We may then find that drunken drivers amount to less than 1 per cent of the driving population yet are responsible for 30 per cent of the accidents. Also, the relative seriousness of particular accidents is ignored. We may find, for example, that 80 per cent of serious accidents involve drunken drivers and so on.

I use this example to highlight the fact that statistics must be used with care and understanding if they are to be of real use in the pursuit of quality. This said, an understanding of basic statistical concepts and methods is essential to the TQ approach.

The normal curve of distribution

Much of statistics is concerned with relationships between variables. In psychology, for example, researchers have attempted to discover whether there is a relationship between birth order and measured IQ and whether certain personality types are more prone to heart attacks than others.

The relationships between certain variables are sometimes surprising, but there is often an underlying order that emerges when large numbers of variables are measured. A commonly used statistical notion is that of the *normal curve of distribution* (often called a bell curve), which asserts that when one particular variable (such as the height of an individual adult) is dependent upon a number of other variables (such as the height of the individual's parents, quality of nutrition as a child and so on), then very large populations will exhibit certain predictable qualities. The standard form of the normal curve is shown in Figure 3.4.

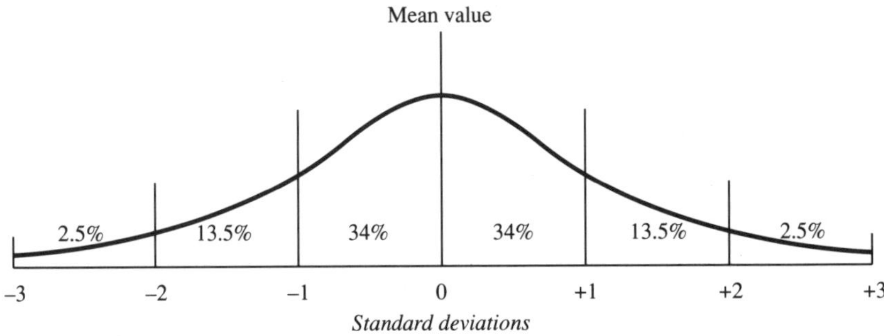

Figure 3.4 *The normal curve of distribution*

As can be seen from Figure 3.4, the curve is sectioned into areas. These represent areas of probability and allow us to predict certain things when a large population (that is a large number of samples) is taken.

When a large number of samples is considered, such as the height of the adult population of the United Kingdom for example, the normal curve of distribution predicts that roughly 66 per cent of males will be within plus or minus one *standard deviation* of the *mean value* of the curve. In real terms this means that 66 per cent of UK men will probably be between 5 feet 4 inches and 5 feet 10 inches in height, a standard deviation being approximately 3 inches. Also, that 95 per cent will be within 2 standard deviations, perhaps 5 feet 1 inch and 6 feet 1 inch. With 2.5 per cent being shorter than 5 feet 1 inch or taller than 6 feet 1 inch, that is within 3 standard deviations from the mean.

This *distribution* will also apply to the female population, although actual heights will be less, perhaps 95 per cent of females being between 4 feet 10 inches and 5 feet 10 inches tall and so on (I have of course guesstimated the actual values purely to illustrate the point). The normal curve of distribution is an example of a *statistical process* that may be used in a number of different ways.

Variation within statistical processes

The range of heights of adults in the UK is an example of variation within a statistical process. The causes of such variations are of very great importance where quality is concerned.

How do such variations arise? There is of course no formal stipulation that prospective parents must be of a particular height before they are allowed to have children! However, individuals tend to seek a partner who is not dramatically taller or shorter than themselves, men commonly seeking shorter partners and women taller ones.

These and other social influences (most people choose a partner who lives within a 10-mile radius of themselves) result in a spread of heights across the UK. In some areas of the country a lot of people are over 6 feet tall and in others they are considerably shorter. In terms of the normal curve of distribution, the effect is to make it flatter (a wider range of heights) than it would be if individuals chose partners completely at random. Let us imagine that a future government imposes a random selection law as far as prospective parenting is concerned, what would be the effect on the distribution of height in the population?

Let us assume that the existing distribution curve looks something like that shown in Figure 3.5.

After a number of generations under the random selection law the curve would probably look more like that illustrated in Figure 3.6.

The second curve is more pointed than the first. This of course does not mean that children will, overall, get taller. Some areas of the UK would produce a taller average population than previously and some areas a shorter average population. The important point to note is that the variation between individuals has been dramatically reduced. The mean

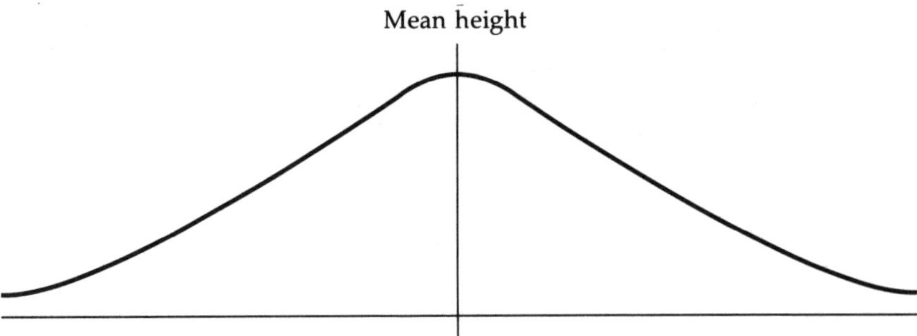

Figure 3.5 *The existing distribution curve showing a wide range of variation*

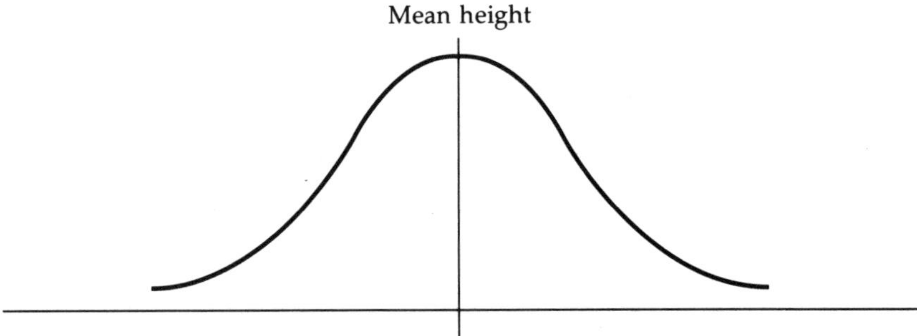

Figure 3.6 *A more pointed curve (less variation) resulting from random selection*

height of the population may not change a great deal, but variation from that mean height will be reduced considerably. The law of proportions and standard deviations will still apply but the actual value of a standard deviation will be reduced.

Of course, in terms of real human populations and real choices of partners it is infinitely more interesting to have a wide variation in people's heights rather than a 'standard person' conformity.

However, the same is not true concerning our expectations of such products as motor cars and TV sets. We prefer a wide range of choices, but once we have made our choice we expect to get what we were promised. We do not expect great variations to occur between different examples of the same product. How pleased would you be if your neighbour's new Ford Fiesta does 60 miles to the gallon while your identical model can manage only 16!

In terms of quality, the aim is to produce an extremely narrow range of variance from a theoretically perfect product or service—a very pointed curve of distribution. We cannot, of course, achieve absolute perfection, nor can we eradicate variance as no two Ford Fiestas will deliver exactly the same levels of fuel consumption, but the difference will be negligible. The aim of quality is to minimize variance from clearly specified customer requirements. This brings us full circle to the question posed at the beginning of this section, how does variance arise?

Special causes of variation

Returning to the example of adult height in the UK, a 'random selection' law would, in time, result in a population that was less varied in height. It would do this by removing some of the special causes of variation in height that currently operate. It would for example mean that the effects of social norms relating to the preferred height range of a prospective partner and the tendency to limit choices to a fairly restricted geographical area would be removed. Random allocation of partners would mean that very tall or very short individuals would be much less likely to be matched together (although this would still be a possibility) and thus dramatic variance would be gradually eliminated. Of course if we were really serious about producing a standard-height population we could decree that people from opposite extremes of the curve of distribution, very tall and very short, partner each other and that random selection was to operate at all other points!

Special causes of variation in any process can usually be eradicated once they have been identified. For example a company producing microprocessors may find that there is a significant increase in faulty components during the summer months. There may be a number of special reasons why this occurs; higher temperatures may affect the delicate machining or assembly processes or perhaps atmospheric pollution levels rise dramatically, again it may be that work areas are inadequately ventilated and people's judgement is impaired. Whatever the special causes, once they are accurately identified, measures can usually be taken to minimize or remove their effects.

Random causes of variation

In contrast to special causes of variation, random causes are more difficult to identify and are impossible to completely eradicate. This is because random causes are inherent in any process and do not produce a clear pattern of errors that can be analysed to identify specific causes. An example from competitive sport may clarify the difficulty.

A world-class sports team may lose an important match to a fairly humble opponent for various reasons. For instance, the team may not have taken their opponents seriously and failed to prepare effectively or a number of key players may have been injured during the game and so on. These are special causes and can be acted upon to prevent recurrence in future. However, it sometimes happens that a world-class team surprisingly loses and *no* satisfactory causes can be identified. The manager then commonly feels as unwell as a tropical bird!

However, unless we accept that events can occur in the absence of causes, there must have been some reason, or set of reasons, that led directly to the surprise defeat. On probing deeper into the possible causes of defeat it may transpire that several of the players, coincidentally, were experiencing minor personal problems that adversely affected their motivation. Although the effect on *each* player may only be slight, the *cumulative* effect results in the game being lost. As a consequence of these findings, the manager may decide to give team members access to a personal counsellor in future in an attempt to prevent the situation arising again. It is impossible, however, to guarantee that the players' personal lives will never adversely affect future performances because too many (random) variables are beyond the manager's control. However, it is possible to set up systems, such as a counselling service, that act as a potential brake to random causes of variation from required performance.

Statistical process control

Statistical process control (SPC) is receiving a great deal of attention in manufacturing industry worldwide. This interest has been stimulated mainly by the success of the Japanese who, chiefly through the influence of Deming, have adopted SPC principles across a wide range of industries.

Process variation

As the title implies, SPC techniques are concerned with the control of variation within a process. We have seen that all processes are subject to fluctuation and this results in varied outcomes, whether this be variation in physical products or in the delivery of a service. For example, every wheel on a car has a different diameter but we would require precision measuring instruments to detect this variation. Also, each time we visit a favourite restaurant the quality of the food we eat and the service we receive is different. No process is absolutely stable over time and variance is inevitable, but if the wheels on our car were quite a few inches or centimetres different in diameter or our meal was 70 per cent smaller than usual, we would have cause to complain.

Acceptable levels of variation

We accept that no two car wheels will be identical to the seventh decimal place or that each steak served at a restaurant will be within one thousandth of an ounce of any other. Such accuracy is theoretically possible to achieve, but it is not required. What *is* required is that we know clearly what amount of variance is acceptable.

As far as cars are concerned, the level of acceptable variance on diameter for a wheel hub would probably be within the region of plus or minus five thousandths of an inch, the steaks probably within plus or minus half an ounce. If we go outside these levels of variance we risk the failure of our component or the dissatisfaction of our diner.

Therefore the first step in implementing SPC is to clearly specify the *limits of acceptable variance, or tolerance,* that we must achieve. It is extremely important that we get this tolerance level right. There are two basic errors possible, each with different consequences. If we set out standards too *low* we will inevitably receive feedback. Our car wheels will not operate effectively and our diners will complain about our meals or not return. A more subtle danger at this stage is that we set our standards *narrower* than is required.

There is a direct relationship between tolerance and cost, the narrower the tolerance, the higher the cost. The tolerance limits on the engine components of a Rolls Royce, for example, are much narrower than they are on mass-produced, bottom-of-the-range vehicles and it has to be paid for. A noisy Rolls Royce engine would be unacceptable, whereas the main requirement of many other cars is that they get us reliably and safely from A to B.

If standards are set too high, costs may become prohibitive, again it is the quality maxim, know your customer's requirements.

Process capability

When appropriate specifications are set (this is very much easier to accomplish with products than it is with services), the next step is to find out whether the existing process is capable of delivering them.

To do this we can use the idea of a normal curve of distribution and probabilities of variance. Let us return for a moment to the example of variation in height across the adult population of the UK. If at some point in the future there were to be a requirement that same sex adults should be no more than plus or minus three inches different in height it is clear that the existing process through which people meet and decide to have children is not capable of achieving that requirement.

The same method of analysis applies to any process. If a manufacturing company wishes to produce goods that consistently meet customers' requirements at competitive prices, they must ensure that their manufacturing process is indeed capable of achieving this aim. All processes are composed of resources and systems, in the case of manufacturing this means that people must be trained effectively, that the machinery used is capable of attaining required standards and that systems and communications actually work. If any of these process components are not to requirements, then the system as a whole is not capable and variation will inevitably go beyond acceptable limits.

Once we have established that our process, whether it be the design and manufacture of television sets or the design and delivery of training courses, is indeed capable of consistently meeting customer specifications, we have the basis for using SPC principles.

Bringing processes within statistical control

As we have already noted there are two fundamental reasons for variation in any process, special causes and random causes. The aim of SPC techniques is to identify each type of cause and to work at eradication or improvement. Special causes of variation are, as we have already noted, capable of eradication. Random causes are an inevitable fact of life and will never be eradicated, that is, there will never be a perfect process. Although this is a somewhat daunting prospect it must not blind us to the fact that the effects of random causes of variation can be systematically reduced. Special causes can be eradicated, random causes must be 'squeezed'. The task of squeezing random causes of variation is the statistical basis for a philosophy of continuous improvement.

As we remove special causes and tighten up on random causes, a process comes into statistical control. Statistical control means that variation, over time, is stabilized within specified and achievable limits. This does not mean that every item produced (or, for instance, every training course run) will be acceptable, but that unacceptable items will be rare and within predicted quantities. SPC is a technique that helps identify whether such unacceptable items are the 'inevitable rarities' or whether they are a signal that something more serious is going wrong with a process.

Control charts

A control chart is a visual means of presenting information about variation within a process. Control charts can be used to monitor the changes that occur within a process, to differentiate between special and random causes of variation and to indicate when corrective action needs to be taken.

In order to do this we need continuous information about the way things are developing; whether the process is remaining in statistical control or whether there are signs that it is wandering away.

The actual construction of control charts is relatively complex and beyond the scope of this book. However, the basic ideas are simple and have direct relevance to the effective performance of all processes.

Control charts plot the way critical aspects of a process vary around a theoretically ideal value. We know that variation is inevitable, but we wish to contain this variation within acceptable limits. To illustrate with an example, imagine that we need to maintain the internal temperature of a gas-fired bakery oven within plus or minus two degrees of the ideal in order that we achieve optimum production speeds and quality of baked products. The two control charts shown in Figures 3.7 and 3.8 indicate that different events are occurring with our oven and that different actions are required.

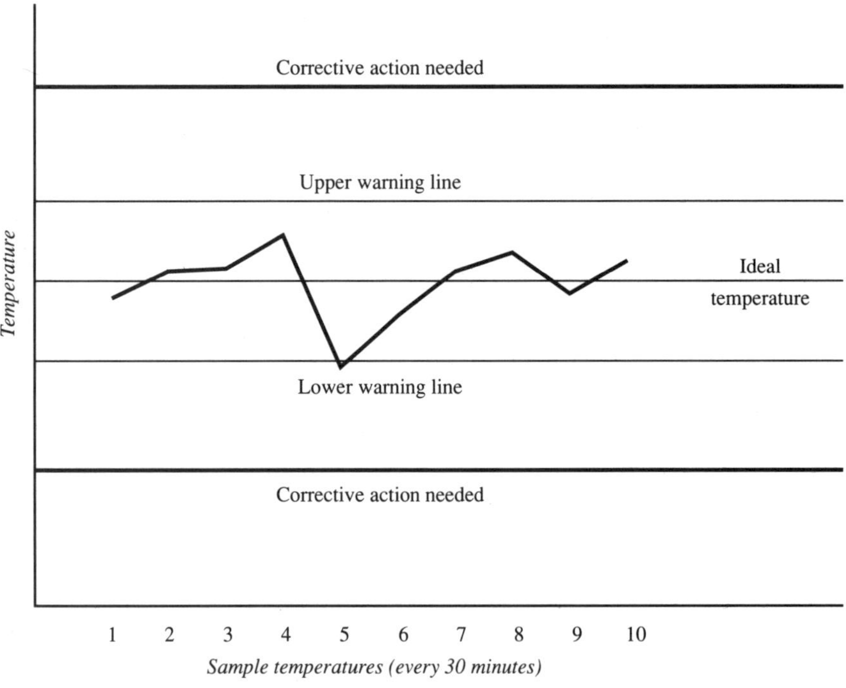

Figure 3.7 *Control chart of oven temperatures, day 1*

In this case the variations about the mean temperature are random and there seems to be no immediate need for action even though the lower warning line was crossed on one occasion. It may be wise, however, to take temperature samples more frequently for a while in order to verify that this deviation was a 'blip' in the system.

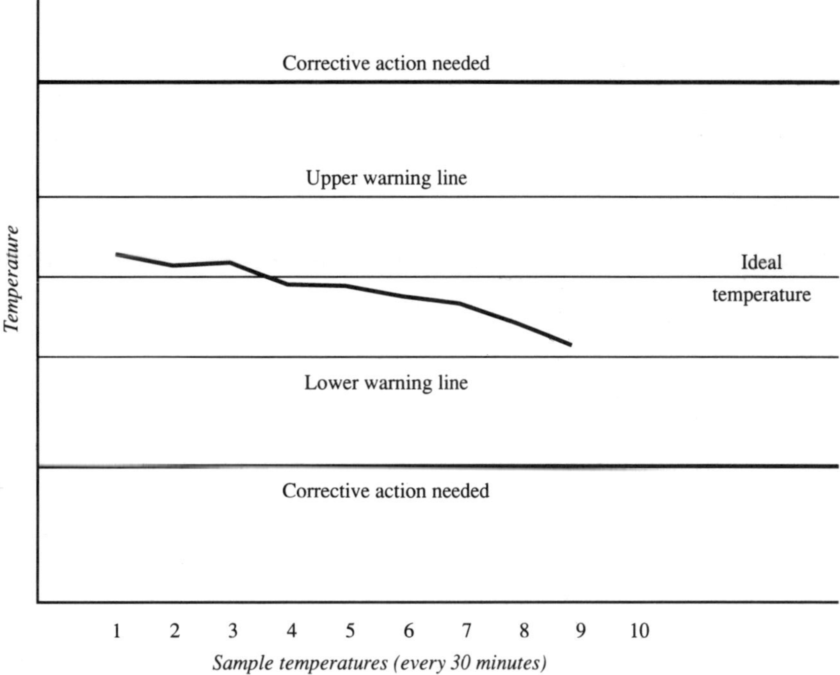

Figure 3.8 *Control chart of oven temperatures, day 2*

In this case, oven temperatures display a definite trend towards the lower warning line and although this has not been reached, there is cause for concern and perhaps action to discover any special causes of variation such as a gas leak or blocking jets.

4 The economics of quality

Quality, as we have noted, primarily means conformance to customer requirements, but not at any price. In order to survive in the real world, every business and service, be it private or public sector funded, must take financial considerations into account. In the business world, financial viability constitutes the bottom line; in publicly funded services, financial responsibility must be of equal importance. Quality means conforming to requirements in a cost-effective manner.

Satisfied customers do not automatically guarantee survival, a motor dealer selling new cars at half trade purchase price would find customers absolutely delighted during the short period of trading time prior to the collapse of the business.

Expenditure and financial investment *per se* is also no guarantee that quality will be enhanced. Quality, as we have already seen, requires clarity and accuracy, this is particularly important in terms of the deployment of financial resources. Expenditure must be directly and cost effectively related to customer satisfaction. The situation described above is (unfortunately for car buyers) somewhat unlikely to occur, but some realistic and common resourcing errors are outlined below.

Resourcing errors

Expenditure that does not lead to direct benefit for the customer

In quality terms, expenditure that does not benefit the customer in any way is a complete waste of resources. There are three principal reasons for this:

- existing customer satisfaction is not increased (it may even be decreased)
- new custom will not be generated
- an alternative (potentially effective) action is not resourced.

Although most organizations implicitly believe that investment expenditure will ultimately be good for business, it is necessary to clearly specify what the direct benefits to customers will be and to compare these with the potential benefits of other viable projects. In my experience, the least sound ideas generate substantial amounts of inconsequential talk during this analysis.

It is also valuable at this stage to carry out some form of cost/benefit analysis, it may be that the 80–20 rule is at work and that 80 per cent of potential benefits to customers will accrue from only 20 per cent of proposed expenditure.

Providing what the customer does not require

Many products and services include elements that the customer either consciously does not require or would not notice were they to be removed or dramatically reduced. This again is a two-fold waste. Unwanted elements add unnecessary (perhaps prohibitive) cost to a product or service and the financial resources thus committed cannot be directed towards the improvement of important elements or the creation of new, desirable ones.

Let us consider our friend the motor car in these terms—I find it a useful training exercise. Is there (a) anything about your car that you consciously do not require and (b) anything you would not miss greatly?

My own response to question (a) would be the ashtrays and cigarette lighter and the automatic choke.

To question (b) my response would be that I would gladly trade in the rev counter and the clock for more useful instruments such as a reliable, easy-to-read compass, a really accurate petrol guage, a way of checking oil and water levels without ruining my clothes or lacerating my hands, a tyre pressure/wear warning and so on. This analysis leads us on to another common error.

Disproportionate expenditure on marginal aspects of the product or service

It is clear that certain aspects of a product or service may be surplus to requirements and that others are of marginal significance in terms of customer satisfaction. It therefore follows that resource allocation must be made with these facts clearly in mind.

We have already noted that Hygiene factors have a limited capability to generate customer satisfaction and that increasing refinement will not bring proportional returns. It is necessary to identify the marginal and critical aspects (as seen by customers) of products and services and ensure that investment and development resources are allocated wisely.

Failure to anticipate customer requirements

Successful organizations seem able to anticipate customer requirements with uncanny accuracy. Of course there is nothing supernatural about their success; they do the research, gather the data, analyse it, discover trends, anticipate problems and generate creative solutions to these problems.

Changes in demography and technology, advances in medicine, the development of world competition and world markets will generate massive opportunities for innovative solutions to be found for the inevitable problems that will occur. Organizations that invest in appropriate research and development functions, and training particularly, will be those who prosper.

The cost of quality

Quality will not happen unless people do certain things. Doing things requires time and time costs money, therefore, in this sense, quality has a cost. However, there is a very big difference between expenditure and investment. Expenditure occurs when financial resources are employed to acquire assets—material and human—whose benefits decrease over time. The purchase of a motor car is a good example. The car, as a resource, is at its prime on the day it is delivered and it deteriorates steadily from that time onwards. The same is essentially true of a computer system or a photocopier.

With investment, the situation is reversed, the costs incurred may bring no immediate benefits and there are often negative effects in the short term. The decision to begin a long-term savings plan, for example, will result in an immediate reduction of expendable income and consequent constraints on possible actions.

In a different context, my own experiences of working in the field of therapy indicates strongly that individuals or couples who wish to change some aspect of their behaviour or relationship experience negative movement in the initial stages of the process. At first, things get worse.

Such negative movement is common to many instances of attempted long-term change and is directly related to the degree to which behaviours, attitudes or beliefs are habitualized. It is similar in many ways to the commonly experienced phenomenon that accompanies adults' attempts to improve their handwriting. Adults who embark on some form of calligraphic self-development almost always find that the immediate effect is to make the handwriting they are already dissatisfied with even worse!

Investment, by definition, is a process that aims to yield results in the long term (as opposed, say, to gambling or speculating). It demands the immediate commitment of resources, changes in the customary and accepted ways of doing things and, in return, it offers immediate negative effects and an uncertain outcome. Little wonder that *real* substantial long-term investment is a rarity.

Quality, like training, is an *investment* rather than an *expenditure*. The shift in direction from the way we do things now to the way we will need to do things in order to achieve quality will require investment in financial and human terms.

Quantifying the cost of quality

In 1979, Philip Crosby wrote a book on quality that has had a substantial impact on the way many American organizations view the relationship between quality and cost. The book was entitled *Quality is Free* and its central argument is that, ultimately, achieving quality costs nothing.

According to Crosby it is not achieving quality that costs money. He argues that the *real* cost of quality is the cost of doing things *wrong*, the cost of *waste*. In contrast, the cost of doing things *right* is not a cost at all, but an investment. The ultimate aim of quality is to eliminate waste, to not do things wrong at any stage in a process. Therefore, if every stage of a process is done absolutely correctly, that is, it conforms to requirements, we are not incurring costs, but accruing value. Real costs are incurred by doing things that do not conform to requirements, they have no return to offer.

It is useful at this stage to specify the costs associated with doing things wrong and the investment required to do things right.

The cost of nonconformance

The cost of nonconformance is considerable and is both tangible and intangible; the lists below are not exhaustive.

The costs of internal nonconformance, that is, nonconforming goods/services identified before they reach the customer, are:

- the time and resources required to design faulty goods and services
- the time and resources required to produce faulty goods and services
- the time and resources required to identify faulty goods and services
- the time and resources required to identify damaged materials that are retrievable
- the time and resources required to retrieve damaged materials
- the purchase cost of damaged materials that are not retrievable
- the time and resources required to dispose of nonretrievable damaged materials
- disruption to constructive activities
- demotivation.

The costs of external nonconformance, that is, nonconforming goods/services that reach the customer, are all those above, plus:

- the time and resources required to receive and respond to customer complaints
- the time and resources required to travel to customer premises
- the time and resources required to identify faults
- the time and resources required to correct faults
- disruption to constructive activities
- demotivation (high)
- customer dissatisfaction (incalculable costs).

The investment required to achieve conformance

The investment required to achieve conformance can be paraphrased in one sentence: *The investment required to achieve conformance is the investment required to* prevent *errors occurring*. The emphasis on the word *prevent* is fundamental.

Errors are possible at various stages in the development and delivery of a product or service. In terms of quality, there are three distinct phases to the process, which may be considered as the quality cycle (see Figure 4.1).

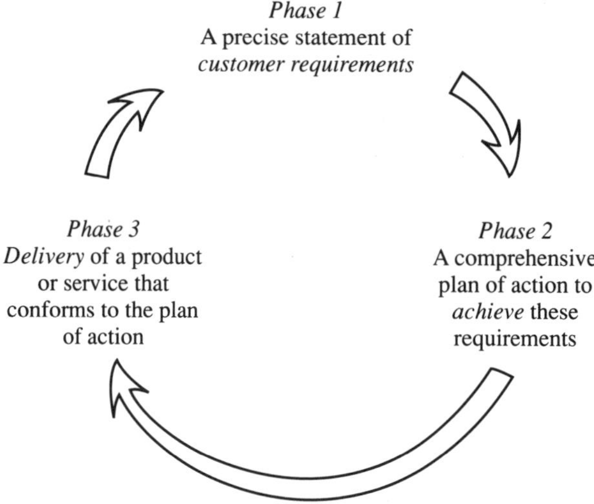

Figure 4.1 *The quality cycle*

The cycle is always driven from the top—customer requirements. In terms of resource investment, this can be identified as shown in Figure 4.1—for each phase, the requirements are that we provide:

- the time and resources needed to *define* precisely what the customer requires
- the time and resources needed to *design* a product or service that conforms to customer requirements in all respects
- the time and resources needed to *deliver* a product or service that conforms to design requirements in all respects.

These then are the three phases of the quality cycle: define, design and deliver.

Serious errors are possible at each phase and resources and systems must be directed towards the anticipation and prevention of such errors rather than detection and rectification of them. A suitable phrase used widely in the field of design engineering applies readily here, 'Think before you ink!'

It is interesting in this context to compare the approach of Japanese and Western car manufacturers to the elimination of the 'teething problems' that inevitably accompany the launch of a new model. No initial design is absolutely perfect and design errors become obvious as manufacture progresses. The Japanese invest a far greater amount of resources 'up front' to combat this than do their counterparts in the West. The Japanese philosophy is to eradicate problems *before* the car reaches the market. Of changes to a new Japanese model, 90 per cent are completed before it is launched, which means that 90 per cent of possible errors are identified and eradicated *before* the car reaches the customer. American manufacturers, in contrast, do far worse, with changes continuing to be made to a new model six months *after* it has been on the market.

The maxim here is 'Don't test your product on the paying customer'.

It is clear from this example that there is a hierarchy of importance among the three phases of the quality cycle. This is sometimes referred to as the quality lever. The first phase of the cycle—definition—is by far the most crucial. If we get this wrong all of what follows is a waste of time.

Sources of error at the definition phase

The avoidance of error at this phase is a fundamental requirement. There are a number of obstacles to be overcome and they are all directly related to clarity and accuracy. Three major sources of error are:

- preventing the customer from defining requirements, which occurs when a product or service is 'sold' to the customer as if it were what is required when, in fact, it is what the supplier is able to supply
- not helping the customer define requirements, which is a common situation, as anyone who works in customer research will confirm (customers frequently need assistance in clarifying their requirements and it is the responsibility of the supplier to facilitate this as customers often find it difficult to articulate precisely what their requirements are, but they know what they do not want when they get it—there is no point blaming the customer for this , as it is a little like being knocked down on a pedestrian crossing: you are technically in the right, but you're still dead)
- defining unverifiable requirements, which occurs when requirements are specified in terms that are open to individual interpretation, such as in the therapeutic context where clients state that they seek 'a better life', but, what is a better life—more leisure, a rewarding job—and how are we to decide when we have actually achieved a better life—it all depends on individual perceptions of what a 'good life' is and if outcomes are open to interpretation, there will almost certainly be differences of interpretation.

There are ways in which the probability of errors at the definition stage can be minimized.

- **don't sell** as it is not a selling opportunity but a priceless information-gathering opportunity
- **avoid doing what it is easy for us to do**—there is a strong temptation to 'bend' customer requirements so that they make life easier for us
- **dig for information**—probe, ask, listen, question, clarify, quantify
- **define requirements in measurable terms** so that there is no room for interpretation—specify clearly, in terms that are capable of being measured, what the requirements are and get agreement.

Sources of error at the design phase

'This is what they want.'

The most common source of error during this phase of the cycle is that customer requirements are forgotten, distorted or compromised to fit in with the capabilities or needs of the supplier. In training terms, this occurs when outcomes capable of being achieved in three days are stretched to five (because it pays more) or vital areas are not adequately covered because 'nobody here knows much about that'.

Every alteration to agreed requirements, no matter how small, leads to some customer dissatisfaction. It is the little things that add up.

Second, there is just plain bad design. I once sat through what was, to all intents and purposes, a one-and-a-half hour lecture on 'the importance of trainee participation in learning'!

There are basic questions that need to be asked at this phase:

- 'Is our design an absolutely accurate reflection of customer requirements?' 'Have we designed a product or service that sticks 100 per cent to the original requirements or has some 'wandering' occurred?'
- 'Have we designed a product or service that is capable of delivering what is required'—in a nutshell, will it work, how do we know, are we sure or are we hoping (there is only one way to find out—try it; the rule is, though, 'if it is humanly possible, try it out on anyone but the paying customer', avoid sending prototypes to the customer wherever possible)?
- 'Have we designed into the product or service any elements that the customer does not require?'—these cost money in terms of development and production and can be omitted and replaced by more of the things that the customer does require, often for less cost
- 'Is the design optimal in economic terms?' and 'can we make cost reductions while still achieving the requirements?'

Sources of error at the delivery phase

Errors at this stage are essentially concerned with sticking to design specifications and the limits of process capability. An excellent design does not guarantee an excellent product or service—a lot of things look good on paper. Just as customer requirements can be compromised during the design phase, design requirements may be compromised during the delivery phase: non-specified materials may be used, short cuts taken, directions ignored, specifications altered and so on. In some cases the process may not actually be physically capable of meeting design requirements: it is pointless designing an aeroplane if your process capability is limited to the production of roller skates!

Questions to consider at this phase include the following.

'Does everyone know we mean business?' In terms of quality, design specifications are not negotiable. I do not of course mean that obvious design mistakes should be adhered to but that deviations from specifications must only be made if customer requirements are in no way compromised. Again an example from manufacturing may be useful. I once worked for a company that manufactured heavy-duty valves for the petrochemical industry. An urgent order was received for a component that called for the use of a particular grade of steel. There was none in stock. The alternatives consisted of a slightly lower grade of steel or a considerably higher grade that cost 20 per cent more. The decision taken was to use the higher grade and to absorb the costs. The long-term reputation of the company was put before reduced profits on this particular order. In all probability (unless we were to be very unlucky), the slightly lower grade of steel would have proved adequate in this isolated case. The view of the chief design engineer however was that 'If the lower grade steel is satisfactory for this order it is satisfactory for all orders and we should therefore lower the existing specification and save ourselves money'. Everyone took the point. If the existing specification is correct (and it was in this case), then it is what is required and compromise is not permissible.

Quality is only possible when everyone is absolutely clear that standards are standards and that detrimental deviations are simply not on the agenda.

'Are our resources—material and human—really capable of meeting design requirements?' Are we being realistic or trusting that 'It'll be all right on the night'? It very seldom *is* all right on the night. Specifying beyond capability is a sure road to ruin and I have the strong feeling that this particular error is responsible for 80 per cent of management ulcers!

'Where are our weak spots?' Unless we have been totally unrealistic in our design specifications, there will be certain aspects of the design that are more difficult to achieve than others. Again the approach must be to identify and *prevent* these weaknesses from being translated into nonconforming products and services.

Is our equipment up to requirements? No? Then replace or re-work it or hire something else. Are our people up to requirements? No? Then re-train them or recruit others (perhaps on a contractual basis). Are our systems up to requirements? No? Then change them, break the rules for the duration of this project (and perhaps for good).

The overriding message must be *'Don't allow the existing status quo to define the produce or service—use customer requirements as an agent for positive change'.*

The cartoon in Figure 4.2 expresses the whole problem in a way that words somehow never can. It did the rounds of design offices in the early seventies, and I send my acknowledgements to the unknown originator—a quality pioneer!

The route to TQM

Inspection cultures

The route to TQM mirrors the inexorable move away from supplier-led approaches to the design and delivery of products and services towards

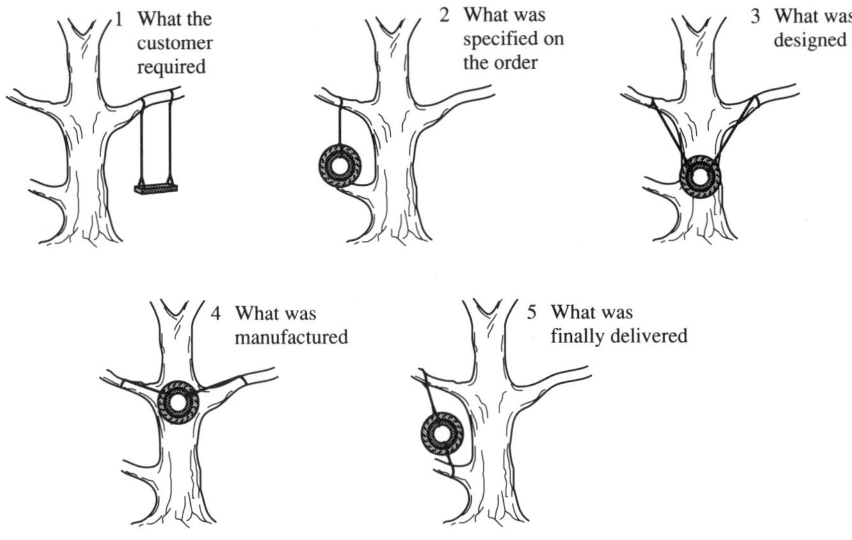

Figure 4.2 *The costs of not applying TQM principles*

a recognition of the increasing power of the customer. It also reflects a fundamental change in the way management views its role in ensuring that quality becomes a reality.

In the supplier-led world managements' perceived responsibility lies fundamentally in the sphere of control. Management systems and strategies are geared to specification and inspection. Products and services are specified with minimum consideration being given to customer requirements, and manufacturing processes are designed with cost optimization as the overriding goal. In this situation power is concentrated in the hands of a very small minority and the role of the majority is merely to implement their decisions and requirements. In all such cases, whether they be organizations, or even nations, this system leads to some form of inspection process being established that is charged with the responsibility of checking whether rules and directions are being followed and that things are acceptable.

This inspection process is essentially a policing and grading one and, *ipso facto*, it is separate from the process of design and manufacture. Such an 'inspection culture' also extends to those who work at the process of manufacture or delivery of a service and managements' role includes the operation of a system of personnel rules and sanctions, including 'time and motion' studies, aimed at establishing worker 'quotas'.

The main point to consider in terms of quality is that such a system is geared towards the *detection* of deviance rather than *prevention*.

Quality control

ISO 8402 (1986) defines quality control as a series of activities '. . . aimed both at monitoring a process and eliminating causes of unsatisfactory performance.'

The important difference between the inspection-based approach and quality control lies in the increased emphasis on prevention rather than detection. In this system elementary process control data will be fed back to first-line workers and supervisors who may have freedom to initiate changes and will be responsible for some level of self-generated quality inspection. Some form of external inspection, however, remains as a final screening mechanism between production and delivery.

Quality assurance

A system of quality assurance will incorporate various statistical approaches to process capability, including SPC and Pareto analysis.

There will be a marked emphasis on prevention rather than detection and a general management philosophy that is focused on the removal of individual and organizational barriers to the achievement of quality. It is common at this stage of the evolutionary process to adopt a systematic approach to problem solving and to involve personnel at all levels.

Such involvement will include customers and may also include external suppliers to the organization. Links with suppliers may be extended to the point that organizations wish to ascertain the capability of their external suppliers to provide goods and services that consistently meet requirements in order that incoming goods inspection may be eliminated. Suppliers who do not meet these requirements may be advised to take specific actions in order to maintain a supplier relationship.

Within the organization, emphasis is shifted towards personal responsibility in meeting requirements and a team-oriented approach to quality development. This commonly results in the formation of departmental and interdepartmental problem solving groups and quality circles.

The cultural changes that accompany such operational changes will include a move away from the traditionally perceived role of management as the 'controllers' of the system and towards a more symbiotic relationship in which nonmanagerial personnel work *with* rather than *for* management.

It is common at this stage for organizations to seek some form of external validation for the quality of products and services they supply. This may take the form of compliance with British Standards requirements (such as BS 5750), recognition as a preferred supplier to a prestigious organization (such as, Marks and Spencer) or the achievement of recognized quality awards (such as, The National Training Awards).

TQM

The final stage of this developmental process is the wholehearted application of quality management principles across the whole organization.

It is common to find that where an organization has adopted some or all of the quality assurance principles outlined above, it is primarily within the design and manufacturing functions. Quality assurance principles are rarely extended to such functions as sales, marketing, administration, personnel and training.

TQM, however, requires that each and every organizational function subscribes and adheres to the principles of quality development outlined previously. The major characteristics of a TQM approach are:

- commitment to the TQ approach extending from the very top of the organization and it being communicated clearly, consistently and highly visibly—this being reflected in systems of recruitment and selection, appraisal, renumeration, recognition and promotion
- management recognizing that the TQ approach is fundamentally a question of organizational culture and that the central challenge involves the development of appropriate attitudes and values throughout the organization
- that the approach to quality development is long term, management recognizing that the TQ approach is not a 'quick fix' and that the various tools and approaches employed will not succeed unless they are embedded in a long-term strategy of problem elimination and continuous development and management being aware that progress will be characteristically incremental
- management recognizing that TQ can be achieved only through effective teamwork and that personal involvement, shared goal setting, effective problem resolution and continuous development of human resources are fundamental components of success, these requirements being reflected in a systematic and continuous investment in training and development throughout the organization
- that the concept of customer and supplier is extended to include all functions and activities within the organization, each functional operation being considered a customer of A and a supplier to B, so each functional operation has the responsibility to:
  —define and communicate its requirements and expectations to internal suppliers
  —define and meet the requirements and expectations of its internal customers
  (It is important to stress that these customer–supplier links extend in all directions throughout the organization therefore requiring, and providing, a comprehensive network of cross-functional communication, each functional operation being actively involved in an overlapping network of quality cycles—see page 77—and the internal customer-supplier relationship also being fluid, the training function, for example, occupying the role of supplier to the sales function in providing induction, product awareness and specialist training and *also* being a customer of the sales department in terms of its need to be kept informed of market trends and developments)
- customers, both internal and external, being provided with effective means of registering dissatisfaction with their suppliers and being

encouraged to do so—such complaints being seen as an essential component of quality development and an opportunity to further improve the service, as problems to be solved rather than opportunities to engage in adversarial activities or blame delegation (the prevailing organizational culture viewing genuine mistakes as being inevitable in a system that strives towards continuous development and innovation)
- staff at all levels within the organization being encouraged to identify and make known any problems preventing them from improving their job performance.
- relationships with external customers and suppliers being comprehensive—customers and suppliers often being involved at the design stage for proposed products and services.

5 The relevance of TQ principles to internal service functions and service sector providers

Internal service functions

The overwhelming majority of recent literature on TQ in this country (a veritable mini-boom in the past four years or so) has focused specifically on aspects of product manufacture and product quality. There are two central reasons why this has occurred.

First, the major threat to our economic security, the reason why we are beginning to take quality seriously, is the rapidly diminishing market share (in terms of home sales and exports) of our manufactured products in comparison with our major competitors. Our competitors' products are often equal or superior in quality and beat us on price. This is, therefore, an immediate, highly visible and comprehensible problem.

Second, the evolution of TQ has taken place within the context of manufacturing and techniques have been developed specifically in relation to manufacturing problems.

These two factors—the immediacy of economic problems and the historical development of TQ principles—has tended to focus attention almost exclusively on first-line functions within manufacturing organizations.

It is increasingly being recognized, however, that *all* functions within an organization impact on product quality, even though some have a more obvious role than others. No organization simply produces products and then waits for customers to come along and purchase them. Products are marketed, advertised, serviced, guaranteed, sold and so on and customer satisfaction is influenced by factors much wider than the quality of the product on offer, although this is obviously of central concern. In recent years, for example, customers have become increasingly concerned to discern the moral, political and ecological positions taken by manufacturing industries. Customers are generally moving towards a position in which their purchasing decisions are a visible reflection of their political and social beliefs. This again is a striking example of the way in which customer needs and customer pressures have influenced the design, construction and manufacture of products and services.

The role of the support service functions

It is salutary to reflect on the fact that within many manufacturing organizations, particularly the medium-sized and larger ones, the number of people involved in the actual *manufacture* of a product often amounts to less than 40 per cent of the total number of staff employed. The remaining personnel are deployed in support service functions such as administration, personnel, training, finance, sales, marketing, design, security, purchasing and so on. If this remaining 60 per cent plus of staff do not impact on product quality, we must ask ourselves what exactly it is that they do.

This question has, in my experience, occupied the minds of the overwhelming majority of first-line staff I have met in the course of my career. The derision that many first-line staff feel towards service and higher management functions is a sad indication of the malaise that continues to restrict our capabilities and will, if we are not prudent enough to do something about it, see us off as a competitive nation.

The role of the service functions within a manufacturing organization is straightforward. It is to positively contribute to the quality of the products and services that the organization provides. By quality we of course mean customer satisfaction. The role of service functions is therefore to positively contribute to customer satisfaction.

Losing sight of the objectives

It is very easy for internal service functions to lose sight of this prime objective and become insular, detached from the realities of customer-oriented operations and concerned primarily with their own existence and perpetuation. Many administrative systems make the abilities of rabbits to increase prolifically look positively amateurish—forms beget forms and systems beget support systems with phenomenal ease. During the time I was employed as a designer in the nuclear research industry, it was postulated that three forms constituted a critical mass and that a chain reaction was inevitable once they came into contact with each other. Having since worked within the further and higher education sectors and, above all others, under the auspices of the (then) Manpower Services Commission, I have come to realize that this estimate is wildly overgenerous.

The reasons for support services becoming detached from customer-oriented activities are various. One major reason is related to the quality of feedback that internal service staff receive concerning their impact on customer satisfaction. If a first-line assembly worker fits an incorrect component into the engine of a motor vehicle, the effects are likely to be quite dramatic and highly visible. The costs associated with internal or external failure may be considerable as customers are either supplied with a nonconforming product or their order may be delayed while reworking is carried out.

In contrast to this situation, the effects of nonconforming service functions are often less obvious yet they can be substantially more damaging in the long term.

The costs of deficiencies in the service functions

It is extremely difficult to calculate the real costs of service deficiencies such as poor recruitment policy, ineffective selection interviewing, bad record keeping, unfair appraisal and reward systems, inappropriate advertising, ineffective management negotiators, incompetent reception staff, ineffective team leaders, untrained decision makers, inadequate problem resolution, inappropriate training strategies and ineffective training staff.

It is also easy to recognize that a first-line operator who inadvertently scratches the paintwork of an almost completed product has a detrimental and quantifiable effect on the organization's profitability. It is more difficult (or perhaps more painful) to accept that ineffective meetings are probably more damaging by an order of magnitude and that inadequate communications are slowly but surely bringing the organization to its knees.

Every employee within an organization impacts on operational cost and operational cost impacts on product cost. Every pound that is wasted and every pound that is overspent inevitably ends up as an increase in the cost of the product and if this increased cost is not balanced by increased customer satisfaction, then quality will be reduced.

Service sector providers

Variation

Variation is common to the vast majority of services. In virtually all sectors, the customer can experience considerable differences in the quality of services provided. Restaurants with comparable prices may differ widely in the range and standard of meals served, general decor, cleanliness and quality of service.

Most small service concerns, such as building firms, plumbers, electricians, accountants, solicitors and so on survive largely on personal recommendations from satisfied customers. It is widely recognized that selecting such a service at random is a pretty risky business as some are much better than others.

This range of variation certainly extends into the education and training sector. Schools, colleges and universities differ tremendously in terms of quality of tuition, levels of educational achievement, absenteeism rates, achievements in sports or arts and so on. Even when variables such as catchment area, socio-economic factors, teacher–pupil ratios and levels of resourcing are, to all intents and purposes, equalized, differences still emerge in the effectiveness of the education provided.

Training is certainly no exception. Variation in the effectiveness of trainers and training organizations is legendary.

Customer requirements and quality

We have already seen that variation is the antithesis of quality. By this of course it is not suggested that *all* cars should be identical, *all* schools should offer an identical curriculum (although moves to this end seem to be afoot at present) or that *every* restaurant should offer the same menu. It is variation *in relation to customer requirements* that must be eradicated if quality is to be achieved. This brings us back to the fundamental postulate of quality: *define customer requirements at the outset.*

What are customer requirements in terms of service industries? I find it useful in training sessions to turn this question on its head and ask, 'What do customers *not* require of service industries?' This exercise is enjoyable, fairly easy to complete and the answers are guaranteed to be true for all customers. Among other things, customers do *not* require:

- a second-rate education for their children
- a central heating system that leaks
- a five-minute wait before someone answers the phone
- to pay 50 per cent more tax than they needed to
- to be given the wrong pills by their doctor
- to be served a meal they did not order
- to wait half an hour in a train that has stopped ten yards from the platform
- to be bored stiff on a training course.

These are some of the many things that customers do *not* require, yet they very often get them. Exercises such as this can be the starting point in a process of clearly identifying common problems within the service sector. The challenge then of course is to deal with such problems effectively.

This is where many service providers misdirect resources. British Rail is an excellent example. As a frequent rail traveller I have noticed that certain aspects of BR's services have changed over the years. In my perception (and it must be remembered that where quality is concerned, customer perception is all there is) BR's service as regards reliability has not improved significantly over the past five years or so and in some cases it has positively declined. What *has* improved however is the quality of BR's apologies for the service. These have improved beyond recognition. I vividly remember an instance in 1981 when I asked a British Rail employee why my train to London had been sitting on the platform at York for 15 minutes longer than it was supposed to. He said, 'Your guess is as good as mine guv'!

A colleague, however, relates a very different experience. He was recently a passenger (or as BR now insists, a customer) on an Intercity train that broke down some miles from its destination. Within 10 minutes the conductor announced the reasons for the stoppage in great technical detail via the PA system and gave the estimated time to re-start the journey, which was 40 minutes. Then came a huge surprise, British Rail employees suddenly appeared with radio phones that were made available to passengers, free of charge, to make any short calls that would help alleviate the consequences of the late arrival of the train.

I have since discovered that this was no freak incident, teams of such personnel are apparently despatched to seriously stricken trains as part of BR's customer care strategy. I can only assume that they are in permanent orbit above tracks waiting for really bad delays to occur, a sort of customer service SAS.

Well intentioned as this is, it is not the way to achieve quality. The customer does not require an unreliable service with attendant apologetic staff; the customer simply wants to depart and arrive at the times promised on the timetable. To instigate such operations as that described above is to go a long way to accepting that train delays are inevitable. This sense of inevitability is further reinforced by such things as having the words 'minutes late' permanently in place on the monitor screens that show arrival and departure times at many stations. These measures generate and support a culture of impotence and when people *believe* that certain things are impossible to control, they *become* impossible to control.

Train delays are *not* inevitable, there is nothing woven into the fabric of the universe that decrees that trains shall not run consistently to time. Trains are delayed because preventable mistakes are not prevented, it is a complex problem, but there is nothing mystical about it. Deploying resources to alleviate the consequences of nonconforming services is simply to treat the symptoms rather than the disease and ultimately to intensify the disease. What is required is that the root causes of nonconformance are clearly identified and systematically eradicated.

Applying TQ techniques—some difficulties

The philosophy of TQ applies as effectively to service industries as it does to manufacturing. The application and relevance of specific techniques, however, demands careful consideration.

There are many similarities between manufacturing and services, but there are also many differences. The *similarities* enable us to see direct opportunities for the immediate application of certain TQ principles and the *differences* present an exciting opportunity to develop new techniques. A brief analysis of the most important similarities and differences is given below.

The similarities and differences between manufacturing and services

The *similarities* are that:

- they are both *processes*, are subject to process variations and process analysis and can be broken down into stages
- they utilize *physical and human resources*
- they must satisfy the requirements of *customers* if they are to survive.

The *differences* are that:

- the *human relations* dimension is characteristically more important in the service sector
- the service process usually involves a much greater element of *customer contact* than the manufacturing process
- the chance of *external failure* occurring is much higher in the service sector

- the *relationship between costs and benefits* is less robust in the service sector (you do not always *get* more when you *pay* more)
- there is characteristically a high level of *variability* between providers of services and between individual elements of a particular provider's service
- *standards* of performance are less clearly defined in the service sector.

The effects of the similarities and differences on the application of TQ principles

The list above includes some of the more important similarities and differences between services and manufacturing and these lead to different requirements in terms of the application of TQ principles. It is well to remember, however, the first point, that both activities are processes and are therefore open to process analysis and process control. The most significant difference is in terms of the importance of human relations in the service sector. Services are characteristically people-to-people interactions rather than people-to-machine, although these are becoming more common as technology advances.

The quality cycle (see page 34) applies directly to the provision of services, although it is clear that the final stage of the cycle, delivery, is of paramount importance. Manufacturing organizations have the opportunity to detect and eradicate errors before a product is passed to the customer (our car, for example, may have undergone three or four re-works before we receive it, but we will never know). The difficulty that faces service organizations, though, is that the final product, the particular service, is 'manufactured' with the customer present, the customer is an active participant in the service process and errors cannot be re-worked without incurring customer dissatisfaction. A spilled meal, a late train, a rude receptionist, an ineffective training session all occur with the customer present and there is very little we can do about it after the event (other than apologize profusely). The immediacy of the effect of errors is further proof that the quality principle of *prevention rather than detection* is extremely important here.

Standards of performance

We have already noted that the lack of appropriate standards of performance is a root cause of many quality problems. This is particularly true of the service sector. Before we consider some of the reasons for this difficulty occurring it is useful to recognize that services can be considered as forming a spectrum of related activities, as shown in Figure 5.1.

Figure 5.1 *The spectrum of service activities*

High role specification and functionality

At the left-hand end of the spectrum we have service activities that may be classified as having a high degree of role specification and functionality. These would include the service activities undertaken by sales assistants, waiting staff and receptionists. Each of these activities may be defined clearly in terms of duties and responsibilities (role specification) and the attitudes, skills and knowledge needed to successfully meet these requirements (functionality).

Thus, high levels of role specification and functionality allow us to clearly analyse and define required standards of performance. To the question, 'What makes a good sales assistant/waiter/receptionist?', we can draw a check-list of appropriate personal attributes and a skills inventory that would be agreeable to the majority of people and could be used as the basis for a training programme in the particular area concerned.

It is also interesting to note that at this end of the spectrum we accept that the person engaged in such activities is, in fact, playing a required role. We do not find it difficult to imagine that the super-polite and patient sales assistant, waiter or receptionist may behave quite differently in his or her personal life or that they may tear their hair out at the end of the working day.

This high level of role specification is often reinforced by the wearing of an appropriate uniform or a standardized mode of dress, appearance and communication style.

Low role specification and functionality

At the other end of the spectrum we have service activities that have a low level of role specification and functionality, these include activities carried out by managers, teachers and trainers. If we repeat the question asked above, 'What makes a good manager, teacher or trainer?', we can expect a lot less consensus and a great deal more debate.

Why is this? One common difficulty is related to the fact that managers, teachers and trainers may achieve results through seemingly disparate methods and approaches. There appears to be no ideal manager, no super teacher or trainer who can act as a template from which we can construct a profile of appropriate qualities and skills that will be guaranteed to be effective across a range of particular situations.

This difficulty stems from an important difference between services and manufacturing, which is that in the service sector, the crucial interactions are people–people rather than people–machine. It is very easy to specify the optimal performance criteria for machine operators, whether they be sitting in front of a computer or a power press. They will need to know the operating principles, limitations and capabilities of their machines, treat them in a certain manner so as not to damage them, carry out regular maintenance functions as required and report any signs of emerging malfunctions before they develop into major faults.

People are different, people are not machines. The management style that works for Mary may be inappropriate for Jane or Tom. Similarly, at the left-hand region of the spectrum we can be reasonably clear about the requirements for our sales assistants, waiters and receptionists because we can be fairly certain of the requirements of the situations in which they operate—very few people come to a restaurant in search of a rude waiter or to a business in search of an incompetent receptionist. At the other end of the spectrum, however, we are in much less certain territory—John may function most effectively with a manager who tells him in great detail exactly what it is that he is expected to do; Mary, in contrast, may be looking for a manager who allows her the freedom to take initiatives and plan her work according to negotiated priorities. Role responsibilities and specific functions are more varied and imprecise at the right-hand region of the spectrum and therefore much more difficult to specify and consequently to develop.

These problems are further exacerbated by the common tendency for the distinction between role and self to become increasingly blurred as we move to the right-hand side of the spectrum. Managers, teachers and trainers generally carry their natural personalities, beliefs and values into their role functions and their management, teaching or training style commonly reflects these variables. This situation contrasts starkly with that of first-line workers in an assembly plant who may invest little if any of their personalities or values in the activities they are required to carry out. This blurring of the distinction between role and self has far-reaching implications for quality in general and for the development of managers, teachers and trainers, in particular.

It was noted in a previous section that quality is based on clarity and accuracy; anything that cannot be quantified cannot be improved. This maxim applies directly to standards of performance in service functions. However, we have seen that service functions can be usefully considered as occupying some position on a spectrum that has relative clarity and agreement at one pole and ambiguity and debate at the other. Unfortunately it is those occupations at the ambiguous end of the spectrum that have the greatest potential influence on our economic security. Improving the effectiveness of our managers, teachers and trainers constitutes the key variable in ensuring our future success.

The ambiguity associated with definitions of effectiveness in these occupations makes the task of applying TQ techniques more difficult, but it does not render it impossible. It does, however, mean that in certain circumstances we may need to review our general obsession with the competence-based, check-list-driven approach to the analysis and appraisal of effective performance. This approach operates extremely well when it is applied to activities that have a clear structure and sequence of operations and are capable of unambiguous description and objective assessment, but there are areas of human performance—fundamentally important areas—that defy analysis in this manner. Human beings are capable of achieving excellence in a wide range of activities that do not lend themselves to sequential analysis and objective description.

It is a fallacy to assume that all human abilities can be translated into a sequence of discrete operations that fall neatly into some algorithmic plan that, if followed, guarantees success. There can never be an infallible programme that, if followed, would consistently produce excellent composers of music, brilliant playwrights or imaginative visual artists. I believe that this situation also, to a certain extent, applies to managers, teachers and trainers. For them there is no infallible check-list of competences to set about achieving. Effective management, teaching and training do not consist of the rigorous application of specific rules in specific situations. If this were the case, the training of managers, teachers and trainers would be a straightforward process, leading either to competence or failure to complete the programme. Anyone who works in these fields will recognize immediately that this is far from being the case.

This does not mean, though, that our task is a hopeless one. I believe that the problem rests not with any lack of ability on our part to recognize what good management, teaching or training is, but with our obsession to break down these performances into a set of discrete skills and competences. Sometimes the whole is indeed greater than the sum of its parts.

A final word on the problem of defining standards of performance in these areas. Think for a moment about all the managers, teachers and trainers that you have worked with or for or been taught or trained by in the past. Were they all of identical competence? Would you employ all of them? I very much doubt it. Now reflect on the criteria you have used to make your judgements.

6 Training—a quality case study

Quality problems in training

In this chapter we will examine some of the more pressing quality problems that face us in the field of training and development. My intention is not to be overly pessimistic in this or to cast blame in any particular direction. I am firmly convinced, however, that the road to quality involves an honest and objective assessment of the provider's (be that an organization or an individual) actual ability to identify and satisfy customer requirements. What follows may not be comfortable reading for anyone involved in the training field, but it must be remembered that complacency is the antithesis of continuous development.

Blaming the customer

My own experiences as a manager, lecturer, trainer, consultant and learner have led me to the firm conclusion that the key to organizational survival—and this is particularly true of the present time—lies in the successful utilization of the training and development function. I have also come to the conclusion that really effective training and development is a very rare bird indeed.

Many of us in the training world have, I suspect, become somewhat institutionalized to the accepted wisdom that the major reason for this country's appallingly low investment in training lies in the 'short-term gains' philosophy of management.

This may be true. If it *is* true, then our task as a training profession is to convince managers that the short-term costs incurred in training and developing staff will be worth while in the long term. How can we go about achieving this?

One obvious approach is to gather together conclusive evidence of organizations that have invested substantially in training and show that this investment has, unarguably, led directly to operational success.

By definition, if we accept that we have a national problem of underfunding training, there will not be many home-grown examples of this kind available for our use (we usually have to import them from Japan, Sweden or West Germany). If there *were* substantial numbers of home-grown examples available, however, we would, essentially, be preaching to the converted.

The question we must therefore ask ourselves is, 'Why are there not many such examples available or at least enough to convince any rational manager that investment in training really pays dividends?'

A common (circular) response is to say, again, that managers only look at short-term results. This response gets us nowhere, this is the classic error of blaming the customer for not buying our services.

Let us, then, look at the problem from the customer's angle. What if we dare suggest that managers in this country are reluctant to commit substantial resources to training because they are far from being convinced that training—and some forms of training in particular—really pays dividends.

Where would they get this idea from? Personal experience? Second-hand reports? Accepted mythology? Training course horror stories? Probably, yes.

I do not believe that the sole reason for the lack of commitment to training in this country is purely the result of management's lack of foresight or the manifestation of some obscure commercial death wish. We must not assume blindly that our potential customers—industry, commerce, public- and private-sector services—are simply being pig-headed and suicidal in their unwillingness to buy our services, as if we were trying, and failing, to sell life jackets to boat owners. Perhaps our customers are far from being convinced that our life jackets will actually keep them afloat.

If potential customers are not buying our products and services then it is we who should own the problem not them.

It is time that we began to look seriously and critically at our products and services in terms of our customers' needs and requirements rather than from the viewpoint of righteous indignation and a tendency to throw other country's training investment figures at them. It is, after all, not inconceivable that training and development in other countries receives more investment because it is more effectively undertaken there.

When I run trainer development courses, I often begin by asking the participants whether they have ever attended a training event that was a complete waste of time. Everyone always says 'yes'. I have personally attended quite a few. Have you?

If we in the training profession are to gain the wholehearted commitment of management to a planned and sustained investment in training, then the onus is on us to prove that we can deliver the goods and deliver them consistently.

What are the goods? The goods are cost-effective training and development services that result in clearly relevant positive outcomes in the actual world of work. In a nutshell, quality training.

Low level of commitment to training

If we are to understand *why* there is a low level of commitment to training in this country, we must undertake an objective analysis of the most significant factors that influence investment decisions. In common with the vast majority of business decisions, the importance attached to training will be perceived as a function of the balance between costs and benefits. In effect, the decision to invest (or not invest) in training can be considered as the resultant of a number of competing forces. These forces can be represented in the form of a force-field diagram, which often helps clarify the actual problems we face when attempting to facilitate some form of change. Figure 6.1 is a representation of the major forces that impact on decisions concerning investment in training.

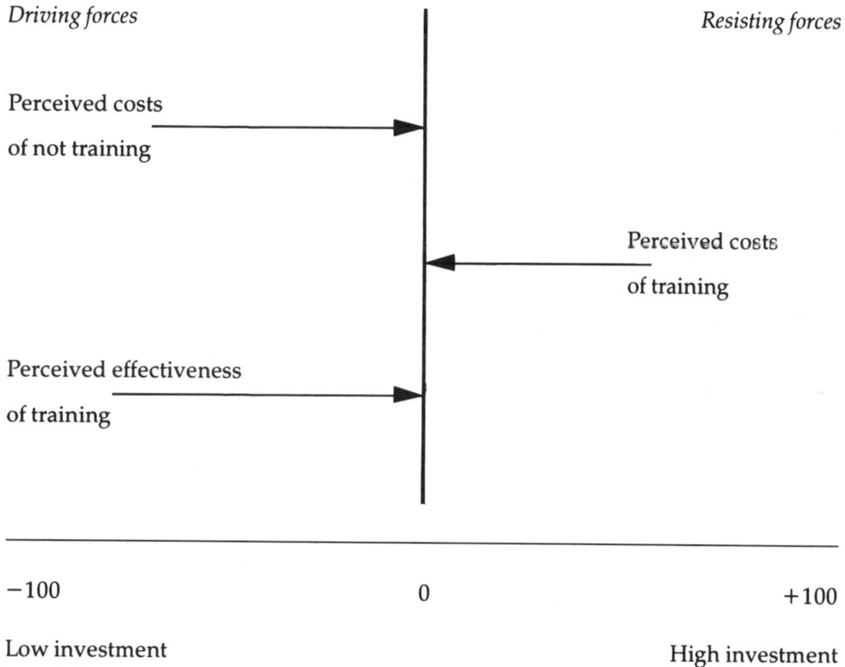

Figure 6.1 *Investment in training—force-field analysis*

All forms of change can be considered in terms of a system of opposing forces, some driving the individual, group or organization in one direction and others that are directly opposing this movement. Movement can occur in one of two directions depending on the relative power of each group of forces. They can result in a move into new territory—this is when real change occurs—or, alternatively, movement may occur in the opposite direction, that is, further into entrenched and habitualized ways of behaving. The alternative situation of course is that both sets of forces cancel each other out and no movement occurs; the status quo is maintained. The forces working towards real change are generally described as *drivers* and those acting against them as *resisters*.

In terms of investment in training, these competing forces can be usefully considered as detailed in Figure 5.2. The reader has perhaps noted that in opposition to the resisting forces associated with 'Perceived costs of training' I have not balanced them with 'Perceived benefits of training'.

Experience has led me to the conclusion that the majority of people (particularly managers and financial decision makers) pay more attention when we talk about costs than when we discuss benefits.

Benefits are hypothetical, arguable, open to interpretation and usually somewhere off in the future; costs are in the here and now and *are* quantifiable. Decisions about investment in training therefore need to be discussed in terms of the costs of not training and the means by which these costs can be reduced. To convince a financial decision maker that not training costs money, however, is not in itself enough. We must also be able to convince that person that we can reduce those costs. This is where the perceived effectiveness of training is important. Investment in training therefore will only increase when we are able to convince decision makers of three things:

- that not training costs money—it costs money now, it will cost money in the future and it can be quantified in terms that can be understood and measured
- that these costs can be systematically reduced by training and that these reductions can be measured and directly linked with training investment
- that this can be achieved in a cost-effective manner, that is, the reduction in the costs of not training will be greater than the costs of carrying the training out.

After all, if we cannot present our case in a practical, down-to-earth way, we should not be surprised when we meet resistance. Presenting training as being the road to some nebulous golden future is all well and good, but in my experience managers are more impressed by some form of argument that involves data that is understandable, measurable and believable.

Not training costs money

The first stage in the process is concerned with the identification and clarification of obvious and hidden costs associated with not training. This is particularly difficult in some areas of proposed training and less so in others. In the case of airline pilots, for instance, the perceived costs of not training are obvious and dramatic, also the perceived efficiency of the training on offer is high. These forces have little difficulty in overcoming the resistance associated with the (considerable) costs involved.

When the consequences of failure, the costs of not training, are immediate, dramatic and highly visible, commitment to training is usually high. Problems with commitment essentially stem from uncertainty in terms of projected costs of not training and concerns about the efficiency of the training on offer.

One major task, therefore, is to help organizations understand the relationship between training and cost reduction. Some of the more obvious costs of not training are:

- re-work/warranty costs
- increasing/stagnant level of customer dissatisfaction/complaints
- reduction/stagnation in market share
- late orders
- recurrent crises
- overtime costs
- costs of scrap
- no systematic reduction of unit costs
- underutilization of existing physical resources
- underutilization of existing human resources
- unneccessary operations and systems
- failure to utilize new technology/new methods and materials
- inspection costs.

Hidden costs include:

- absenteeism (BUPA estimates that 100 million working days are lost each year because people cannot face going to work)
- stress-related sicknesses, including heart disease, diseases of the digestive system and mental illness
- alcoholism
- excessive staff turnover
- inefficient staff recruitment and selection
- wilful sabotage
- resistance to change and progress
- apathy/low morale/no pride in work
- damage to organizational image
- lack of commitment to the organization
- accidents
- avoidable mistakes
- minimal staff suggestions for improvements
- new market opportunities not exploited
- no quality culture generated.

We are often told that many organizations opt for 'poaching' skilled staff rather than investing in training and development themselves. This is an extremely naïve and short-sighted option. Effective training does not simply produce skilled staff; it achieves immeasurably more than that. Systematic, quality training, is the essential component in a process of culture generation and development that maximizes the organization's future possibilities. An organization that does little or no training may poach a skilled worker, but it cannot poach a culture. If an organization lacks a culture that generates true commitment to sustainability and continuous improvement in all its employees, then sooner or later—probably sooner given the nature of change and the competitive context—it will die.

Ensuring that training is effective

Once we have convinced decision makers of the costs of not training we must tackle the problems associated with the perceived effectiveness of training on offer. There is, unfortunately, no magic formula available here. We are in no more of a privileged position than anyone else involved in the process of attempting to convince a prospective buyer. What we must avoid however, is falling into the trap of selling training as a solution to organizational problems under the 'clockwork mouse' scenario. By this I mean that we must not pretend that a training solution merely involves the upskilling and so on of people (take them away and wind them up like clockwork mice and then let them go). If people are changed by training then the organization must change along with them. The organization must welcome, recognize, reward and support the changes that training brings about in individuals and teams. Enthusing and skilling people is a waste of time if they return to the same static, archaic attitudes and systems that have prevailed in the past. Therefore a number of important points must be considered in relation to the potential effectiveness of a training programme. In particular we must:

- avoid exaggerated, undeliverable claims (no overpromising)
- focus on achievable, measurable results
- avoid attempting a training solution where this is not appropriate to the problem
- ensure that those trained will be supported when they return to their work environments
- ensure that training is given public support at the highest levels within the organization
- ensure that any gains resulting from training are publicly recognized/rewarded by the organization
- avoid setting ourselves up for failure by attempting to train those who are essentially untrainable.

These points highlight the fact that for training to be truly effective it must not be perceived to exist in a vacuum. Whether or not training transfers to the work-place will depend on the basic systems of reinforcement (or lack of them) that exist there.

Many organizations do not appreciate this fact. Training is too frequently viewed as being a 'take the staff away and do something to them' type of solution to the problems they face. The organization is not an innocent bystander in terms of the effectiveness of training, it has a vital role to play in recognizing, supporting and consolidating the positive changes that occur. Certainly, there are occasions when training does *not* result in organizational improvement because it is not effectively carried out, but this does not mean that *all* training failures are so caused. While I am attempting to avoid the trap of blaming the customer, the customer does have certain obligations in any transaction. It is rather unfair to blame the car manufacturer for engine failure when we have never checked the oil. If we in training are seduced into believing that this quick fix, 'innoculation' sort of problem solving is indeed possible, then we are deluding ourselves. When we fail to deliver, as we almost inevitably will, our downfall will have been of our own construction.

Having considered the major aspects of the drivers in the training equation we must of course address the problem of the resisting forces.

Unfortunately, the resisting forces associated with the perceived costs of training are often much easier to understand and quantify than the driving forces. Training involves expenditure in terms of money, time and disruption to organizational processes. And in the overwhelming majority of instances, nothing immediately catastrophic will happen to the organization if it does not train staff. Decisions concerning investment in training are essentially decisions concerning the management of risk. If we are to improve our effectiveness in influencing such decisions we must understand how this risk management process operates.

Commitment to training—the management of risk

In order that we are able to understand why people sometimes resist potentially beneficial change, we must understand some basic human tendencies, particularly those associated with the management of risk.

When human beings put themselves voluntarily into a risky situation, particularly when they have the power to do something about it to reduce levels of risk, there is a common tendency to diminish the potential danger of the situation and to maintain the status quo—the 'It won't happen to me, things will work out OK' syndrome. It may be seen quite dramatically in terms of smoking. There is no reasonable doubt that smoking dramatically increases the risk that a person will not enjoy a long life and may, indeed, have a short and painfully terminated one, yet people continue to smoke cigarettes. How do they come to terms with the risk? They come to terms with it precisely because it is a *risk* and not a *certainty*.

If cigarette smoking *invariably* caused death after three years, no one would smoke. But it does not, and it seems that every smoker is personally acquainted with a 97-year-old person who has smoked 400 cigarettes a day since the age of three and who has recently completed a marathon. Some heavy smokers—a *very* small minority—will reach a ripe old age. This is a statistical certainty. The problem is that many other smokers elevate these statistical minorities to the norm, saying things like, 'If it hasn't happened to him it may not happen to me'. Risk takers characteristically ignore statistics or look only where they see what they want to see; prophecies of doom have little effect, particularly when they are overdramatic. Indeed, they may have quite the opposite effect than that intended. What *does* work is if an effective alternative to the risky behaviour is made available. If a tablet was produced tomorrow that totally and harmlessly removed the desire to smoke, then the tobacco industry would find itself in some difficulty.

The same is true of training. Prophecies of doom are, in isolation from credible courses of action, ineffective in producing change. Indeed, they may even harden attitudes. What is required is that training dramatically improves its perceived effectiveness in those areas that are crucial to the future success of our economy. Some of the major weaknesses of training are examined in the following pages.

Variable standards of performance

I doubt if there are very many professions in which customers can experience wider disparities in the effectiveness of provision as they can in the field of training. The standards of competence of training providers and individual trainers varies tremendously. Considering that we are engaged in an endeavour whose aim is the enhancement of human capabilities, it is a source of constant surprise that we are not more frequently charged with the responsibility to heal ourselves before we profess an ability to heal others. The extreme variation (and in my experience it is extreme) has its roots in the same economic, social and organizational factors that give rise to variation in competence across the whole spectrum of work-related activities.

In the not so distant past, less effective middle managers were frequently moved into training to get them out of the way and into a position where their potential to damage the organization would be minimized. Thankfully those days, at least in the more enlightened organizations, have largely disappeared. However, the route by which many training personnel come into the business is often fairly haphazard. The majority of trainers, it seems to me, just 'happen' into it. There is still, in the vast majority of cases, no clear organizational path to training, no mechanism for the effective recruitment and selection of potential trainers, no planned route of occupational experience coupled with appropriate learning that leads naturally and logically into the training and development function, no training qualification that has any real predictive validity in terms of the actual effectiveness of the individual who possesses it. In fact, there is not a great deal on offer that trainers could use as an exemplar in attempting to persuade other occupational groups that their effectiveness is directly related to the systematic training opportunities available to them. It seems to be a classic case of 'Do not do as we do, do as we tell you'.

The past ten years or so have seen a virtual explosion in opportunities for training personnel. The introduction of the Youth Training Scheme, Employment Training, the establishment of a network of Accredited Training Centres and the various other government-funded initiatives such as Pickup, Business Growth Training and so on have meant that opportunities for freelance training and consultancy have proliferated. There has, however, been no parallel investment in the establishment of effective opportunities for potential training providers to develop the capabilities required to meet the real needs of this expanded market. In many cases the gap has been filled by the staff of various further and higher education establishments, often via hastily formed 'Business' or 'Enterprise Units'. Yet it can, and often has, been argued that it is the very lack of appropriate provision by such establishments that has played no mean part in facilitating competitive decline in the first place.

A large number of independent training providers and consultants has emerged as a result of the fertilizing effect of substantial quantities of money being cast upon the fields. In common with the established providers of training services, their effectiveness also varies tremendously. Many freelance consultants readily admit to the fact that they have had little if any formal training for the roles they are required to carry out. That which *is* on offer again suffers from the malaise of unpredictable usefulness. A colleague remarked recently that she had realized abruptly and to her dismay that the vast majority of her training and development experiences as a freelance trainer had consisted of the 'sitting next to' variety that she consistently berated to her students.

Variability is a serious problem affecting customer perception of any service. People have the unfortunate tendency to generalize a negative experience, particularly when it is a relatively new one. First impressions, whether we like it or not, do influence our perceptions strongly. If an organization makes a tentative move towards an investment in training and is unfortunate enough to engage the services of a provider at the wrong end of the effectiveness spectrum, then it is training *per se* that is the greater loser.

Supplier-led approaches

Trainers are very good at doing what they like to do. This is reflected in the individual trainer's style of delivery, the materials and equipment used, the theories and assumptions upon which provision is based and the structure of training sessions. Of course, to a certain extent, this is inevitable and not inherently bad. Training is the sort of occupation that allows a great deal of freedom and personal expression and this is what attracts a lot of people to it in the first place. Trainers usually have a substantial amount of autonomy in terms of the means by which they attempt to achieve their objectives. We must not forget, however, that the function of training is to meet the needs of those being trained rather than those delivering the training. In Chapter 8 we will look in some detail at a framework for understanding the psychological underpinnings of the training process, including the personal needs of the trainer. At this point, however, it may be useful to outline some of the more common manifestations of the supplier-led approach.

Training content

The content of many training events is frequently a reflection of the particular experiences, skills and resources of the training provider(s), rather than being a planned, systematic response to the real needs of the receivers of that training. This is the classic 'package' approach. Of course it is not impossible that what is provided happens to coincide with what is required or, at least, that some overlap occurs. The point is, however, that a substantial proportion of training is designed 'from the inside' and the inevitable result of this approach is that many customers will have only a limited percentage of their genuine needs met. In many instances this may be enough to prevent them from formally registering their discontent, but it hardly turns them into satisfied customers.

My own personal research into customer perceptions of training (particularly training that is not highly procedural in nature) indicates strongly that many people have lowered their expectations of what training can provide. Many people admitted that they attend training events *expecting* to spend some proportion of their time being bored, either by the quality of the presentation or by the fact that what they are being asked to learn or do bears no practical relation to their real needs. I have not done a formal analysis, but I have a strong suspicion that the 80–20 rule is certainly alive and well in this context and that 80 per cent of the benefits gained from the majority of supplier-led training courses comes from only 20 per cent of the content.

Training delivery

Supplier-led training delivery is characterized by trainer-centred or resource-centred approaches. In essence this means that learners have little or no opportunity to influence the ways in which learning situations are planned, structured and delivered. A classic example of this method can be found in the majority of secondary schools (it is less prominent in primary schools) where pupils have minimal or no influence on decisions such as the time of day of particular lessons, the duration of lessons, the sequence of lessons, the content, the teaching methods and so on.

A great deal of research has been undertaken regarding the ways in which different people learn and the results of this research have had (at least in theory) an influence on the ways trainers approach their training responsibilities.

It is now increasingly recognized that individuals have, to some extent, a particular learning preference or learning 'style'. This is borne out by the common observation that two people may approach an identical learning task in different ways. It follows from these discoveries that no single teaching or training approach is able to dovetail into the individual learning preferences of a diverse group of learners.

At this point, however, I would like to focus on the more common manifestations of the trainer-centred approach to the delivery of training. A key requirement for anyone wishing to be effective as a trainer is that they are able to accurately sense and respond to the needs of others and, in particular, that they are able to detect when people are becoming confused, tired or bored. Unfortunately this is not a talent that seems to be widely distributed throughout the population. One of the major reasons for trainers often taking learners past the point where they have effectively switched off is, I believe, an overdependence on resources and structure. If the trainer has prepared 27 overhead projected films, then the group *get* 27 overhead projected films; if the trainer has *brought* 3 videos, the group *watches* 3 videos. If the course programme says group discussion at 11.05 a.m., then a group discussion is what happens at 11.05 a.m. whether it is appropriate or not.

These are fairly obvious, yet strikingly common, problems. However, I am not implying that, as a result, what is required is no structure and no preprepared resources. This approach, again common, is, if anything, more supplier-led than the first. It stems from a philosophy—often espoused with quasi-religious fervour—that 'trainer-centred' means completely and unequivocally wrong and 'learner-centred' is something approaching the secret of the universe.

Completely learner-centred approaches are founded on an (unstated) premise that the learner is, in fact, able to clearly articulate precisely what it is that he or she needs to learn. This, in my opinion, is an extremely naïve notion.

Although frequently sincere and well meaning, each pole of the trainer–learner-centred spectrum is essentially supplier-led because it is based on a personal (and therefore idiosyncratic) assessment of what constitutes a learning opportunity. The trainer-centred trainer is often very keen to ensure that learners get the maximum amount of information presented in the most (to the trainer at least) accessible way. They often work extremely hard at researching information and preparing materials and exercises that, when they are appropriate, bring excellent results. When they are *not* appropriate, however, they become a liability that many resource-oriented trainers find it difficult to free themselves from. Their common response is then to re-work or refine the resources rather than considering whether a highly structured resource-based approach is relevant to the type of learning or type of learners involved in a particular situation.

In contrast, the highly learner-centred trainer tends to 'let learning happen' and, again, when this works, it works very well. When it does not work, however, it can be the most tedious, frustrating and time-wasting experience imaginable. It is also, paradoxically, very highly structured and limiting—the option to 'not negotiate', 'not lay out the room as best suits you' or 'not decide what to learn' is rescinded. Trainers who are locked into this particular end of the spectrum seem to forget that there is nothing inherently wrong with structure and direct teaching. It has an important part to play in all learning and a lot of people appreciate it a great deal.

Perhaps it would be useful for all trainers to keep in their minds a quotation from the psychologist Robert Zend: 'People have one thing in common: they are all different'.

Technology-based delivery

Over the last ten years or so there has been a great deal of activity and quite phenomenal levels of hype associated with the potential uses of computers and, more recently, interactive video in training. I must admit to having only limited experience of either.

My initial experience of computer-based training related to the administration and coordination of a social development project funded by an organization I once worked for that looked at the application of computer-based learning in the acquisition of basic literacy and numeracy skills. I attended a number of workshops where people ostensibly got together to talk about the development of the project. What they actually talked about was computers. It soon became clear to me that it was computer technology that was driving the project and not the learning needs of those who would ultimately use the software developed.

Although there is little doubt that the potential use of computer-based systems for certain types of learning is considerable, there has been a rather hysterical tendency to market it as a panacea for all training ills. This has led to a plethora of poorly conceived and hastily produced materials that have disappointed many trainers and users alike.

In a recent article, a practitioner in the field describes interactive video (IV) in the following terms: 'Half-baked training objectives, ham acting and cheesy patronage make up a good 80 per cent of the genre'. My own, albeit limited, experience and use of IV systems certainly accords with this view. It seems clear to me that difficulties occur when the major driving force behind the development of computer-based training (CBT) and IV systems is along the lines of 'We've got the technology let's see if we can use it for training', rather than being the outcome of a thorough learning or training-oriented analysis.

This supplier-led development strategy is often combined with a marketing approach that focuses strongly on the merits of accessibility and a reduction in unit training costs. Of course these are legitimate concerns as far as the provision of training services are concerned, but there is a danger that this message will appeal mainly to the 'training is an unfortunate cost and inconvenience' school of thought and ultimately move us further away from accepting the reality that training is a long-term continuing investment. If we accept that organizations must continuously adapt to changing customer requirements, we must extend this proviso to organizational functions, too, training included. It is difficult to see how a computer-based training package can achieve this.

In principle, technology-based training systems have a potential role to play in meeting the various needs that emerge in organizations. In practice, much of what has been produced to date is extremely disappointing. The prime reason for this is, I believe, that development has been driven by the suppliers rather than the potential customers. Training is an investment *only* if it is appropriate and effective; it is *not* an investment if its central merits are that it is simply cheap (in the long term) and relatively easy to organize.

Throughput orientation

Correlation and cause

We have already noted in the previous chapter that statistics must be used with understanding and caution if they are to be of real use. This is particularly true with regard to training. A major argument in favour of an increased financial investment in training in this country centres on comparisons with our more successful international competitors. They characteristically spend a far greater percentage of profits on training and development than we do. The argument then runs along the general lines of, if we invest in similar proportions, our competitive position will improve as a direct consequence.

There are a number of points to consider here. First, there is a common tendency to confuse *correlation* with *cause*. When two variables change in unison, all we can say with certainty is that there is a correlation between them. We cannot say with certainty, however, that one causes or influences the other as both may be directly influenced by a third (unknown) variable. Perhaps a practical example will help here.

Educational research in the USA has indicated that there is a positive link between a child's attainments at school and the number, variety and newness of the electrical goods in the child's home. This does not mean, however, that the way to get your child in the best school is to buy three freezers and a computer-controlled microwave. Both variables—attainment at school and quantity of electrical goods—are influenced by a *third* variable: the socio-economic class of the child's parents. It is this factor that ultimately has the real influence on the child's attainments as middle-class parents generally have high aspirations for their children, provide an educationally 'rich' environment at home, are interested in their school progress, often help with homework or employ tutors and so on. The fact that they *also* have a lot of electrical goods is purely coincidental. To focus exclusively on the discovered link between attainment and electrical goods would be to totally misunderstand the real forces operating in the success.

The same is true of cross-cultural comparisons regarding training expenditure. The deployment of increased financial resources to training and development in this country will not *of itself* guarantee success. In order that reliable information can be gained from statistical comparisons, we must be sure that we are comparing like with like. When we say that the Japanese invest x per cent in training as compared to our y per cent, we must be sure that we mean the same things by the term 'training'. There is, for example, a vast difference between a training event attended by people who are there under some form of duress and one in which training is eagerly sought and appreciated; or one in which the training is concise and relevant and another in which this is not the case. Although they may require the same financial investment, the benefits gained will, in all probability, be quite different.

Ideally, training should emerge as a natural consequence of the cultural norms existing within an organization rather than being seen as 'something we have to do if we are to succeed'. The challenge, of course, is to generate the culture in which this will happen. The paradox is that training and development is itself a vital component of that culture-generating process.

The marketing-led training phenomenon

The second point concerning throughput orientation focuses on the tendency for training providers, both inside organizations and external (particularly external), to train anyone who is prepared to turn up or pay for what is on offer. The pragmatic financial reasons for this are obvious and understandable. External training providers cannot force people to attend training events and internal providers work from a philosophy that this is not desirable in most cases. Training providers therefore have to persuade people that what is on offer is worth attending.

This approach almost inevitably leads towards an increasing tendency to become trapped in a marketing-led approach to the provision of training services rather than one based on an accurate analysis of needs and potential benefits. This phenomenon became very clear to me when I was in charge of a training centre responsible for trainer and manager development in relation to government-funded training provision.

We were essentially funded on a results basis and results meant getting people in through the doors. We were therefore required to provide training that people were prepared to attend or accept. We soon found out that what would sell was not usually, in our professional judgement, what was actually needed in order to improve individual and organizational effectiveness. Much of what we provided reflected people's personal interests and enthusiasms rather than being geared to the systematic development of a quality service. Certain provision became our 'bread and butter' in economic terms, guaranteed to attract the numbers required to keep us in business. Counselling skills courses spring to mind as a classic example. There seemed to be an endless supply of trainers and managers who wanted to become counsellors in some form or another. If our experiences are typical of all 55 centres nationally, there must now be more potential counsellors in this country than there are people needing to be counselled.

To be truly effective, training services must respond to more than simple market demand. Providing training is not the same as providing consumer goods or consumer services. In the consumer field the customer is the final arbiter in deciding what products or services to spend money on; in training these considerations must go deeper. I am not of course suggesting that the customers must buy what we tell them to buy, only that we must ensure that what they receive is, in our professional opinion, what it is in their best interests to receive rather than that which is in our best interests to supply.

In many ways the role of the training professional can be likened to that of the physician. An effective physician does not prescribe medication on the basis that patients are prepared to take it or that there are surplus supplies of it in the pharmacy and so it is fairly straightforward to get hold of. Hopefully, the physician effectively diagnoses the situation and then prescribes what is required. This point leads us on to the next major consideration.

Marketing orientation

Whatever we can say about the actual effectiveness of training and development services, one thing is for sure, the claims about effectiveness are of a very high standard. A casual browse through the literature in which training services are advertised, in both the public and private sectors, gives the definite impression that great things are possible in a period of three to five days at an Elizabethan manor or half-way up a mountainside or that the workers without jobs can be trained to do the jobs without workers at the drop of a hat. It is not that simple.

Tom Peters, in his book *Thriving on Chaos*, argues that customer perception of quality is strongly influenced by the images and expectations that potential providers conjure up in customers' minds. I believe that he is absolutely correct. A personal experience may illustrate the point.

Some years ago I was informed by a firm of solicitors acting on my behalf in a house sale/purchase that their total fees for the transactions would not exceed £750. In good faith I left a post-dated cheque with them for that amount. Some weeks after the transactions were completed, I received a letter and a detailed bill of costs from them, together with a cheque for £56. The letter informed me that the total costs of the transactions had amounted to £694 and consequently the £56 was my refund. I telephoned them that day and thanked them for their services and honesty and for the next months acted as an unpaid salesman and PR officer for their firm. I probably directed at least four customers their way who would not otherwise have used them. Why? Because the service they provided had exceeded my expectations. Had the costs been £750 I would have been satisfied, but would not have evangelized for them. Whether this firm purposely included a 'buffer' amount I do not know, but the outcome is directly relevant to Tom Peters' assertion that service providers should aim to 'Underpromise and overdeliver'.

I am not convinced about the underpromise element (I am not sure how this would apply to training, perhaps prospective delegates could be told that a course was three days and then we give them five) but the overdeliver element is certainly an idea to work with.

The central point to consider, however, is that there is a tendency for training providers to do the opposite of what Tom Peters suggests, that is to overpromise and underdeliver. This often takes the form of exaggerated claims that an individual's long-established behaviour patterns can be changed dramatically in short periods of time or that complex organizational problems can be solved by simply filling in the appropriate readers' response card. Instead of looking critically and effectively at improving the real quality of training there has been an almost manic drive towards exotic venues, impressive publicity, trainerspeak, laser-printed everythings and 'delegate packs'.

Of course there is nothing inherently wrong with providing congenial surroundings, elegant and attractively produced handouts and colourful course materials, but we must keep clear in our minds the fact that they are not the central areas into which our quality improvement efforts must be directed. They are certainly not the criteria by which our effectiveness will be judged. It must be remembered that quality is not only concerned with the clarification of customer requirements, this is only the beginning of the process, we must also ensure that we can deliver 100 per cent of what we claim to be able to deliver.

Over the past ten years or so I have, on a strictly informal basis, endeavoured to gain as much information as possible concerning the perceptions of people who have, in some shape or form, recently undertaken a planned training or development experience. It is an educating process, much more so than reading the formal end-of-course evaluation sheets.

I talked to a middle manager in the public sector who had attended a five-day course on 'People management skills', run by a reputable training organization. He said that the course, 'Wasn't too bad—the hotel was nice' (this is a very common response). 'But', he added with a grin, 'the BPB level was pretty high'. This term was new to me, 'BPB?', I said. 'Beautifully Presented Bull', he replied. I asked whether he had passed this information on to the trainers involved. He had not. Let us be warned!

Ineffective feedback mechanisms

Effective, accurate feedback is an essential component of all quality systems. Unless we are able to measure our performance against customer requirements we will be unable to make improvements. It is essential, therefore, that we provide the mechanisms required to generate this information. In principle, there are a number of levels at which an evaluation of training effectiveness can be undertaken:

- an evaluation of training in terms of the achievement of specified aims and objectives
- an evaluation of training in terms of changes in individual work performance
- an evaluation of training in terms of changes in team, group or departmental performance
- an evaluation of training in terms of changes in organizational performance.

There is, unfortunately, an inverse relationship existing between the accuracy with which we are able to determine satisfactory answers to each of these levels and their overall importance.

As regards the first level we can measure results accurately providing that desired outcomes have initially been specified in measurable terms (this is not always the case).

The second level is more difficult in that we are often unable to measure changes because we do not have accurate data concerning performance levels prior to training being carried out (this is less of a problem where practical skill training is concerned because we can often have access to pre-training information such as error or productivity rates and compare these with post-training levels).

The third level is again more complicated to evaluate and in many cases highly subjective (the previous caveat concerning skills training withstanding).

The fourth level is the most important of all *and* the least amenable to direct, accurate cost/benefit analysis as regards the effectiveness of training programmes.

Problems in evaluation of training

In many ways the problem of evaluating training, particularly at the more important and least amenable levels, is similar to the never-ending discussions that surround the evaluation of the effectiveness of therapeutic approaches to the treatment of psychological disorders. Many people get better after periods of therapy, there is little doubt about that, but what is questionable, however, is whether the therapy has anything to do with it. The individual may have improved if no therapy at all had been given. There is no way of finding out for certain. The same applies to training—particularly when it is aimed at those staff who provide internal support and coordination services.

One common constraint imposed on the evaluation of training is to assume that the relationship between training investment and improved organizational effectiveness is a straightforward case of linear cause and effect. I believe that it is more complex. The common approach to the evaluation of training can be represented as shown in Figure 6.2.

Figure 6.2 *A linear approach to the evaluation of training effectiveness*

As we have already noted, this form of evaluation is most appropriate, and most effective, for measuring changes in the work performance of individuals. Above this level, however, the interaction between training investment and improved performance is more complex. At higher levels I believe the interactions are better represented as illustrated in Figure 6.3.

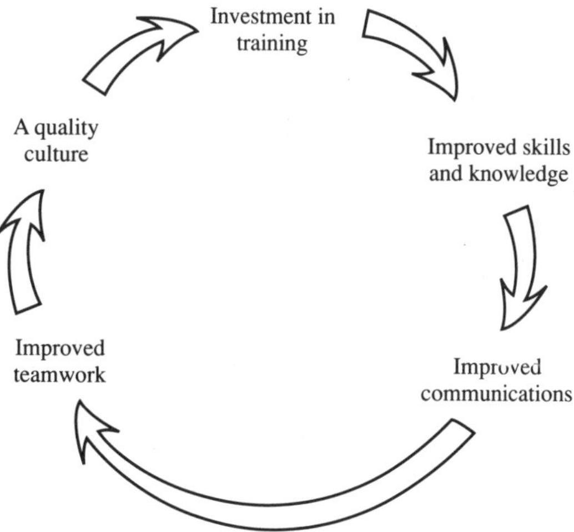

Figure 6.3 *A holistic approach to the evaluation of training effectiveness*

In this model, training can be considered as playing the dual roles of cause *and* effect. Cause in bringing about the development of a quality culture that in turn views training as being an essential organizational investment (effect). What can be seen from the diagram is that training occupies a seminal role in the generation and continuation of a quality culture.

In the vast majority of instances, training must be considered in relation to its role as causal agent in the process of generating a quality culture. In this sense we must look wider than the linear model allows and seek to influence not only individual performance, but also the development of improved communications and teamwork. An expanded view of the role of individual competence is outlined in Chapter 7. At this point, however, attention must be focused on the task of ensuring that the training we deliver will indeed have the effect we seek in planting the seeds of the quality culture. In order to do this, of course, training must be perceived as being of actual value. A quality culture does not arise overnight, it grows slowly and its growth is precarious. Above all else we need to ensure that the training we deliver is perceived as being a positive contribution to the organization's immediate and long-term security. To this end we must ensure that we gain accurate feedback about our customer's perceptions of whether or not we are actually achieving this aim. We must therefore look critically at the current methods used to obtain this vital feedback.

The end-of-course evaluation

Those of us who have a formal responsibility for training are very aware of what the most common process of obtaining customer feedback is—the end-of-course evaluation.

These sessions are, in my experience, at best a process of mutual embarrassment for all concerned and, at worst, an attempt at character assassination or mutual sycophancy.

What is the purpose of an end-of-course evaluation? To determine what? To find out whether the course content, structure and delivery were appropriate to people's needs? Whether we are effective as trainers? Surely we should know most of these things before we start. Could we not monitor the effectiveness of our training as it proceeds?

I am not suggesting that end-of-course evaluations are inherently a waste of time, but, by their very nature, they focus attention on the detection of errors and therefore away from the quality maxim of prevention.

Considering the number of post-training evaluations that have been carried out over the years, it never ceases to amaze me that the same mistakes and faults are identified time and time again. This tends to confirm my suspicion that a large number of such evaluations are rarely, if ever, acted upon—they are chiefly a parting ritual at the end of a period of training.

An evaluation of a number of management training programmes within the further education sector included, as part of its final recommendations, the following points in relation to identified weaknesses:

- that materials used in management training courses should be activity based and directly relevant to course participants' actual work situations
- that different programmes should have equivalent core content in order that accurate comparisons may be made between them

- that levels of achievement in key competences should be assessed
- that the tutors delivering the programmes should have the opportunity to work together in creating materials and approaches.

These are not weaknesses we should have to identify *after* we run a series of training and development programmes. They are obvious prerequisites that must be designed in before we even consider delivering training.

Another important consideration in respect of end-of-course evaluations is concerned with the quality of feedback we receive. It is a very common mistake to measure what is *easy* to measure rather than measuring what *needs* to be measured. Many evaluation sheets are of the 'what session was most/least useful' type or some form of rating scale is applied to variables such as tutor style, quality of materials and so on. There are a number of difficulties with this approach.

First, we have no real way of determining what we mean by, for instance, 'most useful session'—it is, in fact, what the people completing the evaluations mean. To them it may mean 'most useful of the generally useless sessions provided' or 'the one I understood best' or 'most enjoyable' or 'most interesting to me personally' or 'I liked that trainer best' and so on. Another problem is that the majority of these evaluations produce different sets of priorities from different individuals and groups, unless the trainer has got something completely wrong. This cultivates the attitude that 'you cannot please all of the people all of the time' and the idea that the training at least has something for everyone. In this way the evaluations tend to support the status quo and do not act as a direct source of information upon which to base a programme of genuine improvement.

Influencing all of these considerations, of course, is the problem of honesty in completing evaluation sheets or commenting in plenary evaluation sessions. Do we really obtain honest and useful feedback in these ways? I very much doubt it. From personal experience we can all probably recall instances when we have not stated our true feelings either in writing or when asked to comment verbally. Our priorities at the end of a training course may simply be to get home rather than become embroiled in a lengthy and perhaps uncomfortable post mortem.

There are a number of specific problems commonly associated with end-of-course evaluations and some of these are itemized below:

- they provide vague/unusable information
- they are used piecemeal and considered mainly on a 'course by course' basis
- information is not fed into some form of cumulative database and analysed in order that underlying trends and customer priorities may be identified
- information gathered is not integrated within a systematic programme of continuous development
- they are not of sufficient depth and complexity to supply critical information
- the reasons for seeking specific information is not communicated effectively to customers

- they are threatening to trainers and often provoke defence-oriented responses
- they are embarrassing to complete and encourage bland responses
- their emphasis is primarily on what has happened rather than what should happen in future
- they do not supply information regarding the wider needs and requirements of customers including personal and organizational development plans
- they are not an integral part of the course
- they do not measure change or learning.

If end-of-course evaluations are to be of any use they must be constructed and administered in such a way as to supply us with important and valid information that can feed back into the quality cycle and result in genuine improvements being made.

What needs to be done to overcome these problems

If we are seeking information on the relevance of training content *after* training has been undertaken, then there is something very wrong with our methods of training needs analysis. Again this brings us back to the prevailing approach in training of supplier-led provision. There has been far too much training organized and delivered under the 'let us try this and then evaluate it' philosophy. We need to do more of the 'let us find out precisely what is required and supply that' type of training. The process of evaluation is essentially a process of research and in training we do far too much of our research at the wrong end of the quality cycle—that is at or after the delivery stage. We are continuously delivering prototypes rather than soundly researched and well-designed services that meet real needs. It is not impossible to research and deliver training that addresses specific individual and organizational problems in a systematic and effective manner. What is required is that we concentrate our research effort on the definition and design stages of the quality cycle and away from the delivery and post-delivery stages.

7 Tackling quality problems in training—the application of TQ techniques

In order that we may begin to tackle the quality problems that exist in training, we must first determine their root causes. A good place to begin is with the first stage of the quality cycle—definition. I do not mean by this statement that what is required is that we embark on some obscure semantic search for the real meaning of the word 'training'. Rather, I will adopt the approach of the philosopher Ludwig Wittgenstein who asserted that 'the meaning of a word is its use'. Therefore, I will begin this analysis by asking the question, 'What is the function of training—what is training for?'

What business are we in?

Defining training

In order that we can deliver a quality product or service we must be absolutely clear about the needs we are attempting to satisfy. I believe that there is a great deal of confusion in the training world as to the precise nature of the business we are in. This confusion is often apparent when we do embark on the fruitless journey that aims to determine, once and for all, what the real definition of training is. I give below a selection of the more common suggestions:

- training is the process of equipping people with the specific attitudes, skills and knowledge needed to carry out their responsibilities
- training is not education—education seeks to maximize the differences between people, while training aims to standardize individual performance to required levels
- training is the process of integrating personal and organizational goals
- training is the process by which we attempt to close the gap between an individual's present performance levels and desired performance levels
- training is about helping people learn and develop; it should be centred on the learner and it should be fun.

The training spectrum

Training can include all these things but none of them alone accurately describes what the *function* of training is. The first and last definitions indicate the poles of what can be considered as the 'training spectrum'. This spectrum has highly specific, skills-based activities at one end and highly unstructured, 'learner-centred' activities at the other.

Skills-based training

The first is derived from the philosophy of 'scientific management' developed by F.W. Taylor in the United States at the turn of the century. Scientific management is based on the assumption that jobs can be broken down into discrete parts and that there is an optimum way in which any job can be carried out. This philosophy views people as functional units within an operational system that also includes some form of machinery or technology.

These ideas lead naturally to the conclusion that functionality consists of the possession of specific competences. The basis for improving performance, therefore, is to first determine, by rational, logical analysis, the competences and competence levels required to perform particular activities, compare these to the actual competences a person displays and undertake some form of specific training when there is a mismatch.

This approach can and does work in appropriate situations. Skills analysis is an important technique that leads to improved performance in specific areas. However, as we saw in the last chapter, this process of analysis is far easier to conduct in certain areas than it is in others. Another disadvantage of course is that it is primarily deficiency led and pass/fail oriented; a person either does or does not have a specific competence. The actual process of training needs analysis, therefore, is essentially concerned with the identification of failings or weaknesses (often euphemistically stated as being 'areas for further development'). In certain situations this approach poses no real problems. Training for practical skill competences is a good example.

People who undertake training in, say, welding, accept that they have deficient welding skills and that training is the most sensible route to take in order to rectify that deficiency. The situation is very different in the case of occupational areas, such as management, where the systematic analysis approach is concerned to define the 'core competences' required for effective functioning. The vast majority of such analyses come up with variations on the theme that managers need to be effective at organizing, prioritizing, informing, leading, motivating, delegating and so on. This then leads to the concept of organizational skills, leadership skills, motivational skills, interpersonal skills and so forth—competences that managers should possess to certain standards. It should not be difficult to see that being sent on an interpersonal skills course, if we adhere to the competence model, therefore implies that you are deficient in them or that there really are identifiable interpersonal skills that managers should have and that they can be acquired through formal training.

The skills analysis model places the trainer in the position of expert. The trainer, implicitly, knows what the required skills are, how they can be assessed and how they can be developed in the learner. Again this system works extremely well in highly procedural and technical areas. My own experience of being trained within the engineering industry was almost totally of this sort, and it worked. I developed skills and competences from the undoubted experts who taught me. Indeed, their obvious expertise was a positive motivating factor in my learning.

In areas such as management and trainer development, however, the model does not apply so readily. It is very difficult to identify core competences that are absolutely essential to being a successful manager or trainer. There is no difficulty in labelling them, at least in theory, but actually articulating clearly what they are and being able to assess and develop them are very different matters indeed.

Learner-centred training

At the opposite end of the spectrum from the trainer as expert pole, there is the trainer as 'facilitator' view. In this model, the trainer is essentially a catalyst for learning, primarily a resource to be used and consulted as learners see fit.

The facilitator tends to refrain from imposing direction or structure on the learners, but may act as a guide or sounding board if requested to do so. In its more extreme forms, such as 'T' groups or encounter groups, the facilitator may play no functional role whatsoever. The movement towards a learner-centred, facilitative, approach to training has been quite considerable over the past 15 years or so and it attracts a certain amount of missionary zeal in its disciples.

In principle it is an admirably egalitarian ideal and with motivated learners who can clearly identify their needs (rather than their wants, which is what they commonly identify), organize their environment and relate effectively as a goal-oriented group, the approach can produce excellent results. This, however, is far from being a certainty. Although the role of the facilitator is, in theory, a marginal one, in practice it is the facilitator's ability that is probably the most significant factor in achieving real learning.

The approach is based on a number of assumptions that, at surface level seem to be common sense. The major assumption is that:

- people learn best when they choose what to learn and how to learn it.

This statement is, of course, true or at least its opposite—'people learn best when they are forced to learn what we tell them and learn it our way'—is patently *not* true. People *do* learn best when they choose what to learn—that is, when they learn things that interest them and which they find personally satisfying and when the learning environment is in harmony with their own particular learning preference or style. The major danger of adopting this approach in the sphere of training, however, is that learning—any learning—may take precendence over *required* learning.

Training is a functional activity, it has a clear purpose, it is not solely concerned with the efficiency of learning. Training is as concerned with *what* is learned as it is with *how well* it is learned. In other words, *effectiveness* is as important—more important—than efficiency. Learning, *per se*, is not enough.

To be effective, the learning that occurs must facilitate the attainment of organizational goals. I believe that this point is vitally important. Training may be enjoyable, personally fulfilling and rewarding, but if it does not impact on organizational effectiveness, it is a waste of time and money.

In many ways the move toward a learner-centred, facilitative approach to training can be considered as a reaction to the predominantly trainer-centred approaches prevalent 15 to 20 years ago. My own view is that, in many cases, the pendulum has swung too far. Many trainers, it seems to me, have come to see their role as approaching that of individual or group therapist. Although there are undoubtedly similarities between therapy, counselling and training, there are also very significant differences. I believe that these differences have often become blurred and the effectiveness of training has consequently been impaired in many cases.

Training is not therapy or counselling: these are essentially open-ended processes; training is not an open-ended process, but is specifically geared to role requirements in organizational settings. Training is not about personal growth or group harmony, *training is about the process of making organizations more effective in meeting the challenge of change and increasing competition.* This is the bottom line.

I accept that this can, and often does, include such things as personal growth and group harmony but only when they are directly linked to organizational effectiveness. An individual may feel personally fulfilled by a period of training yet remain functionally incompetent in their job. Training groups may evolve strong bonds and a set of shared values, but these may not be appropriate to organizational development and survival.

I firmly believe that the general euphoria surrounding the move towards learner-centred approaches to training has resulted in an overly myopic focus on the individual learner and a subsequent total disregard of the individual's role and responsibilities within the organization.

Quality—the customer is king?

We have already noted that the central emphasis of quality is the customer and it is the customer who defines what quality is.

This maxim poses certain difficulties in the training business. For one thing, our customers often have an extremely vague, misguided or even a totally inappropriate idea of what is really required. Customers often seek a training solution to a problem that actually stems from ineffective recruitment procedures, badly designed systems or, as often occurs, they fail to identify where the real training needs lie. This withstanding, our customers are usually very clear as to the general improvements they would like to see, the specific problems they wish to overcome and the direction in which they wish things to move.

How these customer requirements are best met will vary with specific instances. In some cases (the easy ones) the customer accurately identifies real training needs and selects an appropriate training solution. In other cases (the difficult ones) the customer may fail to appreciate the true causes of problems and select an inappropriate training solution or seek such a solution when none in fact exists. In these cases the training professional has the often arduous task of helping the customer re-frame the way in which he or she views the problems at hand in order that an effective training solution (if in fact this is appropriate) may be utilized.

Who is the customer of training?

This is an important question. The answer we are inclined to give will influence the way in which we approach the training and development function. If quality is directly related to the satisfaction of customer requirements, then an error in accurately identifying who exactly our customer is will inevitably lead us along the path to ruin. Alongside its importance, it is often an extremely complex question. Let us for example consider asking it in relation to compulsory education. Who is the customer of compulsory education?

Is education there to maximize the natural potential and specific inclinations of each individual child according to his or her personal wishes? What if we find that the overwhelming majority of children wish to become artists, poets and musicians or indeed choose (as would any average five-year-old) not to be educated at all?

Should the efforts of education be directed primarily at providing a technically skilled and educated work-force capable of building and strengthening the economy of the country? If we go headlong down this road, what do we all do when we finish work, watch films about the machining of sprockets and listen to songs about double entry bookkeeping?

Is the purpose of education to produce citizens who abide by the conventions of society and conform to its laws? The question here is, who decides what the laws and conventions are to be and who would speak out and challenge them if they were unjust?

The problems inherent in providing a conclusive answer to the question of who is the customer of education is a reflection of the fact that there is not and cannot be a single customer.

There are, in fact, an almost limitless array of possible customers with their own particular needs and requirements. An education system capable of providing a quality service to each would require rather more substantial resourcing than that which exists at present.

Compulsory education will ultimately provide a quality service only to those whose aims and aspirations are compatible with those who have the power to influence the allocation of resources. If a child is passionately interested in following a career in computer-aided design and manufacture he or she will find that there are many more opportunities of obtaining a quality service than if they were equally passionate about Etruscan art.

Training—the two-customer approach

What of training—is the road any easier here? Personally I believe it is. However it is not as simple an analysis as is commonly applied. First, I would wish to repeat that I believe training to be, above all, a functional activity. It has a clear purpose: to develop the effectiveness of organizations by developing the effectiveness of people who operate within a particular context. This, I believe, is where training differs radically from education (if you do not agree, reflect on your feelings concerning the relative merits of sex education and sex training for our children). This is an important point and it leads to the conclusion that there are two major customers of training. First, the people we are attempting to train are clearly our customers: they will have needs and we will have the responsibility of meeting those needs. We can refer to this group as Customer 1.

These needs cannot be considered in isolation from the needs of our second group of customers, who are not present at the training event, these are the people who are affected by Customer 1 in the situation in which they must be functional.

This idea may be clarified by examining the traditional and emerging models of organizational functions.

Traditional model of supplier–customer relationships

In the traditional model of organizations, suppliers appear at the beginning of the manufacturing or service process and customers at the end. The situation may be represented as shown in Figure 7.1.

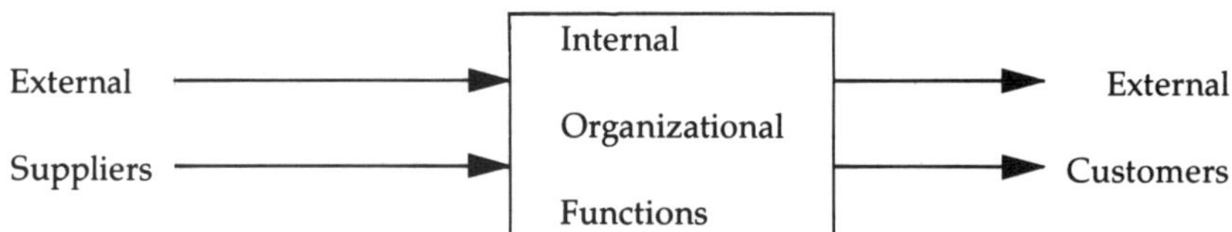

Figure 7.1 The traditional model of supplier–customer relationships in organizations

In this model, the concept of suppliers and customers is essentially one of being external to the functions of the organization. That is, the design, costing and manufacture of products and services. Contact with suppliers and customers is limited to such areas as purchasing, sales, reception and 'front-line' staff.

The quality model of supplier–customer relationships

In the quality model, the concept of supplier and customer is extended to include 'internal' manufacturing and service functions as well. This can be represented as shown in Figure 7.2.

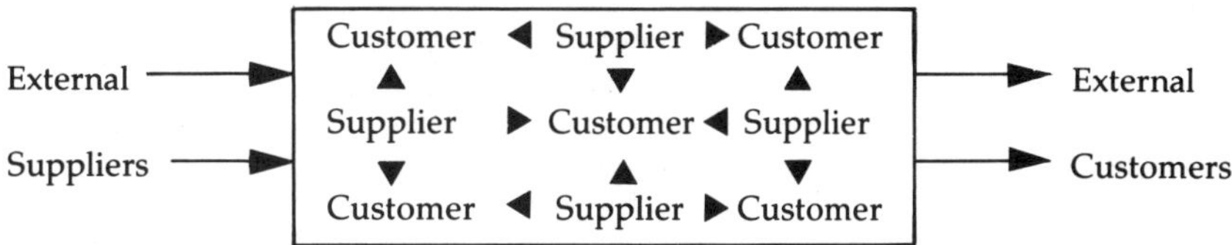

Figure 7.2 *The quality model of supplier–customer relationships in organizations*

In this model each person within the organization acts as a supplier to someone else, that is each person's effectiveness will directly impact on the effectiveness of someone else within the organization.

As the quality of external suppliers directly affects the quality of goods delivered to external customers, so the quality of internal suppliers will affect the quality of services provided to internal customers and, of course, this will also ultimately impact on external customers.

An internal customer may be defined as an individual whose effectiveness is directly influenced by the effectiveness of other(s) within the organization. Thus, an assembly worker's effectiveness will be directly influenced by the quality of work of the machinist who produces the parts to be assembled. The machinist's effectiveness will, in turn, be influenced by the quality of raw materials purchased by the purchasing department and so on.

Within any organization, each person has fundamentally the same job responsibility: to satisfy the requirements of internal customers in terms of the attainment of organizational goals (that is, the ultimate satisfaction of the external customer). In other words everyone's job is to minimize the difficulties presented to those who are directly influenced by their actions. The job of the machinist is to minimize problems related to the assembly of the parts he or she produces. The job of the purchasing officer is to minimize the difficulties of machining parts to be assembled. The job of the purchasing manager is to minimize the chances that inferior materials may be purchased and so on.

When we view job responsibilities in this way, we are making a significant move away from the traditional, rigid, specification-bound view of the past (and, indeed, much of the present) towards the emerging, quality-driven perspective. To consider the machinist as an example. Traditionally, the job of the machinist is to produce parts that conform to drawing specifications. What happens to them after that is somebody else's responsibility. In the emerging view, the machinist enters into dialogue with internal customers and suppliers in an attempt to identify possible improvements in terms of more economic assembly or machining while maintaining functional specifications.

It is well to remember, however, that the relationship between *internal* customers and suppliers does not usually mirror that which exists between *external* customers and suppliers. In the vast majority of instances, external customers have the ultimate choice in terms of the suppliers with which they enter into business.

If I want to go out for a meal, for instance, I have total control over the choice of who will supply me with that meal. As far as quality is concerned I, the customer, have all the votes. The situation is somewhat different in the internal customer–supplier situation, however.

As an internal customer, my effectiveness will be influenced by the quality of my internal suppliers. In the vast majority of instances I will have *no* choice over the selection of these suppliers—assembly workers are not usually involved in the selection of machinists and in the overwhelming majority of instances, subordinates have no say in the selection of their bosses (the Body Shop organization is a rare exception to this dictum). Therefore, although I am a *customer* of these suppliers, my actual ability to influence their effectiveness is, in the overwhelming majority of instances, practically nil. Internal customers therefore are, to a greater or lesser extent (usually greater), 'captive customers' (in the same way that we are 'customers' of the Inland Revenue or British Gas). In the overwhelming majority of cases, the only way I can as an internal customer effectively 'take my custom elsewhere' is to leave the organization and work for a different set of internal suppliers who are better equipped to meet my various needs.

The power in internal customer–supplier relationships is predominantly biased in favour of the supplier. In the case of subordinate–boss relationships, this power bias is institutionalized within the structure and power framework of the organization. In 'horizontal' (theoretically equal) customer–supplier relationships, this power is usually enshrined in the 'you don't fully appreciate the finer complexities of the manufacturing/design/personnel/R&D/finance process' approach to internal customer suggestions for improvements.

The majority of internal relationships are therefore supplier-led and the internal customer usually has little, if any, 'clout' as far as improvements go.

It should be clear from this working definition that the only person in an organization who is, in practical terms, not a captive customer of someone else, will be the person at the very top, the person with ultimate authority. It should also be clear that the effectiveness of the people at the bottom of the traditional organizational hierarchy will be directly influenced by the effectiveness of all those above them—from the chairman down to the person's immediate line supervisor. In order to improve overall organizational effectiveness, therefore, it is necessary to improve the effectiveness of internal supplier–customer networks, with the ultimate emphasis being placed on the improvement of internal suppliers. Internal customers, of course, have a potentially critical role to play in effecting this improvement, but only if their internal suppliers are prepared to enter into a dialogue with them.

Training and supplier–customer relationships

The function of training, therefore, is to facilitate this process of improving the effectiveness of internal supplier–customer networks and the ultimate criterion by which training must be judged is its impact on the internal customer.

That is, training is successful when the effectiveness of an individual's internal customers is enhanced.

Training aimed at top management must be assessed primarily through its impact on the *internal customers* of top management. In theory this will include everyone lower down the organization. In practice, it is middle management that has most direct personal and organizational contact with higher management and it is at this level that the effectiveness of such training may be profitably assessed, and so on throughout the organization.

When we get to the level of training first-line employees, then the criterion for success moves out of the organization to the external customer, who is of course the final arbiter of the organization's whole training endeavour.

It is clear from this analysis that we cannot improve the effectiveness of suppliers by training customers, we will not improve a football manager by training the team—in fact, we may actually produce the opposite result. An improvement in the effectiveness of first-line employees (say in terms of dealing with complaints or machining difficult materials) may, in the long term, prove disastrous in that the root causes of problems are not rectified (that is, actually improving the service or buying in better quality materials) and a competitor ultimately beats us on efficiency or costs.

Training, therefore, must be primarily, though not exclusively, directed at the improvement of internal suppliers and we must not forget that the individuals who ultimately decide whether training has been successful—the internal customers—are usually not on the course with us.

It is important to remember that in training there are always these two customers whose needs we are aiming to satisfy. It is very difficult to ignore the needs of participants, but it is very easy to forget that what happens on a training course is of minimal importance in relation to what happens (or does not happen) back on the farm.

What are our customers' requirements?

Having identified who our customers are, the next step is to clarify their requirements. This process involves analysis at a number of levels—some of these being possible to generalize from and others being specific to particular individuals and contexts.

Customer 1

Let us begin with an analysis of the requirements of Customer 1—the course participants. This process can be considered as operating at three different levels:

- in terms of ethics
- in terms of content and delivery
- in terms of perceived needs.

Ethics

It is the right of all participants to be treated in a way that is not personally demeaning, excessively stressful or in contradiction to their moral or ethical convictions. To this end, course participants should not be made to appear stupid or be coerced into actions they may later regret. I have personally witnessed occasions when forceful trainers have pushed course participants into situations where they have publicly revealed personal information that has subsequently caused them considerable anguish. The more esoteric encounter training proponents are particularly guilty of such actions.

Much constructive learning can be achieved through the use of surprise elements, particularly in terms of experiential exercises, but we must not forget that as trainers we have a responsibility in terms of the nature and degree of manipulation we enter into. There is a line between constructive manipulation and the destructive variety, just as there is between constructive and destructive criticism.

We must also be aware of the fact that we can become desensitized to the threatening aspects of many training experiences. I have noticed over the years that a significant minority of people are terrified by the possibility of having to engage in some form of exercise that will involve video feedback. This affects not only those people who are in occupations where the use of video feedback is unusual or would be of dubious benefit, but includes trainers, teachers, interviewers and personnel staff. All of these occupations have a high 'performance' component attached to their professional responsibilities and, in theory, individuals stand to gain much from this form of feedback. Yet the colour often drains from their faces when the dreaded topic is mentioned.

Oversights and erroneous assumptions are also easy to make. I once used an exercise as part of a negotiating skills course that required course participants to role play opposing teams of lawyers involved in the negotiation of a settlement following the instigation of divorce proceedings by one partner in a marriage. The exercise was well constructed and had many valuable learning opportunities, but what I had not counted on was the fact that one of the course members was acutally in the process of a very painful divorce and obviously found the exercise distressing.

What we must achieve in terms of training exercises is a working balance between 'real life' scenarios that are possibly threatening and artificial constructions that bear little or no relevance to real problems and are, consequently, of minimum value as far as development is concerned.

There is no sure fire way of determining precisely where this balance lies as it is different for different individuals and groups. One of the key skills of the effective trainer is the ability to make such judgements accurately and to manage learning situations in such a way as to highlight the benefits of engaging in exercises that will possibly involve some level of anxiety.

Very early on in my career I spent a short time teaching in a secondary school. Being (then) keen and eager to learn the tricks of the trade, I asked a veteran teacher (who was extremely popular and effective), whether he could give me any tips as to the style of teaching I should employ and the things I should and should not do. His view was that there is no correct style of teaching or any immutable list of dos and don'ts (apart, that is, from legal requirements), but that everything the teacher does will be interpreted by the students in terms of its perceived intentions. His view was that once students are convinced that you have their interests, development and welfare at heart, then all that you ask them to do, even when it is uncomfortable, will be seen as worth while in the long term. I think that this applies equally to the training situation.

Content and delivery

In theory, every person who undertakes a period of training does so with the hope and intention that some useful learning will take place. In reality I believe that many people have come to lower their expectations of what they are actually likely to gain. This is particularly true of the less procedural types of training, such as management, trainer and supervisor development. The onus for this growing cynicism rests with the training profession.

There have been far too many training events and training courses run by ineffective trainers with little or no experience of the realities of the actual work situations in which their course participants have to function. Theories of motivation, learning and human psychology are quoted blindly by trainers who often possess a depth of understanding that extends only as far as an explanation of the slide that fills up an hour of the course. Too often, suggestions are made that are wildly unrealistic and impractical. The headlong rush into the facilitative approach has often culminated in levels of talk, group discussion and discussion of group discussion that make many a philosophical treatise look like a good, relaxing read. I honestly believe that after a day or so of such endeavours no one really remembers what the point being discussed actually was, let alone whether or not some conclusion was reached about it.

Over the past seven years or so I have canvassed the opinions of a large number of course participants as to their ideal expectations of a period of training in terms of actual outcomes. Some of the common responses are:

- to learn how to do my job better
- to learn something that will make my job easier

- to feel more positive about myself and my abilities
- to develop my potential and my promotion/job prospects
- to learn from an expert
- to find out how other people/other organizations tackle the problem I face
- to find out how to solve the big problems I have.

In other words, many people come to a training event in search of answers to the practical problems they face in their work situations. They do not want to hear about obscure psychological theories and lengthy reflective discussion; they want to know what to do on Monday. What they require, therefore, are learning opportunities that are:

- relevant to their work situations
- understandable and capable of being translated into practical action
- supported by evidence of their validity (for example, 'this is what they do at IBM')
- give them feelings of enthusiasm and competence to carry out their responsibilities.

I strongly believe that training should be a highly motivating experience and that, on completion of training, people should be inspired and committed to trying out new ideas and approaches. To this end, effective training should be:

- relevant
- practical
- inspirational
- dynamic
- informative
- solution-centred.

The technique of matched pairs analysis can be usefully applied to the training situation to find out what factors will lead to effective training.

The example given below is taken from an analysis of responses concerning the effectiveness of group-based training. I have used this procedure with approximately 200 course participants involved in trainer, supervisor and management development programmes over the past two years. To be of maximum value, that is to obtain the most useful customer information, the process must be truly customer driven.

The first step, therefore, is to ask course participants to brainstorm a list of factors that, in their opinion, have a direct impact on the effectiveness of a group training event. This commonly results in a list of some 15 to 20 variables that is then reduced, by consensus, to 10. Occasionally separate groups produce identical lists, but there are usually some differences. However, certain factors appear consistently as being important to the success or failure of training. A typical selection is itemized below (the first six factors appear on the majority of lists).

Key factors influencing the effectiveness of group—based training:

- dynamics of the group/group members

- case studies/exercises
- trainer style
- quality and number of handouts
- trainer expertise
- enjoyability
- surroundings/facilities
- travelling distance
- videos
- books/related materials available.

When these variables are incorporated into the matched pairs grid and the analysis undertaken, results are highly consistent between groups. A typical response grid is given in Figure 7.3.

	Number and quality of handouts	*Trainer's expertise*	*Videos*	*Surroundings*	*Travel distance*	*Trainer's style*	*Group members*	*Books available*	*Case studies*	*Enjoyability*	*Score*	*Rank*
Number and quality of handouts		3	5	6	6	6	4	6	5	6	47	3
Trainer's expertise	7		8	8	8	6	8	8	8	7	68	1
Videos	5	2		6	5	4	4	6	6	5	43	6
Surroundings	4	2	4		6	4	4	4	4	4	36	9
Travel distance	4	2	5	4		3	4	4	4	4	34	10
Trainer's style	4	4	6	6	7		7	7	7	6	54	2
Group members	6	2	6	6	6	3		6	5	6	46	4
Books available	4	2	4	6	6	3	4		5	4	38	8
Case studies	5	2	4	6	6	3	5	5		3	39	7
Enjoyability	4	3	5	6	6	4	4	6	7		45	5

Figure 7.3 *Matched pairs analysis—factors in effective training groups*

In the majority of instances, trainer expertise is perceived as being the most important variable influencing the success of a training event. This is often followed by trainer style and enjoyability. Surroundings, travelling distance and, for some reason, videos frequently occupy the bottom rankings.

This is only an initial analysis. We need to know in more specific terms what our customers actually *mean* by such things as trainer expertise, trainer style and so on. The matched pairs grid can again be used for this purpose or a simple brainstorming or initial prioritizing exercise can be carried out. In terms of trainer expertise, when asked to expand on this point, participants commonly come up with variations on the following themes:

- trainers should have a wide range of experience in their particular field
- trainers should not be merely 'course presenters'
- trainers should be able to back up their assertions with facts and figures or reputable research findings
- trainers should have something new to offer, new ideas and new ways of approaching problems and not just rely on the experience and knowledge present within the group
- trainers must have credibility.

On the question of trainer style, the following points are commonly regarded as being important:

- the trainer should be an excellent communicator, that is, ideas and concepts should be explained clearly and in a way that everyone can understand
- the trainer should be able to pace the delivery of the course at the right level
- the trainer should have a sense of humour
- the trainer should be a motivator and be obviously committed to the ideas presented
- the trainer should be interesting
- the trainer should not be sexist or racist
- the trainer should not be egotistical.

'Enjoyability' seems to mean an experience where participants feel they have gained valuable skills and knowledge, have not been excessively threatened or bored, have felt relaxed and able to communicate their opinions, needs and fears.

Customers do not complain often enough, or, at least, they do not complain to the people they *ought* to complain to. This is an unfortunate fact.

The American Consumer Affairs Department estimates that for every customer who complains to an airline, there are up to 25 dissatisfied customers who do not complain. They register their discontent in a number of alternative ways, such as not using the airline again themselves or by telling others not to.

As we have noted already, this problem is particularly difficult in regard to training. It is disturbing to realize that there seems to be a substantial imbalance between the official records of customer comments regarding satisfaction with training and the levels of discontent that people are prepared to admit to in private. End-of-course evaluations are generally positive or very positive and yet we have continuing difficulty in persuading potential customers that training is worth investing money in. There are a number of possible reasons for this. The most obvious is that people do not complete training evaluations honestly. This is a real problem. If participants find it difficult to express dissatisfaction through the channels that exist at present, we must create more effective ones.

It seems from my own limited research that one way of improving things is to have evaluations conducted by someone not connected with the delivery of training or, better still, independent of the delivery organization as a whole. This principle is adopted by the opinion poll industry who take an independent stance in terms of the opinions being researched. When customers are prepared to give honest, critical feedback, what is it that they say? Some common gripes are listed below:

- courses are too long
- large chunks of training content are irrelevant
- some trainers are much more effective than others (this can be particularly problematic in co-tutored courses)
- two weeks later you cannot remember what it was about
- some trainers are extremely tedious
- some trainers are more like entertainers than teachers
- too much discussion, jargon and waffle
- totally impractical ideas
- I did not learn anything new
- 80 per cent of it was a waste of time
- some exercises and role play situations are ridiculous.

Such comments as these rarely appear on the official evaluations of training, yet they have surfaced time and time again during informal research into customer perceptions of training experiences. We cannot afford to ignore them.

Perceived needs

One of the major difficulties we face in the training profession concerns the accurate identification of training *needs* as opposed to training *wants*.

I often feel that, in many ways, we often function not dissimilarly from the old Wild West medicine shows: we purport to have a package of 'cures' for various 'ailments' and we peddle these to our prospective clientele. They, in turn, are charged with the responsibility of identifying the particular illness they suffer from and selecting the appropriate cure. Of course when both parties get it right, or at least appear to get it right, everyone is happy.

This arrangement obviously has severe limitations. To take the medicinal analogy further, much of what was on offer in the old West apparently included some measure of anaesthetic that occasionally relieved the symptoms of whatever complaint the person suffered from and this was registered as a success. We now recognize, of course, that what was *really* required was an effective diagnosis of the actual nature of the ailment, followed by appropriate treatment. I believe that this applies directly to training.

If we are to gain widespread commitment to training and development, we must ensure that the training services we provide can, in fact, influence organizations in a positive way. A key requirement, therefore, is that we train the *right* people in the *right* way. I cannot, in all honesty, see how this requirement can be met by the standard 'everybody's welcome' type of training course, particularly in such crucial areas as management and supervisory development. All that such courses can really hope to achieve is an understanding of the basic responsibilities of the role, that is the responsibilities common to *all* management positions. These would include such functions as financial control, planning, legal obligations and so on—the basic *procedural* aspects of the job. When, however, we venture into areas such as leadership, interpersonal skills, motivation and human resource management, we are in an altogether different situation. Effectiveness in these essentially *process* functions cannot be considered in isolation from the organizational context, that is the particular organizational culture, in which managers must manage.

In an excellent comparative study of two large Japanese and American organizations, Matsushita and ITT. (*The Art of Japanese Management*, by Pascale and Athos), the authors show that management effectiveness is inextricably linked to organizational culture. It is difficult to see how a single training course could be beneficial to managers from both Harold Geneen's ITT *and* the electrical giant headed by Konosuke Matsushita. The basic assumptions, methods of communication, attitudes to achievement and to errors, overt and covert information systems and so on are fundamentally different in each organization. To be effective in each context involves entirely different approaches to the responsibilities of management and, consequently, entirely different attitudes, concepts and skills. It is highly unlikely that an effective manager from either organization could successfully transfer to the other. What would be required in such a hypothetical case is that each manager adopt a new set of basic assumptions and principles. (Whether or not such individual change is feasible, is open to debate.)

Studies such as those comparing Matsushita and ITT are, of course, intended to be dramatic, but they do allow us to see that there are obvious pragmatic limitations to many of the assumptions that underpin 'generalizable' management training.

Trainers are too often convinced that certain assumptions are immutable facts. The theories of Maslow, McGregor and Hertzberg have much to offer us in our understanding of motivational factors at work, but they are not universal truths. Any experienced manager will confirm that, in reality, there are quite a few people in this world who are, for varying reasons, well and truly entrenched in the Theory X slot. If we ignore such facts of experience we will ultimately lose credibility with our customers and be seen as living in an academic dream world.

Alongside the difficulties associated with variations in organizational cultures, we must also tackle the problems that arise as a consequence of inadequate selection procedures for training. All too frequently individuals are sent on training courses without any effective analysis of needs and options being carried out.

Self-selection of training often fares little better. My own experiences in the areas of therapy and counselling have led me to the conclusion that individuals themselves are in no specially privileged position when it comes to accurately identifying what it is that they need in order to feel happier or to improve some aspect of their personal or professional lives. They often do, however, know what they *think* they need, that is, they know what they *want*. This situation occurs in the training context time and time again.

People are often sent on training programmes that are too basic, too advanced, largely irrelevant and so on, and it is the individuals themselves who often select the training that does not address their real weaknesses or is geared to an area of competence in which they already function effectively in terms of organizational requirements, but may have some personal interest in. Areas of *actual* weakness, that is, those aspects of performance that could be significantly improved by training, are frequently dismissed or are perhaps not perceived as weaknesses at all. There is a matrix of possibilities in terms of needs and wants that can be represented as shown in Figure 7.4.

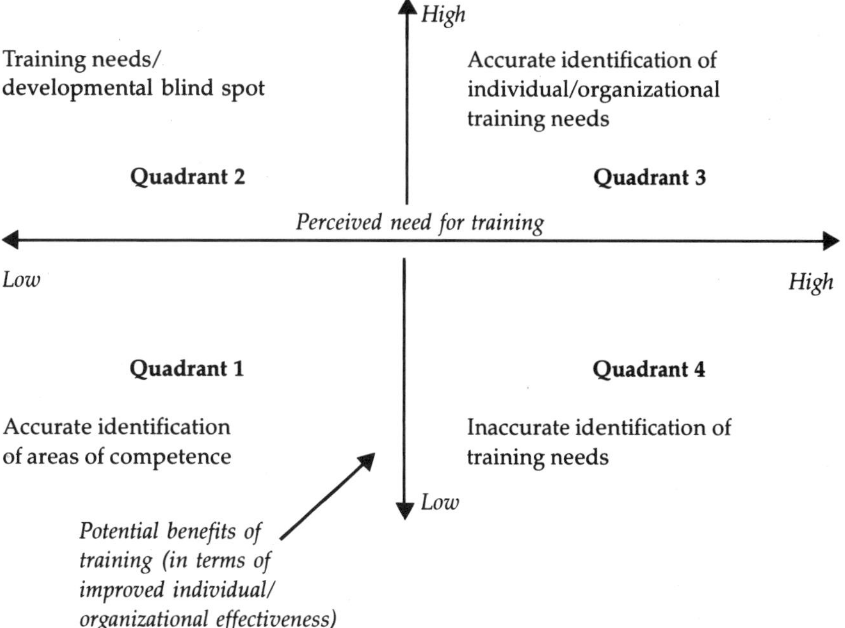

Figure 7.4 *A matrix of the possible relationships between perceived training needs and actual training needs*

The vertical axis represents the potential *functional* benefits of undertaking training in the particular area(s) identified. It is important to note that we are not talking here about potential benefits in relation to the efficiency of training, but with the accuracy of the needs identification process.

Quadrant 1 represents an accurate assessment of individual/organizational competences. The perceived need for training is low and the potential benefits are also low. Quadrant 2 poses a difficult problem at the organizational *and* individual level. We have already discussed the fact that organizations must be helped to see that there is a direct cost attached to *not* training, quantifiable in the short term and usually fatal in the long term. Organizations will only come to accept this view when they see the training process as being an integrated organization-wide activity rather than an isolated interventionist strategy for dealing with short-term difficulties. In many ways the use of the term 'training' in this broad context is less effective than 'development'.

As the major challenge we face in this context is that of convincing decision makers to invest in training, the way in which we present our message is extremely important. I have found that to ask managers the question 'what do you feel will be the likely consequences of not developing your organization?' to be more effective than getting bogged down in general discussions about training and training effectiveness.

At the personal level, Quadrant 2 problems are related to the individual's ability to accurately perceive internal strengths and weaknesses. A training need—let us call it an area of relative incompetence—may be conscious or unconscious. Particular managers, for example, may be aware that they lack the skills and knowledge necessary to make full use of emerging technology in their particular field of operations. They may, however, be totally unaware of the fact that they frequently project an air of superiority and arrogance when dealing with subordinates and equals and that this directly influences cooperation and ultimate effectiveness.

Learning may be a conscious or unconscious process. The great majority of early learning is unconscious and, in many ways, inevitable. Original accents, for example, are learned unconsciously. As we develop, conscious learning takes on an increasingly significant role, although unconscious learning still occurs. Conscious learning is influenced by factors such as levels of intrinsic motivation (that is, the natural interest in the subject being learned), extrinsic motivation (the perceived benefits of learning) and the environment in which the learning takes place.

One of the major difficulties posed by Quadrant 2 is that the *need* to learn is not perceived by the individual concerned. The first step in dealing with this situation, therefore, is to bring this learning need into the individual's attention and proceed from there. In the ideal learning situation, the whole process operates as shown in Figure 7.5.

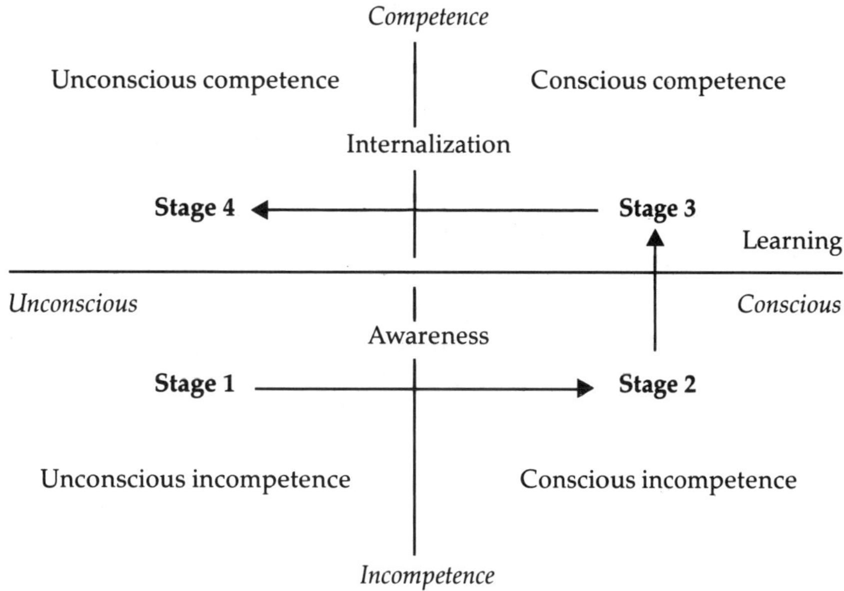

Figure 7.5 *The learning cycle—from unconscious incompetence to unconscious competence*

The transition from Stage 1 to Stage 2 must be facilitated with care. To discover an area of incompetence that may have been hidden for some time can pose a considerable threat to the individual's self-esteem.

Stage 2 represents the 'foundation on which constructive learning can be built and the transition from Stage 2 to Stage 3 represents a successful learning experience.

The transition from Stage 3 to Stage 4 marks the internalization of learning, the point at which learned skills, attitudes and knowledge become an integral and spontaneous component of the individual's normal repertoire of behaviours.

Returning to Figure 7.4 for a moment, Quadrant 3 poses no other problem for the trainer than effectively addressing the training needs that have been correctly identified. This does not mean that all will be plain sailing, but at least we will be sailing in the right direction.

Quadrant 4, again, poses common problems at the level of the organization and the individual. In this situation we are dealing with training *wants* as opposed to genuine training *needs*. An organization may, for example, request training in customer care skills for its front-line staff as a response to increasing levels of customer complaints. However, the training professional may diagnose the problem as being primarily related to bad internal communications and relationships between line management and front-line staff so a customer care programme may actually intensify this problem—poor management staff relationships—

as management would appear to be concluding that the problem rests with front-line staff only.

The problem is essentially a Quadrant 2 problem; an unperceived training need exists. However, there is a perception that *something* needs to be done and this often acts as a springboard to a more accurate perception of the root causes of the difficulties experienced.

At the individual level, Quadrant 4 problems manifest themselves in a number of ways.

- training does not address the individual's real needs
- training is not the appropriate option in terms of the individual's abilities
- training, even if successful, will not impact on functional performance.

A major role of the training professional, therefore, is to help organizations and individuals avoid the problems associated with Quadrants 2 and 4.

Customer 2

In the vast majority of cases, Customer 2—the internal customer—is the real customer of training. Everyone in an organization impacts on the effectiveness of someone else. If they do not, then they are superfluous. Every individual's role in an organization (apart from front-line staff) is to satisfy the requirements of external customers by facilitating the effectiveness of their internal customers.

The analogy with a clockwork mechanism, although not perfect, is useful in clarifying this point. In a mechanical clock, each cog and gear facilitates the operation of another, with the exception of the final cog, which drives the hands of the clock around. We can only improve the clock's performance, that is its accuracy, if we make changes that impact on this final cog. Anything else will be purely cosmetic. If, for example, we remove any number of intermediate cogs and polish them until they glisten, this will not result in a more accurate clock unless there is a knock-on positive effect throughout the system. This also applies within organizations. Training a particular individual or group of individuals will be effective only if it results in knock-on benefits elsewhere, otherwise we are simply 'polishing cogs'.

Effectiveness in any organizational role depends upon the interplay between two major factors:

- individual competence
- external constraints.

Apart from a few notable exceptions, constraints are the result of somebody else's incompetence. For example, the potentially great goal scorer in a football team cannot do his job if the rest of the team cannot or will not give him the ball. Training him to be an even better potential goal scorer will only raise his level of frustration. This type of problem happens a lot in organizations. Training has tended to focus overwhelmingly on developing individual competences without adequate consideration being given to external factors such as the constraints imposed by organizational systems and the limitations of those who directly influence an individual's potential to be effective.

In a way, every person we see before us on a training course is accompanied by two groups of ghosts. The first group is composed of all those people and systems within the organization over which the individual has little or no control that act as a brake to his or her effectiveness. The second group comprises all those people and systems within the organization that he or she affects, or is capable of affecting, for better or worse. The real purpose of training is to help the individual deal effectively with the ghosts. The role of the individual can therefore be represented as shown in Figure 7.6.

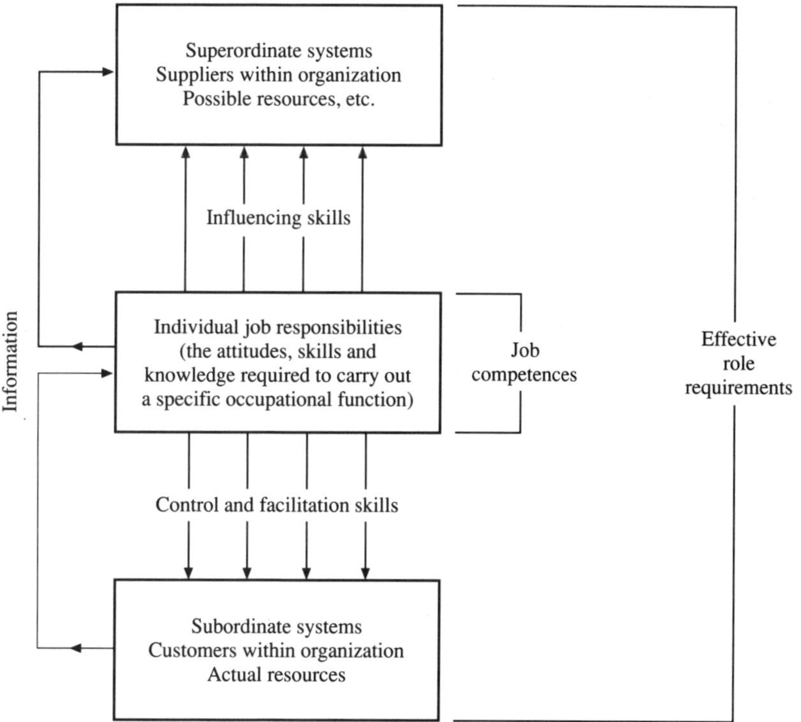

Figure 7.6 *The role of the individual within the organization*

It is clear from Figure 7.6 that the individual's role within the organization is not isolated and static; it is not confined merely to the acquisition and utilization of specific competences. The individual's role is interactive and dynamic. Ideally, it will be geared to development, improvement and change.

Interactions with internal suppliers and superordinate systems can be problematic. To be fruitful, such interactions require tact, diplomacy and influencing skills. Above all else, they require an organizational culture that encourages openness, honesty and a desire to achieve continuous improvement. Such cultures, unfortunately, are very rare.

Interactions with internal customers offer an immense opportunity for possible improvement. The key to development in this area is to help individuals and teams to: *identify those areas of their performance that particularly impact on the effectiveness of their internal customers.*

This is the key task. When we talk about individual competence in a particular occupational area, we are really talking about competence in relation to someone else within the organization who is directly affected by our efforts.

Obviously, therefore, an important route to achieving improved performance is to consult internal customers as to the ways in which we may help them achieve their organizational goals more effectively. This is easier said than done. It means teachers asking students, bosses asking subordinates, doctors asking nursing staff and so on, but we must accept that teachers can and do create barriers to student learning, bosses can and do limit and demotivate subordinates and doctors can and do make nurses' lives more difficult than they need be.

It is important to remember, however, that when we seek such information we are only considering the *interface* between suppliers and customers within organizations. The worker on the assembly line cannot tell the skilled machinist how to be a better machinist. However he or she can help the skilled machinist become a better supplier of machined parts for assembly. This may involve suggestions about batch sizes, priorities and timings or perhaps very minor modifications or particular attention to certain aspects of components that will make assembly more efficient.

Role effectiveness within organizations, therefore, involves more than isolated job competences, it requires an awareness of and an ability to effectively manage the critical interfaces between the functions of internal suppliers and customers.

Training must encompass this broader vision of occupational roles. We must recognize the fact that the individuals, or groups of individuals, that we work with are only a part of a wider network of relationships and functional interdependencies that ultimately define their own, and the organization's, effectiveness.

This perspective is not widely understood or accepted. Training has an immensely important role to play in breaking down the individual and organizational barriers of isolationism and compartmentalization. We can begin this process by ensuring that each person we train, irrespective of their particular function within the organization, is aware of their obligations and responsibilities as internal suppliers and customers.

Effective design

The second phase of the quality cycle, the design phase, is where we construct a comprehensive plan of action to meet the customer requirements we have accurately defined in the first phase.

As we have previously noted, there are a number of possible errors that can be made at this stage. A major difficulty centres on the common tendency for design specifications to wander away from customer requirements in order that life is made easier for the supplier. If we have accurately identified customer requirements in the first phase, however, they must not be compromised. In the words of quality guru Philip Crosby, the standard is 'zero defects'. We must not design defects into our product or service.

I cannot comment on the specific aims and objectives of particular training events—these must be decided by the customer in consultation with the training provider. However, there are underlying principles of good design that apply to all forms of training. These are considered below.

Duration of training

This is directly related to the pace of learning that can be maintained. In general my own research has strongly indicated a preference for learning to be brisk and a dislike of overlong periods of discussion, constant reiteration of points, overexplanation and too many periods of waiting for things to happen.

Primarily, the duration of a training event should be dependent on the time needed to achieve its objectives with learners learning at a reasonable pace. Trainers constantly make assumptions concerning the amount of time it takes for learners to assimilate information, understand concepts and develop skills. In my own opinion many of these assumptions err on the long side. I have very rarely heard anyone complain that the pace of a training event was too fast and people were unable to learn as a direct consequence. People, in my opinion, enjoy a stimulating challenge, enjoy being stretched and achieve a sense of satisfaction when they complete a period of learning that has placed demands on them.

Educational research has shown that there is a direct link between teacher expectations and student attainment. This link has also been detected in research into management effectiveness. Effective managers tend to have higher expectations of their subordinates than less effective managers. It seems that some form of self-fulfilling prophecy is at work, the more we expect the more we get.

I see no reason to believe that this phenomenon does not extend to the field of training. I have seen many training programmes that, to my mind, seem to have been designed as if the client group suffered from some form of learning difficulty and that required excessive amounts of time to be devoted to the discussion of quite basic, uncomplicated ideas.

Perhaps it is time that we raised our expectations of our customers' potential, cut down the waffle, syndicate group discussions and stopped hammering simple ideas into the ground. Who knows, perhaps we, and they, will be pleasantly surprised.

Learning resources

I believe that there is a very real danger (particularly acute in such areas as management development and human relations training) for techniques and approaches to drift inexorably towards the exaggerated and the ridiculous.

Training is a lonely business most of the time and when trainers talk to other trainers, they can come up with some pretty strange ideas if there is nobody around to inject a little reality into the situation. I believe that the main cause of this malaise is the tendency to focus exclusively on the design of course content and lose sight of the link with improved work performance. The course can then become an end in itself. I often have the feeling that certain exercises, games and activities are included for their own sake or because trainers enjoy designing and using them rather than them being included with the enhancement of functional performance clearly in mind.

It is certainly possible to generate valuable insights and develop functional skills through the use of games, role play activities and exercises requiring some form of team participation, but they need to be designed and managed very effectively. Ultimately, the most effective training is that which is carried out in the functional situation, on the job. The more our simulations, games and exercises differ from the realities of the workplace, the greater is the danger that learning will not transfer from one to the other. More importantly, the greater will be the possibility that the credibility of training will be damaged.

I hope that the importance of this point is not lost on the reader. A great deal of damage has been done to the image of training through the use of, frankly, quite idiotic exercises, role playing and games. I had originally intended to catalogue a range of particularly excessive examples, personally experienced and reported by others, in order to reinforce my point here. However, I have come to the conclusion that, in all probability, little would be achieved by doing this. My own experiences of work in such areas as interpersonal skills training have led me to think that a small minority of course attendees are really seeking some form of personal therapy and that a rather larger minority of trainers in this field see themselves as budding therapists. However, I do feel that some form of example is needed in order to clarify the point I am making. A common problem in designing effective learning materials in such areas as management development is the tendency to overdramatize such things as case studies. I once experienced a classic example of this on a course concerned with the role of counselling in the work-place that was run for a group of mainly women supervisors from a large insurance company.

The trainer had devised several case studies that focused on such topics as alcohol and drug abuse at work and sexual harassment. Course participants were asked if anyone had encountered such problems and one or two people gave quite detailed descriptions of colleagues who had experienced drink-related problems (all however said that these instances had occurred in a previous employment). No one (at least no one admitted to it) had experienced drug-related problems or problems associated with sexual harassment at work. However, despite this, the first case study used involved a scenario where a young female employee confesses to her supervisor that she is taking drugs because of the persistent sexual harassment she experiences from a manager.

The group spent a considerable amount of time dealing with this case study, strongly encouraged by the trainer who drew out in much detail the organizational, moral and legal implications involved and the correct procedures to be followed in such a case.

Towards the end of the day, the trainer had allocated a period for 'any other problems' and duly invited course participants to bring forward any particular difficulties they were experiencing. After some initial hesitation, one supervisor very nervously said that she was experiencing a problem with a member of staff and did not know quite how to approach it. 'What is the problem?', asked the trainer. 'Well', came the reply, 'she has a problem with personal hygiene and I don't know how to tell her.' Two other supervisors then said that they also found it difficult to deal with this problem. The trainer's visible dismay at this revelation had to be seen to be believed.

Trainers are often very creative and imaginative people. However, we must not forget that we are in the business of attempting to help people solve their real problems in their real world. Case studies, exercises and problem scenarios *must* be related to the course participants' actual experiences if they are to be effective.

The customer as supplier

I have already noted elsewhere in this book that quality depends primarily on the effective functioning of supplier–customer networks. This is also true of training. We are in the peculiar position in training of obtaining our supplies from our customers. Organizations provide us with the people we are obliged to train and they are then returned to the organizations from whence they came. This is not a common situation in quality terms. To be effective, therefore, our role involves dialogue with our suppliers in order that we can ensure that they do not put unnecessary obstacles in the way of our providing a quality service.

One major way in which this can be achieved is to exert some influence on the composition of the groups we are going to train. This is too often left solely to the discretion of the organization, who commonly make such choices purely on the basis of availability and minimization of disruption to operational processes. Of course these are important considerations and they cannot, in the vast majority of instances, be completely ignored. However, decisions concerning group composition can often be beneficially influenced when decision makers understand the tremendous influence that group makeup has on the effectiveness of training.

If we are to provide a quality training service, we must work with our suppliers at the *design* stage in order that we achieve group compositions that are not excessively heterogeneous in terms of attitude, experience, role responsibility and needs.

Delivering effective training—learning as change

Organizations and organizational practices can be usefully considered in terms of processes and procedures. Training, particularly quality training, is a process of continuous development and change—it is never finished. Within that continuing process of 'change management', various procedures will be employed. Training and development procedures include such diverse activities as training courses of varying duration and depth, coaching sessions, planned work experience, self-directed learning, mentoring, appraisal interviewing, personal counselling and so on.

The majority of my own training and learning experiences over the past ten years or so have been in the fields of management development, trainer training, teacher training and the training of therapists. I have come to see that there are many similarities between what, on the surface, seem to be quite diverse activities. Running a management development programme for a large London Borough, training on trainer development courses, tutoring undergraduate students, lecturing in psychology to student teachers of dance and teaching on a course for prospective therapists—all are, in an important way, concerned with organizational and individual change. Of course the content, style of delivery, aims and objectives of each activity are often very different, but the theme of change, and particularly the effective management of change, occurs repeatedly.

Learning is synonymous with change; failing to learn is failing to change. Individual change can occur in one of three major areas; cognition, emotion or behaviour. Of course each dimension is intimately connected to the other, a change in perception (cognitive change) may lead to a change in behaviour, which results in emotional change. For example, we may change our perceptions of another person, behave towards them in a different way, find that they, in turn, respond differently to us and, as a result of this, our feelings towards them may change. As far as training is concerned, however, practical behavioural change is the sole criterion of effective learning. Unless behaviour changes, nothing has really been learned. If training produces no measurable behaviour change, then what has it achieved? In my opinion, very little, if anything. I have personally attended training courses that have been enjoyable, where I have met interesting people and relaxed, but I could have done that without going on a course.

However, training is not concerned with bringing about just *any* type of change: a successful training experience should change people in some *functionally positive* way. If it does not do this, then, in terms of Customer 2 it has been a waste of time.

We must not forget, however, that change can occur along a spectrum as far as functional performance is concerned. In general terms, the potential change that training can bring about falls into one of three major categories. Change may be:

- **positive** so people are changed in some functionally positive way—they may, for example, make better recruitment decisions, organize

their time more effectively, communicate more effectively or improve their ability to develop staff competences
- **irrelevant** in that nothing happens in relation to functional performance
- **negative** so people are changed in some functionally negative way—they may feel inadequate, depressed, angry, demotivated or engage in inappropriate behaviours or introduce ineffective changes.

Obviously, our role in training is to ensure that the majority of outcomes fall within the first category.

We must ask ourselves, therefore, why it is that some training, particularly management and supervisor training, often fails to achieve significant, durable, positive change? There are myriad possible factors at play—personal and organizational. One major reason is that, in the vast majority of instances of management and supervisory training, the decision whether or not to change rests with the individual concerned. Managers and supervisors do not have to take on board the ideas, methods and practices they are exposed to during a period of training—unless, of course, they are mandatory and monitored and, even then, they may only pay visible lip service.

Management and supervisory training deals with many more intangibles than procedural training, such as the training of airline pilots, surgeons, bricklayers, computer programmers and so on. Procedural training (unless it is very poorly designed or delivered) has the advantage of being clearly relevant to improved functional performance: the driving instructor does not have to convince the learner driver that the brake pedal is worth a try if one wants to stop the car. Managers, trainers, supervisors, lecturers and team leaders, on the other hand, are in a different position as regards the training they receive. By and large nothing immediately dramatic will happen to them if they remain as they are.

The element of persuasion of needing to be convinced is dramatically different between various forms of training. Managers must be convinced that a particular course of action is worth implementing, otherwise nothing much will happen. It is this vitally important area—the gaining of commitment—that forms the core of what we will examine in the remainder of the book. In order that we as trainers may facilitate this commitment, we must have a clear understanding of the psychological, social and structural factors that act to enhance or inhibit its development. We must also examine the possible reasons for our sometimes failing to generate the commitment necessary for significant change to occur.

Facilitating constructive change—why training fails

Training is not an infallible process in terms of facilitating constructive change. On some occasions training is ineffective as a solution for organizational problems because training is not what is required. Some problems are best dealt with through structural or procedural changes and some problems are not problems at all, they are facts and should be dealt with as such. In this discussion of training effectiveness, I will assume that training is an appropriate strategy for the resolution of organizational problems or the development of organizational effectiveness. In short, I will assume that real training needs are being addressed.

Some training is more effective than others, one person may attend a training event aimed at developing particular management skills and come away feeling confident, enthusiastic and committed. Another person, attending a different course with the same aim, may come away feeling that it has been largely a waste of time. Training in general is not a homogenous activity as far as outcomes are concerned and there are many contributory reasons for this. Ultimately, though, failure to procedure change (learning) can be considered in terms of four major factors.

- the trainer
- the learning resources and culture
- learner receptiveness
- quantity and pace of information.

If a period of training produces no positive learning, that is, no constructive change occurs, the cause will always be found within or between these four areas. In terms of individual change theory, these factors may be summarized as follows:

- individuals do not change because they do not appreciate that change is required, do not understand the nature of the change required or do not know how to go about initiating the process of change
- individuals do not change because they cannot see the advantages of change, actively disagree with the need to change or feel that change poses an excessive threat
- individuals are receptive to change, but the pace of change is too fast.

Each of these factors needs to be considered if we are to improve our ability to produce constructive change through the medium of training.

The trainer

In Chapter 8 there is an opportunity to complete an inventory of management/trainer style and to examine a theoretical approach to effective training that includes a trainer profile. To that end I will not deal extensively with trainer qualities or skills at this point. However, I do believe that, ultimately, all three change factors outlined above are heavily dependent on the trainer. I believe it is the trainer's responsibility to ensure that people understand that the purpose of training is to produce constructive change, to improve functional performance in a particular context (if this is not its purpose, what is its purpose?), to explain clearly the benefits of change, what the change is about in specific or general terms, depending on the nature of the situation, and to offer strategies and procedures that help that change occur. These and other important points are discussed in some detail in Chapter 8.

Learning resources and the learning culture

The previous remarks concerning the design of learning resources obviously apply here. In general terms, learning resources must be directly relevant to participants' real-life situations. However, well-designed learning resources alone are, unfortunately, no cast-iron guarantee that positive change will occur.

The effectiveness of resources, like individuals, cannot be considered outside of the context or culture in which they are employed. The learning culture generated during a period of training, therefore, has a profound effect on the quality and type of change that will occur. In many ways it is useful to consider a training group as an organization writ small and the trainer as the chief executive and managing director of that organization. The trainer normally has a considerable amount of influence over the particular structure of a training event in terms of authority, responsibility and the general style in which business is conducted. As with the organization writ large, such factors will be extremely important influences on the development of a particular culture.

All organizations are composed of people, material resources and systems of communication and the organization's norms and practices emerge from the interactions between these major elements. However, the vast majority of organizations do not develop a single unified culture. There is a common tendency for a bifurcation to occur that results in the effective creation of two organizations—the *official organization* and the *unofficial organization*.

The official organization, as the name implies, is the surface or public image that an organization presents to the outside world. In terms of organizations writ large, the official organization is composed of the material, human and financial resources it possesses, its policies as regards purpose, aims and objectives, professed attitudes to its staff and customers, procedures of recruitment, selection, discipline and so on. The official organization is that which is described in the annual report.

The unofficial organization, in contrast, is a set of norms and procedures that emerges from the interactions between people who ostensibly operate in the official organization. However, the norms and procedures in each organization are not synonymous. The official organization describes the way things *should* be, the unofficial organization is the way things *really are*.

For example, in the 'official supermarket', the checkout assistant wears a badge that reads 'customers come first'. However, her manner and nonverbal communication may lead us to the conclusion that, in the 'unofficial supermarket', the badge reads 'customers are a pain in the neck'. The dual nature of many organizations is sometimes referred to as the 'organizational iceberg' (see Figure 7.7).

In many organizations, the division between official and unofficial norms and practices is considerable. In terms of TQ concepts, the greater the division between the two, the less likely it is that quality will be achieved. In order that quality may become a reality, the official and unofficial organizations must become practically indistinguishable, particularly in terms of commonly held beliefs concerning the performance standards required of individuals and groups.

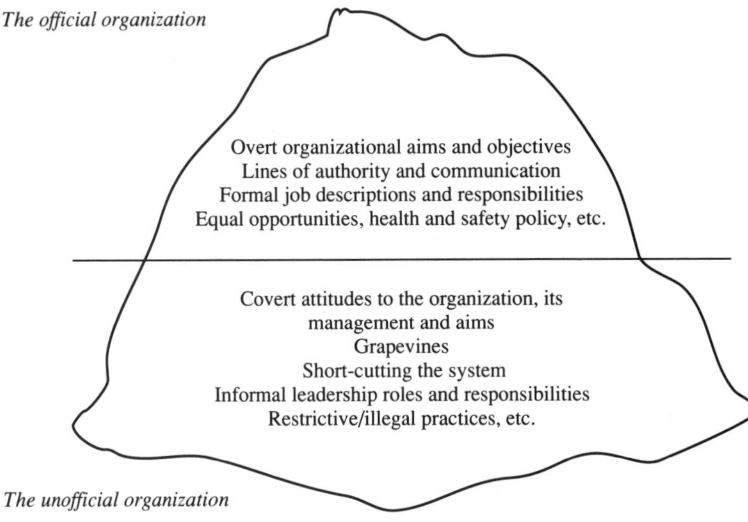

Figure 7.7 *The 'organizational iceberg'*

The phenomenon of the two organizations applies equally well to training and development. As a learner I have experienced situations in which the learning group has developed negative attitudes and values that are not formally expressed to those delivering the learning experience. Not all dissatisfied customers express their feelings through the channels of the official organization. Unfortunately this seems to be far too common a phenomenon as far as training is concerned.

The visual representation of the organizational iceberg can be applied to training as shown in Figure 7.8.

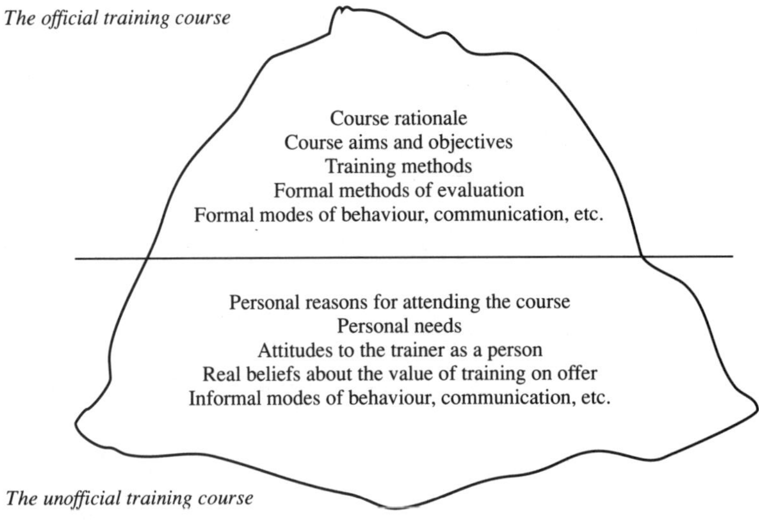

Figure 7.8 *The 'training iceberg'*

In any situation where people are brought together to achieve an aim—an automobile manufacturing plant, a hospital, a restaurant or a training course—there is the possibility that a difference will arise in terms of the aims and values held by those who organize and direct the process and those who are organized and directed: the 'them and us' syndrome.

The vast majority of training courses, especially package courses, are designed and structured in isolation from those who will ultimately form the learning group. There is, therefore, an inevitable element of coercion involved. Decisions concerning the type and location of venue, session content and duration, balance between didactic and interactive learning methods and so on are, in the majority of instances, taken by those who design and deliver the training. These decisions are, of course, made with the facilitation of learning and development clearly in mind, but they are still decisions taken on someone else's behalf. Along with this goes the reality that not all our participants will be willing volunteers. As with the vast majority of similar situations, therefore, people are required to fit into a structure that they have had no opportunity to influence. There may be some space for negotiation in certain areas, but even then the decision that negotiation is possible has been taken by someone else.

These imbalances of power and influence are the seed-bed upon which the 'two cultures' can flourish. Thankfully, the emergence of two cultures is not inevitable and, in Chapter 9 we will consider the major factors that influence whether or not such a phenomenon will arise. First, however we will analyse the major difficulties that need to be managed in relation to the process of training.

The vast majority of trainers recognize that the avoidance of a 'them and us' situation is crucial (*them* being the trainer or trainers and *us* the course participants). This phenomenon can arise in a number of different ways.

First, and I feel that this is the most common division, there is what I term the 'polite syndrome'. Training that is characteristically 'polite' appears, at a surface level, to be no division at all. However, trainer–participant interactions are invariably conducted at the level of the official training course.

Polite training is characterized by 'training course protocol': appropriate trainer–participant behaviours (such as, appropriate dress and etiquette, no overt signs of boredom on either part, etc.), agreement and avoidance of conflict and challenge, everybody 'has a point', nobody ever says anything stupid and everybody is, to a certain extent, kept happy. Polite training evaluations are, characteristically, bland to fair.

The *real* evaluations are reserved for discussion at the unofficial training course level and, if my own limited research findings are not unusual, often differ very considerably indeed. These unofficial evaluations are seldom scathing, they more often reflect a general apathy about what can be expected from many forms of training. The same comments emerge time and time again: 'I learned something from the others on the course', 'Some bits were OK', 'Most of it does not really apply to me', 'It is all right in theory', and so on.

The attainment of quality demands that we find out in detail what our customers *really* think of our services and tackle the problems we discover head on. We must not quash the uneasy feeling that such comments as those above are probably more common than we would wish to believe and we must not, at any cost, consider them to be acceptable, inevitable and unavoidable. They are not. They are, however, problems, not facts, and problems have solutions.

Polite training is a very understandable phenomenon, trainers commonly try to minimize confrontation in order that a more dangerous them and us division is avoided. The reasons for this tendency are both structural and personal.

At the structural level, internal trainers are often in the position of training people who have equal or superior organizational status to themselves and external consultants are playing with their mortgage repayments if they alienate the client group.

At a personal level, training is one of those unfortunate few occupations in which one receives a performance appraisal on almost a daily basis. Whatever we say publicly concerning our desire for honest constructive criticism, it usually hurts when we get it and, like most normal human beings, trainers will attempt to avoid painful experiences.

I believe that the polite syndrome is, in the long term, a dangerous threat to effective training. It is dangerous because it is insidious. It eats away at the true purpose of training and renders it a chummy process based on endless discussion and waffle, compromise at any cost, a reluctance to make assertions and defend them and it tends to push trainers into a role similar to that of the holiday camp redcoat. Polite training is, essentially, an unverbalized contract between trainer and course participants that says 'do not criticize me and I will not criticize you'.

At the other end of the pole we have the antagonistic them and us split that every trainer dreads: the overt declaration of war. I have personally not witnessed this on many occasions, but have heard some terrible stories.

It usually results from the trainer's inability to offer appropriate learning opportunities to an individual or group and/or effectively manage stress and anxiety levels. Once started, such a division is extremely difficult to contain.

This problem commonly arises from such things as personal confrontation between the trainer and a course member that results in a closing of ranks, emphatic trainer assertions which contradict course members' experiences or knowledge, arrogant behaviour and so on. Such divisions invariably result in a general discrediting process by the group of the trainer.

Ideally, the training culture that develops will be an 'us' culture, but not an us culture at any cost. I was recently a guest on a management development residential course that definitely had an us culture in operation. However, after a very long evening session with the group it became obvious that the common goals that united this culture concerned aspects other than management development. This form of training, which a colleague once described as 'Entertraining', often generates quite enthusiastic evaluations.

Quality training is training that fully meets its objectives, it is not simply a process by which people are exposed to new ideas during a pleasant few days away from the pressures of work. Quality training above all else is concerned with generating real commitment to change and development; it is a process of enabling and enthusing.

The existence of an appropriate learning culture is a critical factor in achieving these outcomes. The development of such a culture will be influenced greatly by the management style of those who have, or are perceived to have, power and authority. Whether we like it or not (and I often get the feeling that many of us do not like it), the majority of our course participants want us to lead them in some particular direction and to learn something from us as individuals. I firmly believe that this is our fundamental responsibility. *How* we lead and how we *enable* learning to occur will depend on us and it can be done badly or it can be done well. The trainer is a manager of learning and therefore a manager of change. Training encompasses the fundamental challenges of management. The management role of the trainer involves leadership, negotiation, communication and the ability to create a culture in which commitment becomes a reality. This, I believe, is the most crucial challenge of all.

Learner receptiveness to change

In the preceding section we examined some of the structural and social reasons why training may not achieve real change and saw that the development of group consensus is an extremely powerful means of shaping attitudes and generating commitment to new ideas. Thus, the prevailing culture of a training event will have a direct and powerful effect on the receptiveness of each individual present. However, the generation of a supportive culture does not automatically guarantee that each individual will develop such a commitment. An appropriate culture is a necessary, but not always sufficient, factor in this process. We must also consider factors that influence change at the individual level.

The dynamics of individual change When we take the view that the purpose of training is to change people in some functionally positive way, the dynamic nature of the process becomes more obvious. At the beginning of a training event, participants will have a combination of attitudes, skills and knowledge that constitutes their functional performance in a particular role and context. This may be considered as the starting position of each person, or, in dynamic terms, the current equilibrium. Individuals will, of course, differ in each of these dimensions although very great differences in skill and knowledge can make effective training extremely difficult, particularly when such training is highly procedural. However, there are often large differences in attitude and beliefs among participants whose skills and knowledge are highly homogenous. The possession of high levels of appropriate skill and knowledge are no guarantee that a person will perform to a level of which they are capable in a particular role and context. *Attitude* is the crucial factor here and, as we have already noted, attitude and commitment form the core concerns of quality training.

The aim of quality training is to positively change functional performance, to move a person from one position to another. Such movement does not necessarily imply the acquisition of dramatically different skills or profound knowledge. Often it is a process of harnessing and directing existing skills and knowledge in a particular way and generating the commitment to maximize the use of these abilities in the work-place.

We can extend the dynamics analogy and again use the idea of a force-field diagram to clarify the situation (see Figure 7.9).

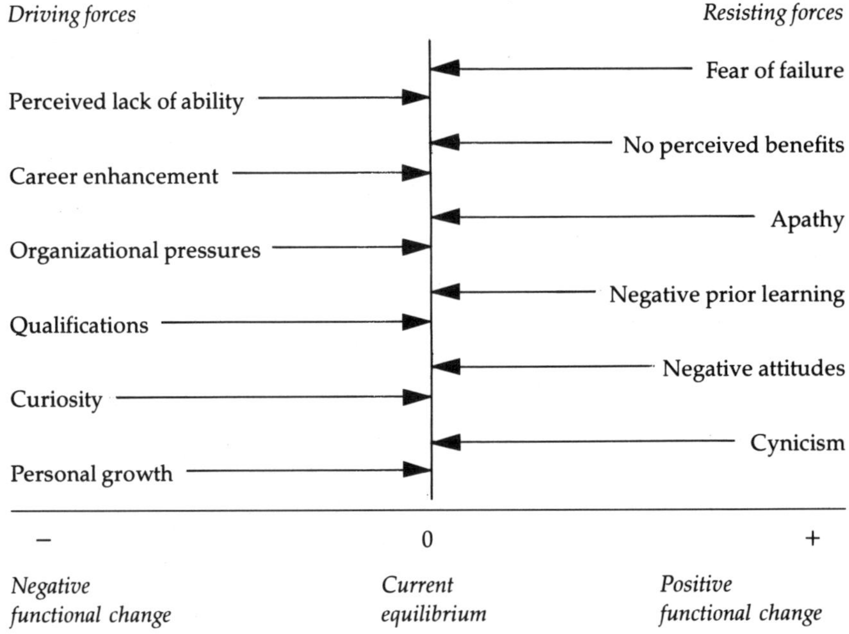

Figure 7.9 *The dynamics of individual change—force-field analysis*

The force-field shown in Figure 7.9 is not exhaustive or applicable to all individuals, but such influences are common. If quality training is to achieve its aim of improved functional performance, the various competing forces have to be taken into consideration. Positive change can be achieved in three ways:

- by harnessing and enhancing driving forces only
- by weakening resisting forces only
- through a combination of the first and second ways.

In general, an approach that utilizes a combination of selling benefits and reducing resistance works best and the key factors are those that operate at the individual rather than organizational level.

As may be seen from the force-field diagram, the resisting forces that aim to maintain current equilibrium are mainly internalized personal attitudes and values that reflect past experiences and current opinions. These are the areas where real change will be encouraged and resisted.

Many of the driving forces are external in nature and commonly originate from organizational rather than personal needs, but internal drivers also exist. These include perceived areas of functional weakness, curiosity and the desire for personal development and growth. The challenge that faces all trainers is that of linking both forms of driver—internal and external—in order that needs may be met at individual and organizational levels.

Another major consideration concerns the relative permanence of change in relation to functional performance. Training has some effect on most people, be it positive or negative, at least in the short term, but the real task is to ensure that positive change endures. This point is particularly important in terms of the development of quality cultures within organizations. Figure 7.10, I hope, clarifies the attitudinal dynamics of the process in relation to the relative permanence of change in the content of training.

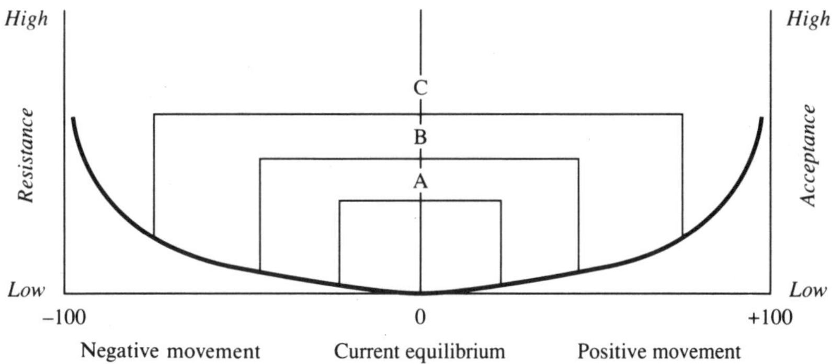

Figure 7.10 *Attitudinal dynamics of individual change*

Although some of our values and attitudes remain very stable over long periods of time—our political, moral or religious convictions—others can be considered to be in a constant state of flux. We do not have exactly the same feelings about our job or our boss from day to day or week to week, for example. There may only be slight variations from a common level or there may be quite dramatic movement from time to time. This phenomenon is known as a state of dynamic equilibrium. Systems that are in dynamic equilibrium, such as many of our attitudes and values, show a marked tendency to oscillate about a mean position, the 'spring-back' effect, and this phenomenon may be usefully applied in the training context.

An individual's reaction to new ideas or new ways of behaving can be represented on a continuum that has highly active acceptance at one pole and highly active resistance at the other. Somewhere between these extreme positions will be the current equilibrium point of each individual before training is carried out. Depending on the context, participants will, hopefully, be somewhere towards the middle of the spectrum—a position of relative neutrality in relation to the training they are to receive. In practice, of course, this is sometimes unfortunately not the position at all.

Depending on such things as course design and content, publicity, recruitment methods, perceived benefit/credibility and so on, participants may arrive already biased towards a particular direction of movement. As can be seen from Figure 7.10, movement in either direction (that is the acceptance of new ideas or entrenchment into established values and attitudes) will correlate with varying levels of acceptance or resistance to meaningful change.

My own experiences in training and development have led me to the conclusion that there is a considerable element of spring-back possible in relation to our attempts at generating sustainable positive change through training. Assuming (as I have done in Figure 7.10) that participants begin a period of training at least with an open mind, that is, they start somewhere towards the centre of the acceptance–resistance spectrum, it often takes a considerable degree of movement to generate change that is sustainable in the long term.

The reasons for this are varied and include such important factors as the amount of support for change that the learner encounters on returning to the work-place (this is a concern that we will address in some depth in Chapter 9). There does, however, appear to be a strong tendency for participants to require considerable on-course movement for measurable positive on-job improvement to be sustained. Commitment to change must be high. The relationship between genuine commitment to change and training experience seems to progress through discernible stages.

Movement that is confined to the area contained within the limits of portion 'A' in Figure 7.10 is temporary and highly likely to spring back to the original position of equilibrium rapidly. This form of training makes people feel mildly positive or mildly negative, but in the short term only, it does no long-term harm or good and is soon forgotten.

Movement that reaches area 'B' in Figure 7.10 has some minor positive or negative effect that is discernible for some time after training is completed.

Area 'C' in the figure, however, represents a critical breakthrough in which significant measurable change occurs in the work-place *and* becomes part of the person's common repertoire of behaviours.

As is clear from the diagram, there is a considerable 'flat area' that needs to be overcome if we are to effectively generate high levels of commitment to change that will ensure that measurable and sustainable benefits occur.

Trainers must recognize that this is far from being an easy task, but it is not an impossible one. Recognizing that significant movement must occur on-course if we are to have any chance of affecting on-job performance helps us become less comfortable with mediocre exercises and activities and highlights the crucial importance of providing relevant experiences during a period of training. The degree of movement that participants experience as a consequence of the training process will be directly related to such factors as those discussed previously; the relevance and quality of training materials and activities, group cohesion, trainer effectiveness, clarity and unity of personal and functional goals and so on. In addition to these largely social and structural factors, much is known regarding the psychological processes that underpin the development, sustainability and changeability of an individual's values, attitudes and beliefs.

Trainers must develop a working knowledge of these processes and utilize them in the achievement of their training goals.

Quantity and pace of information

Obviously, if learning is to be effective, we must ensure that information is delivered at an appropriate depth and pace. The ideal situation is one in which learners are stretched but not overly exhausted. There is no hard and fast rule governing this—individuals and groups vary. Where possible, however, we should aim to ensure that the groups we train have at least a common baseline of relevant knowledge and experience that we can build on. Trainers must constantly monitor the non-verbal signals that indicate whether the pace of information is too fast or too slow, some common indicators are given on page 109.

Can we deliver?

Applying the principles of TQM to the analysis and design of training is a fairly straightforward process. The real challenge is making it happen. The aim of adopting a quality approach to training is to provide a service that meets customers' requirements every time, to minimize variation in standards and to deliver what we promised we would deliver. Our aim, therefore, is to bring the training process into statistical control. Not to attempt to make it perfect, but to achieve standards of performance that remain within the limits determined by the customers' requirements. We therefore need to be clearly aware of what *is* acceptable and what is *not* acceptable, from the customers' point of view. Once these parameters are defined, we can begin to determine the special and random causes of variation that must be controlled if we are to achieve our aims.

Special causes of variation in training effectiveness

Our previous analysis of customer requirements is a sound basis upon which we can begin an identification of special causes of variation in training.

The major factors so far identified include:

- trainer expertise
- trainer experience
- trainer credibility
- trainer style
- event content
- event length
- event structure
- learning materials
- exercises
- length of sessions
- trainer mix (on co-tutored courses)
- surroundings.

This list is not exhaustive, but it does include some of the major special factors that are responsible for variation in training effectiveness. Because they are special causes we can specify beforehand what standards are required in terms of each of the variables outlined above and see that these standards are met. There must be no compromise on this.

Random causes of variation in training effectiveness

Random causes of variation present us with a more difficult challenge. Unlike special causes, random causes of variation are an inevitable fact of life for all processes. Nothing is perfect. We can, at least in theory, eliminate special causes of variation, but all we can do with random causes is to work at squeezing their effects out of the system as much as possible by continuously improving what we do.

Some of the major sources of random variation in training effectiveness are:

- group mix and group dynamics
- personal problems (trainers and participants)
- attention spans
- climactic/environmental changes
- equipment failure
- health problems (trainers and participants)
- personal goals of participants
- abilities of participants.

These factors are, by their very nature, beyond our complete control. What we can do, however, is to monitor the adverse effects that such factors have on training and attempt some remedial action before things go beyond acceptable limits. In other words, we are employing the notion of control charts in the context of training. Control charts, as we have already noted, allow us to detect trends in the operational characteristics of processes by monitoring and measuring certain critical variables over a period of time.

In order that we may apply this principle to the training context, we must determine what variables we intend to monitor and the methods by which we may measure them.

The central variables we must monitor as training progresses are:

- assimilation of learning
- levels of enthusiasm and interest.

These variables are often interlinked as interest and enthusiasm generally correlate well with levels of understanding. The better we learn, the more enthusiastic we become. The challenge, then, is to measure whether these variables are remaining within acceptable levels.

In terms of assimilation of learning, there are a number of well-used formal methods of evaluating effectiveness in existence. Written or oral tests of some form, phase tests and skill development indicators and so on. These are commonly used in the context of procedural training, but are rarely, if ever, used in such contexts as management development. The general tendency to avoid, at all costs, any hint of 'schoolish' procedures and processes means that such things are usually considered beyond the pale. We must, therefore, use more subtle measures, which essentially means that trainers must be very astute at picking up the non-verbal correlates of confusion, boredom and dissatisfaction. Competence in this particular area seems to vary considerably. I have seen trainers take groups along a journey that begins with indications of mild disagreement and passes through ever-escalating levels until it culminates in total participative withdrawal or actual physical desertion of the course. I have also witnessed occasions where trainers have reduced individuals and groups to levels of mental and physical immobility that border on those more usually achieved through cryogenic means.

What is particularly disturbing about these instances is that the trainer very often seems to have no perception that such situations are developing, nor registers any of the early warning signals and therefore does not take corrective action. In other words, the trainer allows the process to go completely out of statistical control.

What, then, *are* the warning signals? There is no exhaustive list, but some common indicators that things are not going well are:

- a lack of spontaneous participation from the group
- few, if any, questions, extrapolations or ideas from the group
- 90 per cent of the questions from only 10 per cent of the group members
- intergroup communication increases (closing ranks)
- non-verbal signals, including:
  - —symbolic withdrawal from group/trainer, such as, leaning back, crossed arms, stern appearance
  - —lack of eye contact with trainer
  - —increased eye contact with other participants (closing ranks)
  - —yawning, sighing, sniggering and so on
  - —fidgeting, staring
  - —dozing, sleeping.

I have seen all these warning signals ignored by trainers who simply press on with their delivery as if everything in the garden was rosy. I believe that a major reason for this is not related to a lack of perceptual sensitivity, but to a lack of knowledge or confidence as to the appropriate action to take in such circumstances. There are a number of strategies available.

Intervention strategies:

- stop, take a break, even when it is not scheduled in the course programme
- change the pace of delivery, going slower or faster
- change the structure of the training—use a participative activity where one was not planned or deliver a talk rather than an activity if others have not gone well or it is obvious that people are tired of 'getting into groups'; stop using the overhead projector; start using the overhead projector; put a video on
- have a question period—this can be open or directed and it is sometimes useful to start the ball rolling by addressing a question to a particular individual and then asking others for their views on what is said
- cut the session short—move on to something else, even if you have not covered everything, returning to missed points later (it is amazing how many trainers find it difficult to do this)
- have a negotiated change in the programme—consult with the group as to any changes they could suggest, while still meeting course aims
- use humour—this can be a great tension reliever, but it must be handled effectively (I once heard a colleague say to a particularly reticent group 'Shall we all join hands and see if we can make contact with the living?' and it worked—for him!)
- relax the group by stopping and saying that it seems a good idea to let people have a chance to air any fears or misapprehensions that may have developed as the course has progressed, which can be made more effective by changing surroundings, moving rooms, going outside or whatever
- confront the signals, bring things out into the open, say that you are picking up a lot of negative signals and would like to do something to tackle the source of these signals
- change the dynamics of the group—perhaps cliques have formed that need to be dealt with, although, obviously, this must be done with subtlety; careful consideration as to the formation of task-centred groups and so on can have dramatic positive effects.

These are some of the options available to the trainer who detects the beginnings of trouble and wishes to avoid an inevitable escalation. They are fairly straightforward techniques and require courage rather than expertise.

Quality improvement techniques

Improving customer information bases

The only way to improve quality is by getting closer to our customers. We must discover what their real needs are, we must find out precisely what they like and dislike about the services we provide and we must become effective at anticipating what their future needs will be. We can only achieve these objectives if we have effective relationships with our customers and we have effective methods of obtaining the critical information we need.

The bedrock of quality improvement, therefore, is to *strengthen relationships and communications with customers*. In training terms this means getting closer to Customer 1 and Customer 2. In terms of external training providers and consultants this means that we must strengthen our links with the organizations we occasionally provide services for—on an unpaid basis if necessary (the investment will be worthwhile in the long term).

We must broaden our understanding of the cultures and systems in which people work and understand the context in which our efforts are set. We must also have a working understanding of the markets in which these organizations operate and the central challenges that face them now and in the longer term. We must, if we are to succeed, convince them that training and development are an indispensable component of long-term survival.

As far as internal training services are concerned, the same applies. A major weakness of many training departments is a tendency towards ivory tower isolationism. Internal trainers, above all, should have at least a working familiarity with the functions and responsibilities of each major department within the organization, detailed knowledge of the organization's overall aspirations and strategies and an understanding of the ways in which both factors interact.

We must develop effective databases of customer information in order that we can identify trends, anticipate problems and opportunities and become increasingly proactive with the services we provide. We cannot achieve these outcomes if we limit our customer contact to the design and delivery of short-term training services alone.

We must build up a comprehensive dossier of information that allows us to pinpoint those areas where training and development expenditure will be most likely to deliver visible returns for the organization. Simple exhortations to invest in training because the Germans and Japanese do will not have much effect if that is the *only* reason we are able to come up with.

Successful organizations are successful because they keep in touch with existing customer needs and anticipate future needs and they do this by means of thorough research. It is not a simple, easy, cheap or quick process, but it pays enormous dividends and it is taken extremely seriously.

The Fuji Xerox company in the US has a sales data research system that requires sales staff to spend, on average, one third of their working hours updating information on their customers and analysing trends with their immediate line manager. They are not simply driving around making cold calls and hoping for the best; they are analysing data to determine *which* copiers to sell, to *whom*, at what *price*, for what *reasons* and *when*.

The initial task in compiling databases is to decide on the type of data to be used. In terms of determining existing and potential training needs this could include:

- total number of employees
- breakdown in terms of sex and age
- breakdown in terms of skilled/unskilled
- breakdown in terms of years of service
- average amount of training per employee/per category
- areas of high turnover of employees
- areas where recruitment problems are acute
- sickness rate and type of sickness
- accident rate and type of accident
- installation of new technology
- plans to install new technology
- market share
- industrial relations indicators
- possible effects of forthcoming legislation
- possible effects of demographic changes
- possible effects of technological developments.

As can be seen from this initial list, the collection of data presents the training provider with a formidable challenge and it requires that a relationship of considerable trust is developed with the organization concerned.

Nobody said that the attainment of quality was easy to achieve. Without accurate, meaningful data, the services we provide are, essentially, shots in the dark. We must base our services on a more substantial and professional footing if we are to succeed.

Increased focus on error prevention

Without wishing to flog the point to death regarding variable standards of performance in training, there is a tendency to witness the same mistakes occurring again and again. They are predominantly special causes of variation, as we saw earlier, and they are largely avoidable. Among other things we must ensure that the training we intend to deliver is designed in such a way as to avoid being:

- boring
- repetitive
- largely irrelevant

- insulting
- too high a standard
- too low a standard
- full of jargon
- largely academic
- old hat
- full of waffle
- unconvincing.

This means that the trainers who deliver the training need, among other things, to be:

- experienced in the particular area concerned
- adequately knowledgeable in the areas required
- able to 'speak the language' of the participants
- credible with participants
- able to translate concepts into practical, usable ideas
- enthusiastic and committed
- innovative and quick thinking.

Again, nobody said that achieving quality would be easy!

Improving relationships with suppliers

We have previously noted that in training we are commonly in the unusual position of obtaining our most important supplies from our customers—Customer 1 is usually sent to us by Customer 2. To this end, the improved relationships with customers advocated in the section above should also include, where necessary, attempts at influencing the homogeneity of training groups and the suitability of individuals who are nominated for training. Too often in training we are confronted with groups of individuals who have immense differences in experience, knowledge, ability, natural inclination, personality and confidence. I have, on too many occasions, attempted to train individuals who are completely out of their depth on a particular course and are painfully aware of the fact (or everyone else is). The trainer's role in such instances is reduced to damage limitation to the person and a frantic search for opportunities to build on anything positive. This, though, is not training, at least not in my view.

If we are to be effective, we must be clear about baseline requirements in terms of participant's experience, role responsibilities and potential to benefit from the training on offer. Training should aim to motivate and inform, to better equip individuals to carry out their broad responsibilities in the contexts in which they operate. It is difficult to envisage how this can be achieved if the individual sent on a management development course actually has no discernible management responsibilities, no real authority and little natural inclination for the subject.

Improving relationships with suppliers is an integral component of quality enhancement. We must become more effective at influencing the process of selection and identification of training suitability at its earliest stage, that is, within organizations, if we are to improve our results and, consequently, our perceived effectiveness. Too often we are charged with the responsibility of improving the performance of individual employees who are unsuited to the role requirements they are expected to carry out. I have long been convinced that a significant majority of performance difficulties stem from woefully inadequate selection procedures rather than being symptoms of failure in training and development. There are limits to what individuals can be trained to achieve. To ignore this fact, or to hold the mythical view that *anyone* is capable of *anything* is to set people up for failure and, ultimately, to prevent them from achieving their true potential in more suitable areas of work.

As training professionals, we must extend our sphere of influence into the critical area of selection and identification of training suitability. If we do not, if we continue with the implied philosophy that we can train anyone who is prepared to turn up, then we also are setting *ourselves* up for inevitable failure.

Training resource suppliers

Improving our links (and therefore our possible influence) with suppliers certainly extends to the area of training resources. It is difficult to find a better example of a supplier-oriented market than this.

Take the production of training videos for example. This market seems to be predominantly within the control of frustrated directors of comedy classics. Although these videos are often highly creative, the ideas about what constitutes an effective learning resource often leave a lot to be desired. They are good entertainment—there is no doubt about that—but what do they really achieve in terms of actual improved performance?

I have previously discussed what appears to me to be severe limitations in much of the computer-based learning and interactive video materials produced to date. These failings stem primarily from a supplier-led approach to design and manufacture. Nobody talks to the customers.

If the manufacturers of commonly used training resources were prepared to talk to us, what useful suggestions could we give them? A few ideas are outlined below.

Training videos

We have had enough of the comic approach. People are becoming increasingly weary of the doctor's surgery scenario and the imbecilic manager, trainer and supervisor. It would be extremely useful, however, to have a compilation of *real* managers, trainers and supervisors talking about the *real* problems they face in their day-to-day work. The phenomenal interest shown in the 'Troubleshooter' series of programmes presented by Sir John Harvey-Jones shown on BBC Television attests to the fact that people are actually extremely interested in real programmes about real industries and real problems.

This could so easily be extended to the training context. An enterprising video production company could engage the temporary services of real managers, trainers, sales staff and supervisors and ask them such questions as, 'What are the major obstacles you have to overcome in order to be effective in your job?', 'What is the biggest mistake you have made?',

'What is the best advice you have been given?', 'How do you set your targets and priorities?', 'Who is the best boss you have worked for?', 'How do you deal with really difficult people?', 'What do you really think about appraisal systems?', 'How do you deal with the stresses of the job?'. These videos could be sector specific, for example, management in local government, in the voluntary sector, in hi-tech areas, in engineering, volume manufacturing, in the health service, in small companies, in banking, construction, insurance, haulage, the media and so on. After all, 99 per cent of what people learn about being effective in their jobs is learned from experience, often by modelling the effectiveness of others. Perhaps there is a role for Nellie after all!

When W. Edwards Deming begins his legendary process of helping organizations (which include Ford US, General Motors and Xerox) take on board his 14-step plan to quality, he begins with front-line workers. Not, I hasten to add, in any attempt to berate them for their performance levels or to threaten their future security, but to ask them how they are prevented from doing the jobs they know they can do. He commonly addresses large groups of workers, with no management present, and promises them that they will not be penalized for speaking their minds. He has this frank discussion video recorded and plays it back to top management. They are commonly astounded at what is happening in their organizations and at the level of concern and wealth of potential that exists within their front-line employees. What Deming actually produces in this process is a superb training video—something that is real, dramatic and educating.

This can be capitalized on. Take, for example, the topic of motivation at work. This is usually dealt with in management training via liberal helpings of Maslow, *et al.* Why not ask real people in a range of real jobs what it is that motivates them to work hard, what stops them doing so, what worries them and so on? The potential is enormous.

Effective trainers do not need scripted, obvious, ham-acted video materials. Any trainers worth their salt would have material for almost unlimited applications from a range of 50 honest interviews.

Case studies and role playing exercises

Prepared versions of case studies and role playing exercises usually appear in book form. Some are very good, but most have at least a few aspects that do not fit well with the context they are to be used for. Perhaps the names used (Lucinda and Gavin appear in one I recently saw) are inappropriate for a particular situation or the *setting* of the incident would detract from its validity. In book form there is little that can be done.

Why not, therefore, produce a compendium of case studies and role playing on a floppy disk? With word processing capability, trainers would be able to pick and mix from the database and amend or add as required. Again, if case studies and so on were grouped into occupational categories and industrial and commercial contexts, this would decrease the time required to locate a suitable basis from which an original case study or role playing exercise could be constructed.

Training hardware

Some suggested improvements.

Overhead projectors Add an attachable peel back opaque film that allows overhead projected slides to be revealed part by part; a remote control on-off switch; make the venting horizontal or downward directed so that papers are not blown away; provide quieter fans and vertically adjustable front and rear feet.

Flipchart pads Make them 10 per cent larger in each direction, perforated at the top for easy removal; reduce the number of sheets per pad by 25 per cent; make them from reversible, recycled paper with an adhesive strip at the top at the back; number the sheets; add a discrete warning note six sheets from the end.

Overhead projector/flipchart pens Make them retractable; have three colours in one pen; make refills available; make them magnetic.

Flipchart stands Give them an adjustable face; provide a spring-loaded retaining bar with hooks (instead of the existing bar and screw-on retainers); rubber suction pads on the feet; vertical magnetic/metal strips each side with graduations; make it stable *without* moving to arrange the legs at excessive angles; provide self-contained illumination.

Quality circles

These initial suggestions for improvement were the result of a small group of trainers spending a short time brainstorming ideas. In effect they formed a temporary *quality circle*—a group of volunteers engaged in a process of suggesting improvements to existing products and services.

Many organizations have experimented with quality circles—with varying levels of success. The key factors involved in the effectiveness of quality circles include genuine authority being invested in group members, action on sound suggestions, long-term commitment—as opposed to short-term gimmick approaches—and management accepting responsibility for action where this is required. In general terms, quality circles will only succeed in an organizational culture that genuinely seeks to solve problems and improve products and services. They cannot be 'bolted on' to an inappropriate culture. When this is attempted, they usually fizzle out over a period of months, leaving disillusionment and demotivation in their wake.

Systematic quality improvement

There is a sequence of operations generally associated with systematic quality improvement. This sequence can usefully be presented as a series of basic questions.

1 'What do we want to improve?'

This is the basic starting point. Areas for improvement are ideally identified from customer-generated information, but they may also be identified by the suppliers of goods and services. Cost-reduction projects, for example, would fall into this category. If, however, the improvement area is directly related to changes in the final product or service, that is, that delivered to the external customer, care must be taken to avoid the errors outlined on pages 35–37.

Let us assume, as a working example, that a training organization wishes to improve some aspect of its mailshot advertising programme. A number of possible options are available including:

- a customer (internal and external) survey to determine current views, including an assessment of critical requirements
- an assessment of the impact that this area has on customers
- an assessment of how much improvement is needed
- an assessment of the possible benefits of this improvement.

2 'Where are we now?'

This is the data collection and problem identification stage. As much information as possible is collected that is relevant to the improvement area under consideration in order that it can be studied from a number of perspectives. One particular problem is then chosen for action.

In terms of our example, the problem may be related to any of the perspectives taken, for example, the design of mailshot materials, the cost of production, the speed of design to production processes, the suitability and scope of mailshot targets and so on. A statement of customer requirements is obtained (from internal or external customers) and a clear problem statement is written.

3 'Where do we want to be?'

When a clear problem statement has been originated, a realistic, theoretically achievable and beneficial improvement target is set out.

4 'What are the root causes of the problem?'

This is a process of cause and effect analysis that is aimed at discovering the root causes of the problem under consideration. It is extremely important at this stage that it is *root* problems that are, in fact, identified, otherwise we may be likely to tackle mere symptoms rather than underlying causes.

Many quality experts recommend that a cause and effect diagram is used in this process. These diagrams are sometimes referred to as fishbone diagrams or Ishikawa diagrams after their originator, Professor Ishikawa. These diagrams usually approach the analysis of problems under a number of headings. A common technique (it is sometimes referred to as the Four M), it analyses problems in terms of manpower, methods, materials and machinery. Let us assume that a major problem, identified in Stage 2, concerns the excessive time taken to turn design specifications into actual printed materials ready to be mailed out. The diagram could look like that shown in Figure 7.11.

Such analysis usually takes the form of a brainstorming session and it continues until no further ideas are forthcoming. There then follows a process of identifying those root problems that we can, in fact, do something about and those with the most impact on the desired outcome are then selected for action.

5 'What action can we take?'

Once root causes have been identified, there follows a process of examining the possible actions that could be taken in order to eliminate them or reduce their effects to within acceptable limits. There are a number of points to take into consideration here.

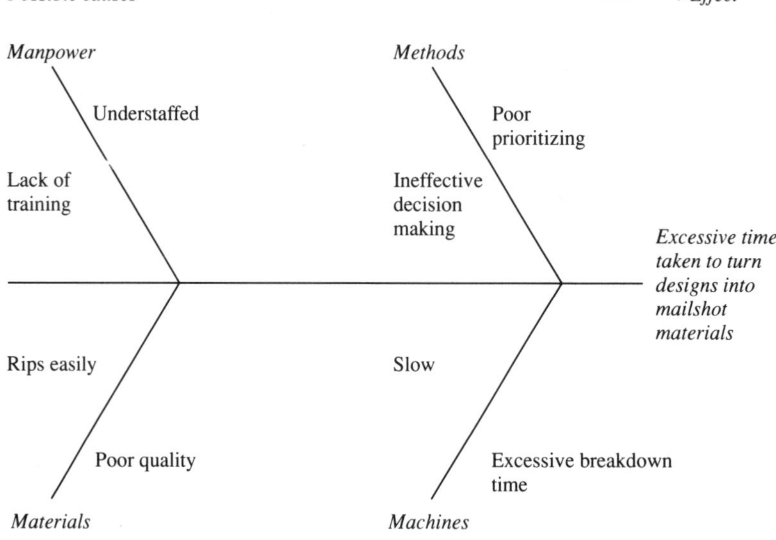

Figure 7.11 *Cause and effect analysis of excessive turnover time for design of material to mailshot*

- these possible actions must be capable of achieving the outcome(s) identified in Stage 3
- they must be cost effective in the long term
- they must not create significant difficulties elsewhere.

6 'Who does what, when?' This is the stage at which an action plan is drawn up. This action plan will include specific tasks to be achieved, state who is responsible, the likely problems to be overcome and the cooperation needed to achieve a solution.

7 'How can we tell if it is working?' The action plan is then implemented and monitored for results. These results are compared to the desired results specified at Stage 3. Additional measures must be taken if results do not meet requirements. Stages 4, 5 and 6 are repeated.

8 'How can we ensure that the problem will not recur?' Once the results specified at Stage 3 are achieved, procedures, training and other necessary measures are taken to ensure that the problem does not recur. Action specified at Stage 5 becomes part of the normal work process in this area.

9 'What have we learned?' Lessons regarding the improvement process, problem solving and teamwork are analysed and good points noted. Areas where difficulties and holdups occurred are analysed for improved performance in future quality improvement projects.

Thus the whole process is a learning activity involving the systematic identification of quality improvement areas, problem identification and analysis, action planning, problem solving, project monitoring, teamwork and change in existing work practices. The final stage offers participants the opportunity to reflect on the experience and to suggest methods by which the whole process can be refined for future application.

The quality improvement model has considerable potential in the area of training and development. This potential will be examined in some detail in Chapter 9.

8 TQ—the human dimension

So far in this book I have concentrated on the 'systems' dimension of quality—the procedures and techniques that underpin the TQ approach. It is, however, a mistake to think that quality is itself merely the application of a set of procedures. Quality is not a system; quality does not come from machines or statistical analyses. Although these are important adjuncts to the process, ultimately, quality comes only from people.

Quality is essentially about attitudes, organizational cultures and a belief in continuous improvement. A quality culture cannot be legislated for or prescribed by the organization; it can only be encouraged, nurtured and developed over time. To understand quality, therefore, demands that we attempt to better understand the nature of individual psychology and the dynamics of group and intergroup behaviour, because quality is ultimately about the development and management of people.

In this chapter I will begin by outlining an approach to understanding the psychology of individual and group behaviour. This is followed by an application of these principles to the design and delivery of training events, the development of organizational cultures and the analysis of individual trainer styles.

Understanding personality and behaviour—psychological theories

Some words of caution. The psychologist Thomas Szasz wrote, 'There is no psychology; there is only biography and autobiography'. These, I believe, are wise words indeed.

Psychology is a peculiar subject, if it is a subject at all. In many ways psychology can be considered as being a range of loosely connected studies linked together by, in Wittgenstein's terms, a form of 'family resemblance'. At the extremities of the subject we have the Jungian or Freudian view of human beings as deep and mystical entities, while, at the other end, we have the radical behaviourists and the artificial intelligence models of the cognitive movement, who appear to view us as some form of vertical computing rat. If we were to put together two psychologists from each end of the spectrum it would be extremely unlikely that they would have anything mutually coherent to say to each other.

Szasz's point is that psychological theories are, inevitably, a reflection of a particular psychologist's understanding of the way things are. In essence, they are assertions of the form, 'this is what *I* think'. As such, they will have a particular appeal to some and none to others.

Of course there *are* psychological theories that are ostensibly founded on experimental evidence and objective analysis. There is, however, a price to be paid for this objectivity and that price is relevance. Experimental psychology (real experimental psychology, that is, not the pop variety) is limited to the study of extremely mundane aspects of human experience by the fact that human beings and human interactions are incredibly complex. When experimental psychologists do venture into the murky waters of real interest, what commonly happens is that interesting and provocative assertions are made, a controversy ensues and further studies do not support the initial one or, indeed, suggest that the opposite is true. This leads to security of tenure for academic psychologists and the generation of endless and pointless research programmes. Having, during the course of my formal education in psychology, believed in turn at least some aspect of almost every theory presented to me, I have since given up the notion that any of them are, in any fundamental sense, 'true'. Like religious beliefs (in my own opinion, that is), they are true if we believe they are true. What does appear to be true, however, is that we all do adhere to some form of psychological theory, however vague, incoherent or unsubstantiated such a theory may be. We are, it appears, all psychologists.

My experience in management, training, counselling and therapy have led me to the conclusion that pragmatism is the best arbiter of truth concerning particular psychological theories. If it works, use it; if it does not, try something else.

A framework for understanding personality and behaviour

Having made the rejoinder above, I do believe that some psychological theories are more relevant than others in relation to management, training and development. The prime requisites of any potentially useful theory are that it is understandable, has validity in terms of an individual's experiences of the world, leads to helpful insights concerning past behaviours and suggests ways in which future actions may be made more productive. Obviously this is a tall order for any theory and, as I have already indicated above, the final choice is left to the individual manager or trainer concerned.

The basic framework outlined below is not new. It is based on the theory of personality and communication founded by Dr Eric Berne and commonly known as *Transactional Analysis* (TA). However, I have taken the basic framework and, from it, developed a practical, action-based approach to an understanding of management and training practices and also to the development of organizational cultures. I have called this approach *Training Action Analysis* (TAA) and *Management Action Analysis* (MAA).

Before we explore the foundations of this approach it would be most useful if you now set aside a period of 20 to 30 minutes in order to complete the self-analysis inventory on pages 174 to 177 (the scoring sheet is on page 178). It would be most useful if the inventory were completed with the minimum amount of distraction and the maximum amount of honesty.

Welcome back! I hope you found the inventory interesting. You now have the choice of either reading the following sections, which explain the theoretical foundation on which the inventory is based (I strongly advise this), or, if you cannot resist it, immediately transfer your initial scores (see p. 178) to the analysis score sheet on page 179 and then skip to page 136, returning to this section later. Which option you choose may give you further insights into your preferred style of behaviour.

TA—the basic framework

The theory of TA was founded by Eric Berne, a Canadian psychotherapist who practised mainly in the US. Berne originally trained in Freudian psychoanalysis and spent many years in the role of analysand (the process by which prospective psychoanalysts are themselves psychoanalysed before they are allowed to practise as fully licenced analysts).

Berne did not complete this process successfully and, in 1956, he parted company with psychoanalysis after a period of 15 years of study, although he continued to work with mentally disturbed patients. He was then 46 years old.

During the four years that followed, Berne concentrated his attention on the process of intuition—a subject that had intrigued him for some time. He found that by 'forgetting all the jazz' he had learned in psychiatry and by 'listening to what the patients were saying', he was able to make more effective diagnoses and to become a more effective helper. He gradually developed his ideas into a comprehensive body of theory and practical applications that he called Transactional Analysis.

The theory that Berne developed is, in fact, wide-ranging and complex and later writers have added to the foundations that he laid in his seminal book, *Transactional Analysis in Psychotherapy* (Souvenir Press, 1975). All this may have become a subject of interest to a restricted audience of psychiatrists and academics had Berne not written, in 1964, a book that became an international best seller. This book was called *Games People Play*. It captured the interest of millions across the world (it was reprinted 16 times in the UK alone between 1968 and 1979). There are a number of reasons for its phenomenal success: it is well written; although complex, it is easy to understand; it makes extensive use of metaphor, analogy and ordinary language; but, above all else, it makes for fascinating reading because it rings true. Very many people feel that the theories detailed in the book make sense of their experiences, help them understand their feelings, thoughts and actions and offer them ways in which they can perhaps try alternative behaviours or alternative approaches to the difficulties they face in their personal and working lives.

It is fair to say that, despite this response, TA does not carry a great deal of 'weight' in the established fields of academic psychology and there are a number of reasons for this. Berne wrote many of his books, particularly *Games People Play* and those that followed (including *A Layman's Guide to Psychiatry* (Penguin, 1971), *Sex in Human Loving* (Penguin, 1973) and *What do You Say After You Say Hello?* (Corgi, 1975) using everyday language rather than an academically 'respectable' style. He also purposely included many 'Americanisms', such as the idea of 'OK'ness (as used in *I'm OK, You're OK* by Thomas Harris (Pan, 1978). He also committed the sin of writing psychology books that became best sellers!

It is also fair to say that, following the phenomenal success of *Games People Play*, much of the theory was sensationalized in various magazines and vigorously adopted by the 'Here's the final answer' pop psychology marketeers. This, of course, further alienated the academics.

TA theory has evolved consistently since Berne's death in 1970 and media and general interest has cooled considerably since the heady years of the sixties and seventies.

Although the term TA is used to describe the whole theory, the analysis of transactions (communications between individuals) is based on the prior analysis of personality that Berne called *Structural Analysis*.

The structural analysis of personality

The structural analysis of personality is the foundation on which the whole of TA theory is built. The idea behind structural anlaysis is, like the overwhelming majority of other good ideas, fundamentally a simple one.

If we closely observe a person's social behaviour over a period of time, say during a conversation at a party or perhaps over a period of 15 minutes during a group discussion on a training course, it becomes clear that such things as modes of speech, body language, interest and attitudes do not remain constant, but tend to fluctuate over time.

Berne postulated that these outwardly visible signs of change reflect changes in internal psychological processes. He called these internal processes *ego states* and the changes in these processes were referred to as changes of ego state.

Ego states are essentially ways of reacting to the external world. For example, we may react to a particular event with anxiety, indifference, anger, affection or enthusiasm. Each reaction, according to Berne, is a symptom of an underlying ego state. Berne also noted that there are limitations to the range of changes an individual goes through and he therefore came to the conclusion that there must be a limited number of ego states available. Structural analysis refers to the process of attempting to define the ways in which these ego states are structured within the personality.

The ego states

An ego state comprises a set of perceptions and emotions that result in certain forms of behaviour—ways of viewing the world and ways of reacting to events in the world. There are essentially three different ego states present within the personality of a mature individual and they function very differently from each other. They may sometimes work in unison, but, more commonly, they produce internal tensions and a sense of uncertainty about decisions and behaviours. The sense of uncertainty that characteristically results from the conflicts between internal ego states can often be detected in the frequently heard phrase, 'I've got mixed feelings about . . .' An examination of the nature of these primary ego states will explain why feelings of uncertainty and confusion are such a common human experience.

Berne based his theory of structural analysis on three obvious assertions:

1 that everyone has had parents (or substitute parents, caregivers or whatever) and that everyone will have internalized (learned consciously or unconsciously) some of the views and behaviours of those parents or parent figures
2 that everyone is capable of behaving in a rational and objective way; that is, everyone is capable of behaving according to the realities of a situation rather than reacting irrationally or purely in terms of their emotions or conditioning
3 that everyone was younger than they are now and sometimes they may react to situations in the way they reacted to similar situations in the past.

These assumptions led Berne to the conclusion that an individual's personality can be considered to be composed of three primary ego states. He called these ego states 'Parent', 'Adult' and 'Child'. In his writing, Berne used initial capital letters to distinguish ego states from actual parents, adults and children and I will use his convention here to avoid confusion. Also, when discussing the Parent, Adult and Child ego states, I will simply refer to them as the Parent, Adult and Child.

First order structural analysis

The Parent The Parent comprises a set of attitudes, values, beliefs and behaviours that we have learned from significant authority figures in our lives. Obviously, when we are young children, almost every person we meet is a potential authority figure, but our perceived parent(s) play a particularly important role in our lives and in the formation of our personalities.

Parents (real parents, that is) often teach their children formal values such as what is right and wrong (from their point of view), how to behave at the table, with elders, with guests and so on. Not all of what we learn, though, is learned in this formal, taught, way. Think, for example, about the common practice, particularly evident in British culture, of formality in public places. I cannot remember anyone ever instructing me not to sit right next to the only other passenger on a bus or to always sit at the opposite end of a park bench if someone else is sitting at the other end or never to start a conversation with other passengers when travelling on the tube, yet I would find it embarrassing to do any of these things. Anyone who has travelled in other countries will testify to the fact that this is not an intrinsic aspect of human psychology—it is particular to this country. Such norms are learned unconsciously, in the same way that we learn the accent we speak with (unless we are trained out of doing so at some point). Therefore, and this is particularly true of our early lives, we unconsciously take on board many of the values and attitudes that are implied by our parent(s)' behaviours. They are not only our formal teachers but also our informal role models.

According to TA theory, the Parent comprises all those values, attitudes and behaviours we have learned from significant others in the past and when we act from our Parent, we are acting according to them.

The Adult The Adult aspect of our personality comprises our ability to obtain and process actual information. Its central characteristics are objectivity, information seeking, analysis and deduction. The Adult operates in the here and now and it attempts to deal with difficulties through the application of a problem-solving approach. The Adult differs from the Parent in that it has no pre-conceived values, it simply processes information and decides on an appropriate course of action. The Adult does not equate with being grown up or intelligent, it is simply the psychological state that allows us to put aside our prejudices, personal needs and emotions and to attempt to see a situation as objectively as we are able.

The Child The Child is concerned primarily with emotions and emotional needs. In TA theory, the Child is representative of the actual child we were at the age of about six or seven. The Child in us can be spontaneous, intuitive, creative, rebellious, selfish, whingeing, cruel, polite, frightened, stubborn, loving and a host more typically child-like ways of thinking, feeling and behaving.

The three ego states identified in first order structural analysis are commonly represented as three circles arranged vertically. It is important however to note that the arrangement most commonly used—Parent at the top, Adult in the middle and Child at the bottom—do not in any way imply that a hierarchy exists. The first letter of each ego state is used for identification purposes and the diagram is sometimes referred to as the PAC model for this reason (see Figure 8.1).

This, then, is the basic structure of personality as described by Berne. Perhaps you can identify times in the past few weeks when you recognize that you have behaved in terms of one, two or all of these ego states. Have you, for example, had a heated exchange with someone? If the incident arose because the other person would not do what you wanted to do, then you probably resorted to your Child and threw a tantrum or sulked or felt sorry for yourself or stormed off and indulged yourself somehow.

If the incident arose because the other person had not done what you wanted them to do, then you probably went into your Parent and criticized them, told them in no uncertain terms what their failings were or

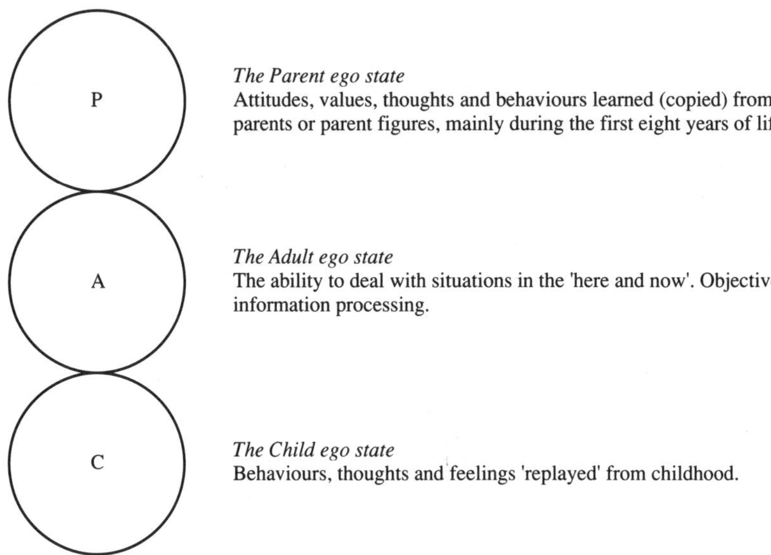

Figure 8.1 *First order structural analysis (the PAC model)*

felt that if you need something done you have to do it yourself or felt that nobody around here but you does anything.

If in the past weeks you can look back on an incident in which you resolved a difficulty with someone without resorting to emotional means, then you probably were using your Adult to see what was at the root of the difficulty, to approach it calmly and rationally and to work out a mutually acceptable solution.

In the course of normal, day-to-day life, we commonly switch rapidly between the different ego states and, in the vast majority of instances, these switches are not obvious to us, but we can become attuned to them with practice. I use the TA model as a basis for much of the interpersonal skills elements of management and trainer training and part of this work usually involves helping participants to become aware of their own ego states and to recognize the ego states of others.

A useful exercise involves participants recording the thoughts and feelings they experienced from the time they received joining instructions and outline details of the training involved until they actually arrived at the training centre and met other participants and the trainer(s). Here is a fairly typical response from a participant we shall call Elaine. I have included the relevant ego state identification in brackets at appropriate points in the text. Obviously, in the actual situation, this can be an individual or group exercise.

Elaine's thoughts and feelings on joining the management development programme

When I first received the joining instructions and the course outline I felt a little apprehensive (Child). There seemed to be a lot to cover in the three days and I wondered whether I could do it (Child). However, when I read the accompanying notes and the main areas we were to cover, I could see that a great deal of it was relevant to the problems I have experienced over the past six months (Adult). The bits about delegation seemed particularly useful because I know I do not do enough delegating and I should do more (Parent).

On the way over to the centre this morning I met Kay and found out she was coming instead of someone else who was ill. This made me feel a lot better as we had worked together in accounts a few years ago and got on very well. We had a really good laugh about our nerves before we got here (Child).

When I got into the training room, I saw the video camera in the corner and my heart really sank (Child), but I thought to myself, you volunteered for this course, you knew you were going to be videoed, so this attitude is really silly (Adult). Anyway, I thought, you are here now so you have got to do it (Parent).

Exercises such as these help us appreciate that ego states are a psychological reality and not a theoretical abstraction. The main point of relevance to trainers and managers, however, is not that such exercises as those above may be interesting and revealing, but to identify their practical implications in terms of the ways in which such knowledge may be used to make training and management more effective in achieving organizational goals.

In order to move towards this position, we must first explore the ego states in more depth. This involves a process called the functional analysis of ego states.

Functional analysis of ego states

Functional analysis is an exploration of the ways in which we use ego states in everyday life. For example, our Parent can be used in a number of ways: to protect ourselves and others, to criticize ourselves and others or to be sympathetic to ourselves and others. Similarly, our Child can be used to please ourselves or to do what others want us to do. Our Adult, being rational and unemotional, only operates in the here and now, so it can only be used to process information in an objective way.

TA theorists have concluded that there are five major functions carried out between the three ego states: two within the Parent: two within the Child and one within the Adult. The two Parent functions are commonly known as the *controlling (or critical) Parent* and the *nurturing Parent.*

The controlling Parent ego function Parents (real parents again) commonly spend a considerable amount of time controlling (or attempting to control) their children. They also spend varying amounts of time criticizing them for various behaviours (or lack of them). Here are some controlling Parent comments that you can hear in almost any family with children under the age of eight or so: 'Stop that', 'Stand up straight', 'Don't eat so fast', 'Don't touch that', 'Pull your socks up', 'Don't speak with your mouth full', 'That was very naughty', 'Eat your vegetables', 'Why don't you . . .', 'You should . . .', 'You ought to . . .', 'You must . . .', 'You will, or else', 'Come here, right now', 'I'm not allowing you to do that', 'Did you hear what I said?', 'Bad', 'Wrong', 'Go to your room'.

As a child, unless you were brought up by extra-terrestrials, you were probably at the receiving end of your fair share of such comments as these. If you are a parent, you probably dish them out on a fairly regular basis. A certain amount of controlling Parent behaviours are almost inevitable and are often absolutely appropriate. If little Suzy is about to push her metal fork into the live terminal of the kitchen socket, then a child-centred discussion on pros and cons may not be very productive. Each ego function has positive and negative possibilities. In general terms, controlling Parent behaviours stem from a desire to control or exercise authority over others.

The nurturing Parent ego function Unless you were particularly unfortunate as a child, as well as being subjected to the controlling Parent you probably also experienced a variety of nurturing Parent behaviours.

Being allowed to stay in bed when you were mildly ill, drinking all the glucose drink you wanted to drink, not having to eat your vegetables, being comforted when you did not do well at school exams (not too common), being hugged, having help with your homework, getting the expensive thing you really wanted for your birthday and so on. In general terms, nurturing Parent behaviours stem from a desire to help and care for others.

The Adult ego function The Adult is the source of such uniquely human abilities as concept formation, analysis, logical problem solving and the prediction of future events on the basis of statistical probability.

The function of the Adult is to differentiate fact from opinion, to scrutinize the logic of a deduction and to plan courses of action that are optimally suited to the achievement of a desired goal. The Adult is objective, rational and logical.

When differences of opinion arise in work or personal situations, the Adult is not concerned with the control or nurturing of others, but simply with an identification of the logistics of the difficulty and the formation of a rational and logically consistent solution. As you will probably appreciate, this approach will only work if all parties concerned are also prepared to view their differences in this objective, detached manner.

The Child ego function The Child reflects the turmoil and emotions of actual childhood: the mental energy, the insatiable curiosity, the sense of wonder, the enthusiasm, the imagination, the naïvety, the fears, the irrationality, the rebelliousness and the desire to please and be good—all the emotions, intuitions and emerging thought patterns that characterize the first six or seven years of our lives.

The Child is an extremely important aspect of our personality. Like the Parent, it is highly emotional in nature, but whereas the Parent is 'other person'-centred, that is, concerned with the control or nurturing of others, the Child is essentially self-centred. The Parent is 'You'-oriented, the Child 'I'-oriented.

There are two functions carried out by the Child. Berne characterized these functions as the *free (or natural) Child*, and the *adapted Child*.

The free Child ego function The free Child is imaginative, spontaneous, fun loving, rebellious, risk taking, explosive and obsessive. It is the source of much of our emotional energy. The free Child gives vent to its emotions and its needs and is the state in which we are completely in touch with our genuine feelings. Berne suggested that genuine feelings include joy, anger, frustration, and sadness. Those feelings, in fact, that are capable of being experienced by a child under the age of one year. He contrasted these natural feelings with other, conditioned, feelings such as guilt and anxiety, which he associated with the other function of this Ego State, the adapted Child.

The adapted Child ego function If the free Child characterizes complete autonomy, the adapted Child signifies its opposite—submission. We all, to some extent, modify our free Child wants and needs in relation to the requirements and conventions of the outside world. We learn to eat with a spoon rather than with our hands (which is easier and more convenient) in order to meet the wishes of our parents who may withhold our food until we do so. We conform to seemingly idiotic requirements and conventions such as going to bed when we are not tired and being made to get up when we are. We learn that certain behaviours are likely to get us what we want and others are not. We learn to wait, to cope with frustrations and to act in a manner that will gain the approval of those adults who have authority over us. It is during this period of adaptation (from about one year onwards) that we begin to experience feelings such as guilt, anxiety, resentment and the need to please others.

These five ego functions are broadly represented by Figure 8.2.

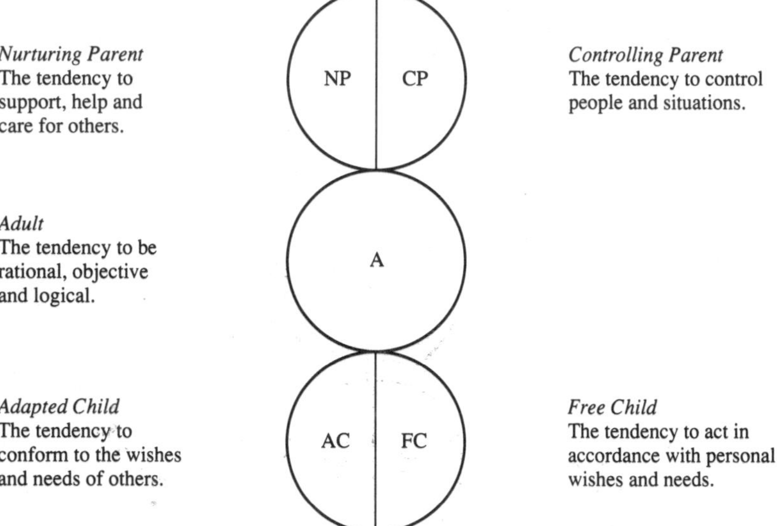

Figure 8.2 *A functional analysis of ego states*

The distribution of ego states within the personality

In theory, each ego function has an appropriate part to play in our lives and a well-balanced individual will display the full range of ego behaviours in appropriate situations. For example, in a situation where someone has been injured and you are the only person present who has specific training in first aid, it would be appropriate to operate from controlling Parent and take charge. Equally, it would be appropriate to operate from nurturing Parent in a situation where someone has received tragic news. In a crisis, where corrective action must be taken in a short time span, operating from Adult would be the most effective response. If someone else has more knowledge or experience of a particular situation than we do, it would be appropriate to operate from adapted Child and accept their advice. In a situation where a team needs to be committed to a course of action it would be appropriate for the leader to operate from free Child and display his or her own commitment vigorously and enthusiastically. In some situations of course it would be appropriate to switch rapidly between ego functions in order to achieve an aim.

There are many examples of these situations in the everyday interactions between managers and staff, trainers and learners. However, they tend to occur in short periods of time and often pass unnoticed. In order to illustrate this point, I have taken an example of ego switching from part of a short science fiction story I read many years ago (unfortunately the title page and identity of the author have long since disappeared and so I cannot give acknowledgement).

In this particular scene, the crew of a small spaceship have collided with an asteriod and are in danger of 'burning up in the methane atmosphere of Zandos 31'. The captain is unconscious and panic has broken out among the six remaining crew members. At this point, the navigator, Riggs, tries to bring things under control. This particular extract is interesting in that it clarifies the role of ego functions in the context of decision making and problem solving. The dialogue (with attendant ego functions) goes like this:

Riggs Shut up! Everybody just shut up and calm down! (controlling Parent). We're getting nowhere like this. I estimate we've got four and a half minutes until we hit it. (Adult)

Murphy, run a simulation, quick. (controlling Parent)

Murphy OK. (adapted Child)

Got it. (Adult)

Riggs What's it say? (Adult)

Murphy Ditch the fuel. (Adult)

Riggs All of it? (Adult)

Murphy The lot. (Adult)

Riggs Damn it! (free Child)

OK. (adapted Child)

Harris, ditch the fuel. (controlling Parent)

Harris I don't know Riggs, this don't feel good to me . . . (free Child)

Riggs Look. I don't want to fry and I don't want any of you to fry (nurturing Parent) this is the only chance we got (Adult). Come on! We can do it, we've survived worse than this! (free Child)

Harris OK Riggs, it's your call. (adapted Child)

Naturally Riggs has made the correct decision and nobody 'gets fried' (at least not at this point). Although fictitious, the dialogue illustrates the interplay of ego functions at different points in the decision making process. Riggs uses his controlling Parent to calm things down in order that the problem can be addressed and to gain information from Murphy. His Adult is used to clarify the situation and to assess it. His free Child reacts emotionally to the news that they must dump the fuel, but his adapted Child allows him to accept it. Harris' reaction, which is also free Child, is countered by Riggs resorting to a combination of nurturing Parent, Adult and free Child. This is a very important combination that has direct relevance to the real-life situations that trainers and managers face every day and we will explore it in some depth in this chapter.

In the story, Riggs is effective because he has access to *all* his ego functions and uses them at appropriate points to resolve the problems he faces. In real-life situations this, unfortunately, is not always the case. Although in theory everyone has the possibility of utilizing each ego function, in practice individuals often resort to a single function or a combination of only two or three. This phenomenon is known in TA terms as *exclusion*, that is, the tendency to operate from a single or limited set of ego functions.

The excluding personality

It is not uncommon to meet individuals who have a strong tendency to utilize only one of the available ego functions across a wide range of situations. I attach no value judgements to this, it is simply a statement of observation. Such individuals are, above all else, predictable.

In terms of the five ego functions, the excluding personality may exhibit any one of the following:

- a strong tendency to say 'no' to requests or suggestions
- a strong tendency to say 'yes'
- a strong tendency to ask questions before saying either 'yes' or 'no'
- a strong tendency to be concerned about others
- a strong tendency to take risks.

Each behaviour is characteristic of one particular ego function—the other four are effectively excluded out. The major characteristics of these five excluding personalities are outlined below.

The excluding controlling Parent Individuals who are very high in controlling Parent are typically distrustful and critical of the overwhelming majority of others and often resort to elaborate means of checking and monitoring performance and actions. They will typically be strong on leading from the front and show very high levels of conviction to beliefs, values and standards. They are very resistant to views that they do not perceive as being in tune with their own and argue vehemently, and sometimes illogically, against such views. They engage in a good deal of 'blame delegation' and find it very difficult to admit to any responsibility for failure, which is usually attributed to the weaknesses or inabilities of others.

Their tenacity and total commitment to ideals can act as an inspiration to others. When their beliefs are (functionally speaking) correct, they provide dynamic leadership that often brings dramatic results. When their beliefs are (functionally speaking) incorrect, they frequently plough relentlessly on to disaster while dismissing the views of those who have a more effective grasp of the realities of the situation.

Individuals high in controlling Parent will be drawn to occupations that offer opportunities to exercise authority and power, such as politics, the judiciary, the police, management or (secondary school) teaching. This does not mean that *all* people engaged in these occupations are, therefore, raging egotists. People may be drawn to such occupations for very different reasons, but one common reason is the opportunity to exercise control, which exists in them.

The excluding nurturing Parent Individuals who are very high in nurturing Parent are focused primarily on others and the satisfaction of their needs. Their perceived role in life is to give rather than to receive and they are at their happiest when they have someone or something to care for. They are very concerned with the emotional needs of others and may become overpowering in terms of their constant 'How are you, you look unwell?' type of behaviours. Although they can be a significant source of comfort and support to others, particularly during periods of emotional stress, they may also act (usually unconsciously) as a barrier to the development of others through overprotection and a tendency to build dependence and helplessness.

Individuals high in nurturing Parent will be drawn to the 'caring' professions, such as nursing, social work, voluntary work, counselling and (primary school) teaching.

The excluding Adult Individuals very high in Adult tend to see the whole of life as a problem of logic. Emotion plays a characteristically small part in their lives and they find great difficulty in dealing with emotional problems. They are characteristically excellent organizers, extremely thorough and totally reliable. They usually possess high levels of concentration and low distractability, they are completely at ease with numbers, information and data and enjoy (if that is the appropriate word) analysis and deduction.

They prefer to work with things rather than people and are therefore drawn to such occupational areas as computing, scientific research, mechanical engineering, accountancy and fiscal management.

The excluding free Child Individuals very high in free Child are commonly charismatic, spontaneous, risk taking, irresponsible and unreliable. They are extremely emotional and prone to emotional turmoil.

They are enthusiastic, creative, disorganized and can be (when interested) very hardworking. They have a low boredom threshold, high distractability, a tendency to procrastination and the potential to convince and enthuse others.

Their need for excitement, autonomy, risk and change draws them towards occupations such as the arts, advertising, financial dealing, selling, management and politics.

The excluding adapted Child Individuals very high in adapted Child have a strong drive to seek situations in which they feel secure and safe. They like structure and stability. They prefer to carry out established procedures rather than having large amounts of autonomy. They are not good decision makers. They are generally well-organized, prone to bouts of self-doubt and acutely sensitive to the comments of others. They are reliable, conscientious and hardworking. They prefer to work as part of a team and react well to strong leadership as they rarely make suggestions, preferring to keep a 'low profile' approach to their work. They make excellent 'foot soldiers' and can be relied upon to carry out instructions to the letter. They are most comfortable working in anonymous positions, ideally in large bureaucratic organizations.

Speech and behaviour indicators of ego functions

There are characteristic speech and behaviour patterns displayed when an individual is using a particular ego function. The frequency of use of these patterns of speech and behaviour indicates the extent to which an individual has access to the full range of ego functions.

Controlling Parent *Typical words*: No!, stop, can't, got, should, ought, must, fault, responsibility, disgusting, appalling, useless, stupid, bad, wrong, dirty.
Typical phrases: 'You've got to', 'I don't believe it!', 'Listen to me when I'm talking', 'Going to sort this out once and for all', 'When I was your age', 'How many times do I have to tell you!', 'What you need to do is', 'I told you, didn't I?', 'Have I got to do everything myself?'
Typical behaviours: Tense, explosive, tight-lipped, hands on hips, frowning, glaring, pointing/wagging index finger, exhaling loudly, tapping fingers/feet in frustration.

Nurturing Parent *Typical words*: Careful, hurt, care, consideration, pity, love, happy, sad, unwell, tired, concerned, help.
Typical phrases: 'Oh dear', 'How are you?', 'Let me help you', 'Take care of yourself', 'You look tired', 'I'll do it for you', 'You relax', 'You poor thing', 'If there's anything I can do', 'Never mind', 'It'll be all right, I'm sure'.
Typical behaviours: Smiling, actively listening, many 'mmms' and head nods, many facial gestures, sympathetic eye contact, prepares food/drinks for others frequently, touches others frequently.

Adult *Typical words*: Facts, evidence, logical, clarify, sensible, rational, precise, irrelevant, what, why, when, where, how.
Typical phrases: 'How do you know that?', 'Let's not get emotional', 'Let's get to the facts', 'The facts are . . .', 'That's merely an opinion', 'I can't

see the logic in that', 'What point are you trying to make?', 'There's not enough information to decide', 'Let's try to be objective'.
Typical behaviours: Precise, not animated, purposeful, intensely interested, direct, searching eye contact, few facial gestures, slow head nods, steady voice, tone and pitch.

Free Child *Typical words*: Yes!, great!, brilliant!, fantastic, fun, smashing, now, boring, grotty/naff (or other current derivative).
Typical phrases: 'I can't wait', 'It's brilliant', 'Let's do it', 'I don't care', 'So what', 'I can't be bothered', 'I'm going', 'I'm bored with it'.
Typical behaviours: Very animated when excited, wide-eyed, many facial gestures, rapid head nods, talking loudly, talking very fast, giggling, pouting, may be clumsy, easily distracted.

Adapted Child *Typical words*: Yes, OK, sorry, pardon, oops, all right, sure.
Typical phrases: 'I'm sorry', 'Of course I will', 'Right away', 'I'm hopeless', 'What do you think we should do?', 'You're right', 'I can't', 'What do you want to do?', 'Can you help me?', 'When will you be back', 'What shall I do if . . .'
Typical actions: Being polite, differential, careful, anxious, self-deprecating, controlled, embarrassed.

The completely excluded personality is a rarity. However, there are many examples of prominent figures, past and present, who provide substantial evidence that the theory has validity. Some examples are:

- *controlling Parent* Margaret Thatcher ('The lady's not for turning')
- *free Child* President John F. Kennedy (risk taker extraordinary)
- *nurturing Parent* Mother Theresa of Calcutta.

It is, by definition, unlikely that individuals extremely high in Adult or, especially, adapted Child would strive for positions of prominence. It is, therefore, difficult to offer clear examples of well-known individuals who fall into either category. We do, however, have an interesting political situation at present that may be illustrative. Both the current Prime Minister, John Major, and the current Leader of the Opposition, Neil Kinnock, display a strong tendency towards particular ego functions.

Mr Major displays many of the characteristics of the excluding Adult. He is rarely accused of being overemotional or charismatic. His reaction to the mortar bombing of 10 Downing Street was classic excluding Adult: 'I think it would be wise to move to another room gentlemen'. That comment could have been uttered by the ultimate embodiment of Adult, Mr Spock of 'Star Trek'.

Mr Kinnock, on the other hand, is frequently criticized for his lack of leadership qualities and his inability to maintain a set of beliefs and values over time. He is also accused of being highly manipulable, characteristics of the adapted Child.

Although both leaders appear to have access to fairly strong secondary ego functions (nurturing Parent for Mr Major and free Child for Mr Kinnock), it appears that the British electorate ultimately has to choose between two individuals who display a strong tendency towards Adult and adapted Child behaviours respectively.

Mapping personality characteristics—the egoGram

We have already noted that individuals with completely excluding personalities are rare. However, it is also rare to find an individual who does not have some preference to use a particular group of ego functions rather than others. There are many individuals, for example, who can be rational and caring, but find difficulty in asserting themselves or in allowing themselves freedom to do what *they* want to do rather than what *others* want. We could describe such individuals as having a strong Adult, nurturing Parent and adapted Child, but a weak controlling Parent and free Child. Many people experience situations in which they act rashly or impetuously and later regret these actions deeply. They could be described as having strong and conflicting free Child and adapted Child tendencies as such individuals commonly experience considerable levels of guilt feelings about past actions.

Each individual, therefore, can be considered as having an 'ego profile', a particular set of ego function preferences that can be represented diagramatically. Such a diagram is often referred to as an egoGram. EgoGrams can be constructed by observing others, or indeed ourselves, and noting how often particular ego functions are used. This frequency can then be represented as a histogram or Pareto diagram or as a profile constructed from measured points (one form of representing an egoGram is shown in Figure 8.3).

It can be a revealing exercise to construct our own egoGram (that is, our own view of how we see our particular ego function preferences) and to compare our diagram with one constructed by someone who knows us well. The results are often extremely interesting.

Let us begin such an exercise by examining the egoGram of a fictitious trainer, Chris. Let us assume that Chris has undergone a series of psychometric tests (similar to the inventory you completed at the beginning of this section), plus in-depth interviews and observations during training sessions. These test results and observations are recorded and represented in diagram form as shown in Figure 8.3).

It is clear from the diagram that Chris' most frequently used ego function is nurturing Parent, followed by adapted Child and Adult. Controlling Parent occupies the lowest frequency of use, with free Child functions also being low. If this profile is an accurate reflection of the way Chris typically operates across a range of situations, we can make some educated predictions about strengths and weaknesses.

Chris is probably someone who would be described as being caring, warm and helpful. Chris' training style would, in all probability, be highly participative in nature and the majority of learners who Chris works with would find little to criticize in terms of general approach and desire to help. Some, however, may find Chris' approach to be a little indecisive and Chris may experience difficulty in exercising effective control on occasions.

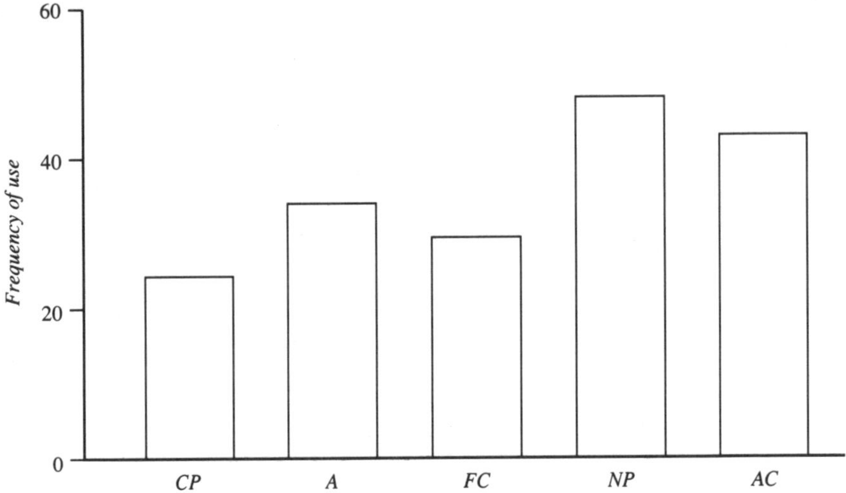

Figure 8.3 Chris' egoGram

The relative lack of free Child functions may mean that Chris often takes on more responsibility for learning than is wise and tends to place own needs behind the expressed needs of others. A programme of personal development for Chris would probably focus on developing the positive aspects of the controlling Parent and the free Child.

This analysis, although fictitious, gives an indication of the potential use of egoGrams in terms of training, management and personal development.

It would be useful to analyse the responses you made to the personality inventory included at the beginning of this section now. Transfer your individual scores onto the analysis sheet on page 179. Add each of the five columns vertically to produce five separate scores and transfer these scores *in order* into the boxes below.

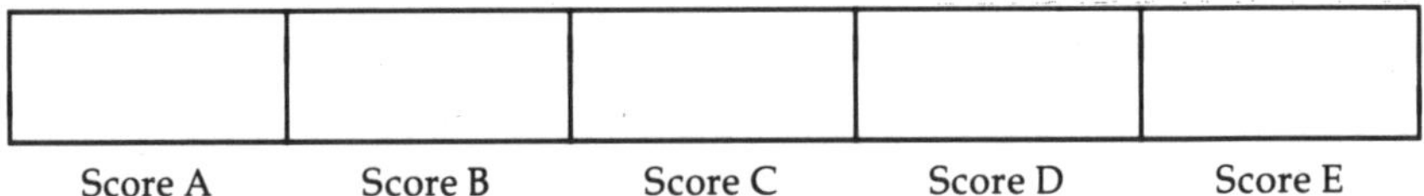

Score A Score B Score C Score D Score E

Score A represents your score for controlling Parent.
Score B represents your score for Adult.
Score C represents your score for free Child.
Score D represents your score for nurturing Parent.
Score E represents your score for adapted Child.

It is well to remember that these scores are taken from a single, unsupervised inventory and therefore the results obtained will be subject to a number of possible distortions. However, as the aim of the exercise is *not* to offer deep and meaningful insights into your personality, but to introduce a method that may be useful in the context of training and self-development, I hope that it has proved interesting and productive.

The final scores obtained can now be transferred to the egoGram form shown in Figure 8.4.

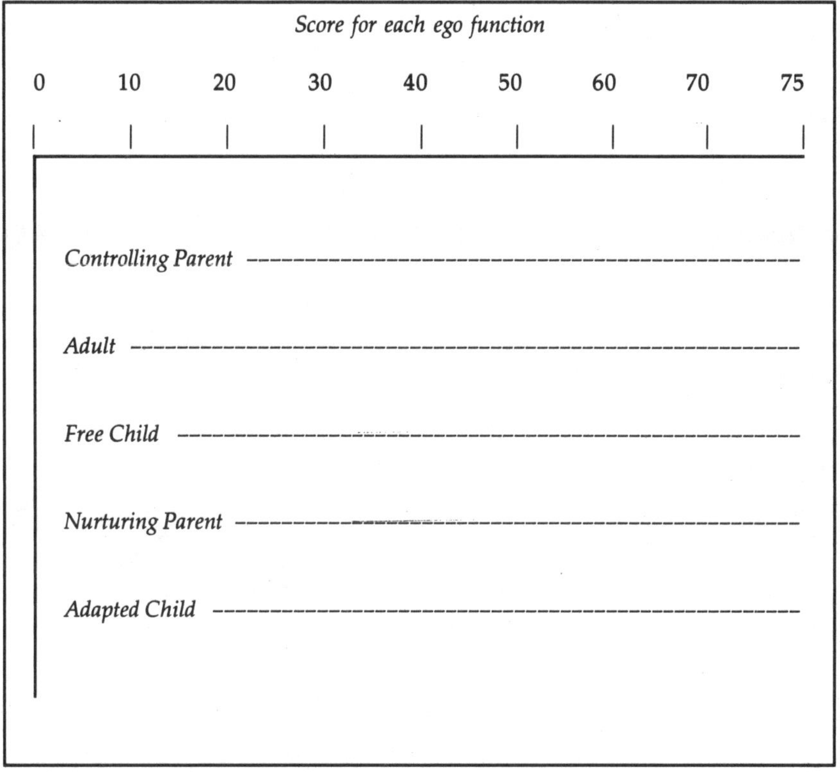

Figure 8.4 *EgoGram form*

Interpretation of scores The maximum score obtainable on any dimension is 72 and the minimum obtainable score is 12. I have used variations of this inventory with some 600 or so trainers, teachers, trainee teachers and managers over the past 4 years. The cumulative data indicate the following for each dimension measured:

- a score of between 12 and 24 is very *low*, with only 2 or 3 per cent of respondents scoring between these points
- a score of between 24 and 34 is *low*, with approximately 15 per cent of respondents scoring between these points
- a score of between 34 and 48 is *average*, with approximately 65 per cent of respondents scoring between these points
- a score of between 48 and 62 is *high*, with approximately 15 per cent of respondents scoring between these points
- a score of between 62 and 72 is *very high*, with only 2 or 3 per cent of respondents scoring between these points.

The shape of the egoGram (the egoGram profile) can also provide useful insights into individual personality. A fairly level profile indicates a number of things. First, it indicates that an individual has access to the full repertoire of ego functions. However, this is not the end of the story. A fairly level profile with scores averaging around the 38 mark indicates an individual who would probably be considered as being calm and flexible. In contrast to this, a fairly level profile with scores averaging above 60 indicates a person who may often display fairly dramatic shifts in behaviour and attitude. Such a person would probably be considered volatile and unpredictable. The general message is that emotional intensity is represented by the area under the ego curve, the greater the area the greater the emotional intensity and vice versa.

In all probability your egoGram profile is not a perfect horizontal line, but indicates that one, or perhaps two, ego functions tend to dominate. Some ego combinations are more common than others. The Adult can be included in almost any dominant combination, for example, Adult plus controlling Parent (such individuals commonly control others through the power and logic of their arguments).

Free Child plus Adult is potentially an extremely productive combination, particularly when each function is present to a significant degree. It is essentially a blend of creative and rational tendencies, vision and logic, art and science. Many great philosophers and scientists throughout history have, if their biographers are to be trusted, displayed behaviours that indicate that these tendencies were present to a significant degree—Albert Einstein, Leonardo da Vinci and Ludwig Wittgenstein being prime examples.

Other combinations of dominant ego functions are very uncommon, for example, controlling Parent and nurturing Parent.

In the following section we will examine the implications of various combinations of ego functioning in relation to the design and delivery of training and the development of organizational cultures.

Applications of the ego function framework to the analysis of training design, training delivery and the development of organizational cultures

Tom Peters has rightly observed that 'Organizations are people'. Organizations are human constructions and it is therefore reasonable to expect that they will reflect human variables and human complexities. Human beings are characterized by the tensions between rationality and emotion and progress usually occurs when there is a synthesis of both facets of our personalities—the practical and the imaginative, the tried and tested and the innovative, the facts and figures and the gut feeling. In the ego function model, these primary drives are associated with the Adult and the free Child: analysis and synthesis.

Each of the five ego functions may be translated into a set of observable actions and behaviours and these actions and behaviours can be analysed and quantified. This process constitutes the basis of *Training Action Analysis* (TAA) and *Management Action Analysis* (MAA).

The five key actions (5KA)

We have already seen that an individual's behaviour can be categorized in terms of the five ego functions. In practical terms, these ego functions can be translated into five discrete, observable actions. These actions, which I refer to as the *five key actions* (5KA), form a framework that may be used to analyse training and management processes (the 5KA framework). The five key actions are:

- **controlling** (from the controlling Parent)
- **informing** (from the Adult)
- **enthusing** (from the free Child)
- **supporting** (from the nurturing Parent)
- **adapting** (from the adapted Child).

These actions can be considered in terms of self and others. Some common applications are outlined in Table 8.1.

	Self	*Others*
Controlling	Discipline Time Eating/drinking Exercise Emotions	Discipline Standards Safety Finances Workload
Informing	Reading Listening Asking Thinking Experimenting	Telling Showing Coaching Guiding Correcting
Enthusing	Curiosity Optimism Fun Humour	Commitment Sense of mission Persuasion Dynamism
Supporting	Rest Self-praise Self-respect	Praise Help Empathy
Adapting	Strengths Weaknesses Limitations	Rights Expertise Needs

Table 8.1 *Some applications of the five key actions to self and others*

Analysing training design using the 5KA framework

The 5KA framework can be used to identify the particular orientation of design that underpins a period of training or learning. In general terms, training design and training delivery (which I will term training style) can be considered as occupying a particular point on a spectrum that has a highly directive style at one pole and a highly consultative style at the other.

This spectrum of training styles can be represented in terms of the five key actions outlined below (see Figure 8.5).

Directive		*Adaptive*
I----	--	----I
Control/inform	Enthuse	Support/adapt

Figure 8.5 *The spectrum of training styles*

At the directive end of the spectrum we have training that is designed and delivered using a *control/inform* (C/I) philosophy. It is probably fair to say that, until the mid seventies, most training in this country was C/I-oriented. This model essentially puts the trainer into the role of expert. The trainer determines training objectives, decides training content, structures the training event and delivers it. The key actions most often used in this type of training are controlling and informing.

The late seventies and early eighties saw the rapid growth of learner-centred training philosophies and an abrupt shift to the other end of the spectrum: *Adapt/Support* (A/S) oriented training. This model places the trainer in the role of facilitator. The trainer acts as a resource for the learners, remains nondirective and generally aims to provide a nurturing environment. The key actions most often used are adapting and supporting.

Although—as with the case of the excluding personality—training programmes are seldom completely C/I- or A/S-oriented, they can be very much biased in one particular direction. Some common indicators of C/I- and A/S-oriented training design are listed below.

Indicators of C/I-oriented training design

- Task-oriented.
- Learners not consulted during analysis and design stages.
- Systematic participant selection procedures in place.
- Specific training aims.
- Desired learning outcomes specified before training commences.
- Highly structured training programme.
- Oriented towards the acquisition of specific skills and knowledge.
- Extensive use of predesigned resources.
- Interchangeability of trainers poses no major problems.
- Significant quantities of back-up materials included (notes, handouts, manuals, etc.).

Indicators of A/S-oriented training design

- Relationship-oriented.
- Learners may be consulted during analysis and design stages.
- No systematic participant selection procedures in place.
- Generalized training aims.

- Desired learning outcomes not specified clearly before training commences.
- Loosely structured training programme.
- Oriented towards discussion.
- Limited use of predesigned resources.
- Interchangeability of trainers poses problems.
- Few back-up materials included.

Applications of C/I- and A/S-oriented training

Each orientation has its particular field of application. C/I-oriented training design can be extremely effective when required learning can be specified precisely and in behavioural terms. The acquisition of specific skills and knowledge and the execution of fixed procedures are good examples. Much of the training of airline pilots, welders and doctors would come within this category.

A/S-oriented training design, in its more extreme forms, is more problematic. In many ways this design is best suited to group problem solving, team building and consensus seeking. It can be extremely effective in situations where a desired aim can be specified (such as reducing customer complaints by 50 per cent or increasing productivity by 5 per cent), but the means of attaining such an outcome are not known. Effective use of A/S-oriented training is heavily dependent on the intrinsic skills, knowledge and attitudes of the group participants.

C/I-oriented training design is best suited to context-independent learning. That is, learning that is applicable to a range of situations. For example, we do not train airline pilots to fly only one specific aeroplane on one route or welders to use only one specific set of welding equipment to weld one type of material.

Conversely, A/S-oriented training is best suited to context-specific learning, that is, learning that is applicable to a single or limited set of situations. These points may be clarified by the use of suitable examples.

I was once responsible for designing and delivering a one-year training course aimed at converting skilled mechanics, fitters and machinists into mechanical equipment designers. The course was very much C/I-oriented, involving precourse selection and suitability testing, a resource-based approach to instruction, systematic and specific evaluations of learning progress and structured exercises.

Course participants were recruited from a range of background situations and, on successful completion of the course, went into equally diverse sectors of the mechanical design market. This diversity of background experience and uncertain final destination posed few real problems as the skills and knowledge to be acquired during the course were built on fundamental knowledge and principles that *all* participants possessed to a required degree, independent of the particular contexts in which they were acquired.

Similarly, the skills and knowledge acquired through the training programme were highly generalizable within the field of mechanical engineering design.

An A/S-oriented training design was inappropriate as the specifics of what was required to be learned (in order to meet the requirements of employment into the design field) were well-established and clearly recognized. These specifics were also accepted as being credible by course participants.

In contrast to this situation, on another occasion I was involved in a short training programme for managers and supervisors in the public sector. The aim of the training was to help these staff develop a more 'commercially oriented' approach within their areas of responsibility.

The training was highly A/S-oriented. There were no selection criteria, other than position within the hierarchy (and availability), a flexible structure, few prepared resources and little back-up material. My role was essentially to offer suggestions, give specific information on similar projects and existing research and to act as a catalyst and sounding board to the group.

The courses of action proposed, problems expected and assistance required were established by group discussion and general information sharing. The actions proposed were, however, highly specific to the context in which these managers and supervisors operated and tackled problems relevant to their particular resource and staffing situations, legal obligations and organizational culture. The approaches and actions developed were highly unlikely to be effective in situations that differed significantly from those pertaining to the group.

Each training orientation has possible advantages and disadvantages.

Possible advantages of a C/I training orientation Training standards, expectations and outcomes are clearly stated so training can be evaluated clearly in terms of desired and actual learning outcomes. Pretraining requirements are clearly understood so pretraining selection criteria improve the probability of success. Little time is wasted on irrelevancies and continuous improvements in training design/delivery result in improved cost/benefit ratios. Technology/based training systems can be incorporated.

Possible disadvantages of a C/I training orientation Training may not respond to environmental changes or be slow to respond (may become obsolete) and, therefore, may not be sensitive to improvement feedback from participants. Overdependency on systems and resources can mean that the training may become dehumanized. The training encourages conformity rather than creativity so precourse selection criteria may exclude some potentially competent participants. Training may become unstimulating and limited to skill/knowledge competences.

Possible advantages of an A/S training orientation It encourages participation and 'ownership' of learning. There are high levels of personal support from the trainer and trainer/learner rapport should be high. There are high levels of negotiation on training content, delivery methods and learning outcomes. This style encourages creativity and group cohesion. It is enjoyable.

Possible disadvantages of an A/S training orientation Learners may achieve little of practical use, with time being wasted on interpersonal irrelevancies. Impractical strategies may be formulated and learners may see the process as a waste of time. The trainer may see the main responsibility being group cohesion rather than constructive change, so suggestions may not be challenged or analysed effectively, threatening issues may not be confronted and 'groupthink' may occur.

Each training orientation has its limitations. C/I orientation can easily lead to rigidity, inflexibility and the sanctity of the curriculum, while A/S-oriented training can easily become amorphous, bland and inconsequential.

The key action missing from both is, of course, enthusing. C/I-oriented training renders it unnecessary and A/S-oriented training largely precludes the leadership role.

Delivering training—individual trainer styles

Although there are certain established prerequisites, every trainer's style of delivery differs in idiosyncratic ways. Some may make extensive and effective use of humour, while others rarely, if ever, use it in the context of training. Some trainers prepare visual aids, handouts and course notes with meticulous precision, while others seem to fly by the seats of their pants. One of the major attractions of training is that it offers us the opportunity to stamp our own personalities firmly on the work we do. Each trainer's style will, in effect, be a reflection of his or her individual personality, that is, the range of ego functions that the trainer is able to bring to the training situation.

As trainers are normal human beings, we can expect that they will display a fairly normal distribution of personality differences. Of course it must be said that trainers are not a random group of individuals; we share certain psychological qualities, such as a tendency towards extroversion rather than introversion and so on to a greater extent than would a randomly selected group. However, we are not (thank heavens) clones of each other and, at each end of the normal curve of distribution of trainers, we find substantial differences in terms of training philosophy and training style. Different trainers have a tendency to favour different combinations of uses of the five key actions outlined earlier and these differences will be reflected in their individual training styles.

During my 17 years' involvement within the field of education and training, I have been fortunate to witness a very wide range of teaching and training styles and I have learned something from all of them. I have often noticed a tendency for one or two key actions to have a major influence on the style a particular teacher or trainer adopts and, on certain occasions, I have seen teachers and trainers who are effectively locked into a single dominant approach.

I give below a resumé of what appear to me to be the main advantages and disadvantages of adopting a single-action approach to the structure and delivery of training. Most of my observations are taken from situations where learners and trainers/teachers have an ongoing relationship over a relatively extended period of time rather than a one- or two-day course. I have also included some typical comments from learners, mostly overheard!

The controlling approach

Positive effects Learners know where they are in terms of discipline, standards and expectations. Aspects such as rules of attendance, starting and finishing times, behaviour, health and safety and so on are highly stressed and rigorously enforced. Training standards and expectations are clearly stated. The training environment is clean and ordered and there is a general sense of purposefulness. Reviews of progress are carried out regularly. Reports are commonly up to date.

Negative effects Some learners may feel dominated, powerless and overcontrolled and rebel or leave. Training programmes may become rigid and inflexible. There may be few opportunities for learners to negotiate changes in the programme. Review sessions tend to be faults-oriented and may be excessively demotivating to the learner. Learners are unlikely to approach their trainer for help with personal problems that may affect their progress.

Some comments from learners 'She's hard but you know where you stand'; 'I hate him'; 'She never gives any praise'; 'He makes you get on with it'; 'There's no messing about in her section/class'; 'He never admits he's wrong.'

The supporting approach

Positive effects Learners receive high levels of personal support from their trainer. There is a generally caring, friendly atmosphere. Learners rarely feel pressurized. Trainer/learner rapport is commonly high. There are high levels of learner influence on the training programme.

Negative effects There may be an overemphasis on personal problems, with the training suffering. Discipline can sometimes be erratic. The trainer may tend to oversupport learners and not allow them to learn from their mistakes. There can be a tendency to overpraise. Progress review sessions tend to avoid confronting issues that may lead to disagreement between learner and trainer.

Some comments from learners 'She's lovely'; 'He gets on my nerves'; 'She'll always listen to your problems'; 'He always wants to know how you are'; 'She's a very nice person, but . . .'

The informing approach

Positive effects The trainer is highly knowledgeable about the subject. Training materials and resources are meticulously prepared and there are lots of explanatory materials. There is regular measurement of achievement and prompt marking and returning of learners' work. Administration is excellent. The trainer is not easily distracted from the subject.

Negative effects There is very little person-to-person contact between trainer and learners. There is little, if any, humour or 'light relief'. The training is unlikely to be spontaneous or creative. There is a preponderance of formal training methods. Learners are unlikely to approach the trainer for help with personal problems.

Some comments from learners 'She knows her stuff'; 'He knows his stuff, but he can't teach'; 'She doesn't have favourites'; 'He's terminally boring'; 'I wonder if she ever laughs.'

The enthusing approach

Positive effects There are high levels of commitment and personal enthusiasm from the trainer. There are good interpersonal skills. It is a creative training style, spontaneous. There is good use made of humour and light relief. A wide variety of training methods are used.

Negative effects Such trainers are often poor at administration, marking learners' work and returning it promptly. They may have unrealistic expectations of learners and may go too fast. They may spend too much time on what interests them most and be easily distracted from the subject.

Some comments from learners 'She's great'; 'He can't stick to the point'; 'She's on an ego trip'; 'I love his lessons'; 'He really makes the subject interesting'; 'I'm still waiting for my assignment to be marked.'

The adapting approach

Positive effects High levels of negotiation are included in the training programme. The trainer is prepared to expend a great deal of effort to identify and meet learners' needs. The trainer conscious of their own weaknesses and strives to continually improve their performance. The trainer actively seeks feedback from learners regarding the content and delivery of the training.

Negative effects The trainer may become dominated by the learners, being excessively anxious to please and suffer dramatic shifts in self-confidence. The trainer may not confront interpersonal problems until they reach serious proportions. The trainer may resist any leadership role, although learners would benefit from this on occasions. The trainer is easily led off the subject during training sessions.

Some comments from learners 'She lets you do what you want to'; 'He can't control us'; 'She always listens to what we ask'; 'He never disciplines anyone'; 'She won't tell you what your weaknesses are.'

It should be clear from this that each approach has certain advantages and certain pitfalls to watch for. A major failing of the single action approach is that its effectiveness is limited to learners who naturally have a complimentary learning style to the particular training style employed or are prepared to *adopt* a complimentary style in order to successfully complete the training.

For example, the controlling approach works best with learners who have a strong tendency to adapt or a bona fide reason to adapt, such as, to gain a prized certificate or highly marketable skills and knowledge. It will not be so effective with those learners who tend to challenge authority or question the reasons that underpin particular activities.

A supporting approach works best with those learners who need high levels of encouragement and assurance and have a desire to feel liked by the trainer. For those learners who are self-motivated or task- and information-oriented, excessive amounts of support actions may prove to be counterproductive.

An informing approach works best with learners who are task-oriented, independent and self-motivated. It is less effective with learners who are lacking in confidence and have a need to relate to the trainer as a person.

An enthusing approach works best with learners who are capable of responding to a stimulating message and then go on to achieve results mainly under their own steam. It is less effective with those learners who need ongoing support and guidance to achieve results.

An adapting approach works best when learners have the basic capabilities to achieve what needs to be achieved and simply require the space and facilitation necessary to bring the various strands together. It is less effective with learners who lack the vital skills or knowledge necessary to lead to a successful learning outcome. Of course the learners, or indeed the trainer, may not realize that required skills or knowledge are lacking.

Using the 5KA framework to design effective training

The 5KA framework can be used as a basis for the design and delivery of effective training interventions. However, we must not lose sight of the fact that effectiveness in training—that is, effectiveness in achieving constructive organizational change—is dependent on a number of variables. The quality of training input is obviously a key factor in achieving success, but it is not the only one. Whether or not a successfully delivered training programme is actually translated into beneficial organizational change will depend on various factors within the structure of the organization and its systems. These factors will be considered in some detail in Chapter 9.

In terms of training, the 5KA framework can be used at all stages of the quality cycle: definition, design and delivery. The framework forms the basis of a five-dimensional check-list that covers the most important factors influencing effective training interventions.

The check-list comprises a series of fundamental questions that must be addressed before training decisions are made and training interventions designed. The key questions are:

1 What must be *controlled,* such as budget, duration, content, client group?
2 What *information* must be obtained and transmitted at the definition stage, during the design stage, during the delivery stage, after training has been delivered?
3 What *support* must be given before training begins, during training, after training has been completed?
4 Who must be *enthused* before training begins, during training, after training has been completed?
5 What must we *adapt* to before training begins, during training, after training has been completed?

Well-researched answers to these important questions will lay a sound foundation on which effective training interventions can be designed, delivered and followed through.

It is clear that this process requires that a substantial amount of research is undertaken before any training decisions are made. In my own experience, such an in-depth analysis is rarely, if ever, carried out. This, I feel, is one of the major reasons for training often failing to deliver what is required in terms of measurable results. In my own view, training decisions are often based on erroneous assumptions, inadequate data and are made without due consideration of the post-training actions that need to occur in order that the potential benefits of a period of training are translated into actual operational benefits. Too often our clients effectively slot us into one or other end of the training spectrum. That is, we are most commonly perceived in one of two ways: as an expert in training diagnostics or as a course provider.

When we are placed in the role of expert we are commonly charged with the responsibility of analysing a particular problem and designing a training solution. This is the 'You're the training expert, you tell us what we need to do' approach. In other words, we are pushed firmly to the control end of the training spectrum.

When we are placed in the course provider role, we are effectively shifted to the other end—adapt. This is the 'We want you to run a two-day time management course for our supervisors' approach.

The first approach is 'You tell us what we need' and the second is 'We'll tell you what we need'.

Of course both approaches may result in a successful outcome: we may indeed have the expertise and ability to diagnose exactly what training intervention is required in a particular situation *and* be capable of providing it. A client may effectively identify a training need that can be met by a standard course. Both procedures are, however, clearly not collaborative or negotiated procedures. They tend to separate the training process from the work situation and they place training providers firmly centre stage in terms of responsibility for the ultimate success or otherwise of a training intervention. This is a naïve and unfair assumption. As we will see in the following section, the ultimate effectiveness of training, that is its effectiveness in bringing about constructive organizational change, depends on a wide range of factors.

The approach advocated here is to avoid the central weaknesses of the C/I and S/A training strategies and to adopt instead what is most effective in both. This approach can be considered as *negotiated training*.

It must be emphasized, however, that the approach advocated here is one of genuine negotiation. It is probably true to say that the vast majority of trainers would agree that a negotiated training programme offers the optimum possibility of success. I often wonder, however, how much of the many so-called negotiated programmes are actually what they purport to be. Most negotiated learning is carried out between trainers and course participants, that is, trainers and Customer 1. Occasionally negotiations are carried out between trainers and those who have organizational authority over prospective course participants—Customer 2. Rarely do negotiations address the requirements and responsibilities of *both* customers. This, I feel, is a serious deficiency of many training interventions. In terms of the spectrum of training activities outlined previously, the negotiated training approach aims to avoid the pitfalls of both the directive and adaptive approaches while adopting the potential benefits to be obtained from each. Its position along the spectrum is as shown in Figure 8.6.

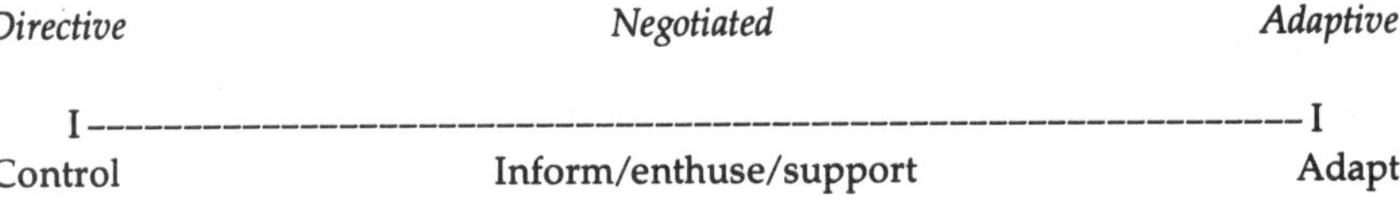

Figure 8.6 *The negotiated approach to training*

The approach draws heavily on three key activities: informing, enthusing and supporting. I have found that combining these three activities constitute the basis of effectiveness across a wide range of situations, including management, teaching and training.

In terms of the training analysis procedures outlined above, the negotiated approach advocates that the majority of attention is paid to answering questions 2, 3 and 4. A more detailed exposition of the Negotiated Training philosophy is given in the final section of the book.

Developing an effective group culture

I have made frequent reference to the importance of organizational culture in the development of quality. We have already noted that quality cannot be legislated for or guaranteed as a direct consequence of adhering to a set of principles and procedures. Principles and procedures enable us to identify and monitor the key variables involved in quality, but they alone cannot guarantee that quality will actually be achieved and that continuous improvement will occur. Ultimately, quality comes only from people. Quality is about attitudes and values and attitudes and values are both a cause and an effect of organizational cultures.

Many writers have reflected on the nature of organizational cultures and attempted to identify the central characteristics that distinguish one from another. That great differences do exist is beyond doubt. For example, the culture of ITT under the leadership of Harold Geneen differed greatly from that of Hewlett Packard or the Matsushita Electric Company.

Organizational cultures are, of course, group cultures. Albeit often involving very large groups they are still the product of an interaction between people, systems and physical resources. We have already noted that organizations may develop more than a single integrated culture (the organizational iceberg phenomenon noted in Chapter 7) and that this has direct relevance for the design and delivery of group-based training. It is useful, therefore, to consider those factors that characterize effective groups.

Group cultures can usefully be considered in terms of three central variables:

- power
- relationships
- achievement.

Some groups are characterized by a power or authority culture. They are frequently hierarchical in structure and function through directives and orders. Groups within the armed forces would be included within this type of culture.

Other groups may be characterized by a culture that values and nurtures interpersonal relationships, consensus seeking and general harmony. In my own experience, this type of culture is characteristic of many voluntary sector organizations.

Finally, groups may be characterized by a culture which places the achievement of a set goal or task above considerations such as authority and relationships.

Scientific and medical research groups often display this form of orientation.

The majority of groups, particularly work groups, will in all probability have a culture which includes influences from each of these 'pure' orientations. However, as with the excluding personality, strong biases toward a particular orientation are not uncommon.

Characteristics of effective groups

Effective groups are characterized by achievement, individual responsibility and a sense of team unity. Effective groups, therefore, are able to successfully balance three critical variables:

- getting things done
- developing and utilizing the abilities of individuals
- creating and maintaining group unity.

This balancing act lies at the heart of the effective management of *all* groups. It is not uncommon, however, to find that groups (under the influence of the manager or group leader) have a tendency to focus on one or two factors only. This leads to problems in the long term. Managers and group leaders who are primarily task-oriented may fail to take adequate measures to develop and utilize the abilities of individual team members or to generate a culture of cooperation and mutual support. On the other hand, managers and team leaders who are primarily 'people'-oriented may find that, although there is a good deal of cooperation and harmony present, not very much actually gets done.

The quality model demands that all three factors are recognized as being essential to the successful operation of teams and form the basis of continuous improvement. The interrelationship between these three factors is often represented (for example, by Adair) as a configuration of overlapping circles (see Figure 8.7).

The effective training group can be expected to conform to this general model of effective group operation. It will be useful therefore to consider each of the variables in turn.

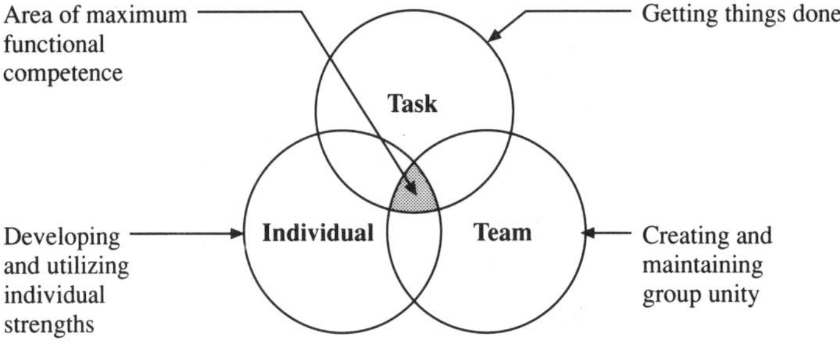

Figure 8.7 Critical factors in effective groups

Getting things done A training group is, in many ways, a task-centred group: it is there for a purpose. That purpose is to develop abilities that are capable of being translated into improved organizational effectiveness. Trainers aim to develop these abilities through various learning opportunities. In training terms, therefore, the task, that is, the things that need to be done, will include trainer input, discussion, feedback, structured and unstructured exercises and the attainment of key training objectives.

Developing and utilizing the abilities of individuals This is obviously a key training objective. Trainers must be aware of individual needs and individual competences and use this knowledge to the benefit of both the individual and the group.

Creating and maintaining group unity Ideally, the training process should be such that a sense of group identity is created and maintained. This requires that the trainer be skilled in such areas as vision building, group dynamics and conflict resolution.

The challenge, of course, is to bring all this together in what is usually a fairly short time span. In order to achieve this, trainers must be aware of the factors that encourage the development of highly integrated groups. My own experiences as a manager, trainer and consultant have led me to the conclusion that effective groups, irrespective of size, share certain characteristics. These characteristics are related to three important variables:

- information
- trust
- shared values.

Information Effective groups are characterized by effective communications. In organizational terms, this means that important, accurate, up-to-date information passes freely within and between departments and is not withheld or restricted to a top-down flow. Effective groups have little need for rumour networks or grapevines.

In terms of training groups, this means that important information concerning training aims and objectives must be clearly communicated along with the intended methodology for achieving these aims and objectives. This communication must also include the rights and responsibilities of all concerned, trainer included.

Manipulation and subterfuge must be avoided. This does not mean that trainers cannot use experiential exercises that may put learners under some form of limited stress or may challenge preconceived views (from which valuable learning can accrue). However, it must be stated clearly at the outset of training that a number of learning techniques will be employed, including confrontation and challenge.

Trust It should be clear from the preceding section that the levels of trust in the group will be directly related to the quality of information available. Trust is a direct consequence of honesty. Trust is demonstrated by a willingness to treat individuals on a basis of equality, to share rather than withhold relevant information, to mean what one says, to assist and ask for assistance, to listen and to respond to the views of others and to demonstrate a desire to maintain the integrity of the group and its members.

Shared values When quality information is available and levels of trust are high, the development of shared values is a relatively straightforward process. However, it does require a leader or vision maker who is able to provide direction and coordinate group resources. I firmly believe that, in the training context, this role is primarily the responsibility of the trainer.

The establishment of a system of shared values and a commitment to action lies at the heart of the quality culture and training must be at the forefront of this process of culture development.

Effective trainer behaviours

It should be clear that the three variables which characterize effective groups are directly related to the three key activities of negotiated training:

- informing—communicating honestly and effectively
- supporting—facilitating individual development
- enthusing—creating a sense of vision, unity and commitment within the group.

These three activities characterize effective performance in management, teaching and training across a wide range of contexts. Effective managers, teachers and trainers show a marked tendency to use the positive aspects of the Adult, nurturing Parent and free Child ego functions and to avoid their negative potentials. Controlling Parent and adapted Child functions are used appropriately and sparingly. They work from a basis of earned commitment rather than ordered compliance. In terms of egoGram profiles, therefore, the effective trainer can be expected to display something in the region of an 80 per cent preference towards these types of behaviours. This situation can be represented diagramatically as shown in Figure 8.8.

Obviously the figures in Figure 8.8 are not absolutely precise, they are intended to indicate the approximate range and frequency of behaviours

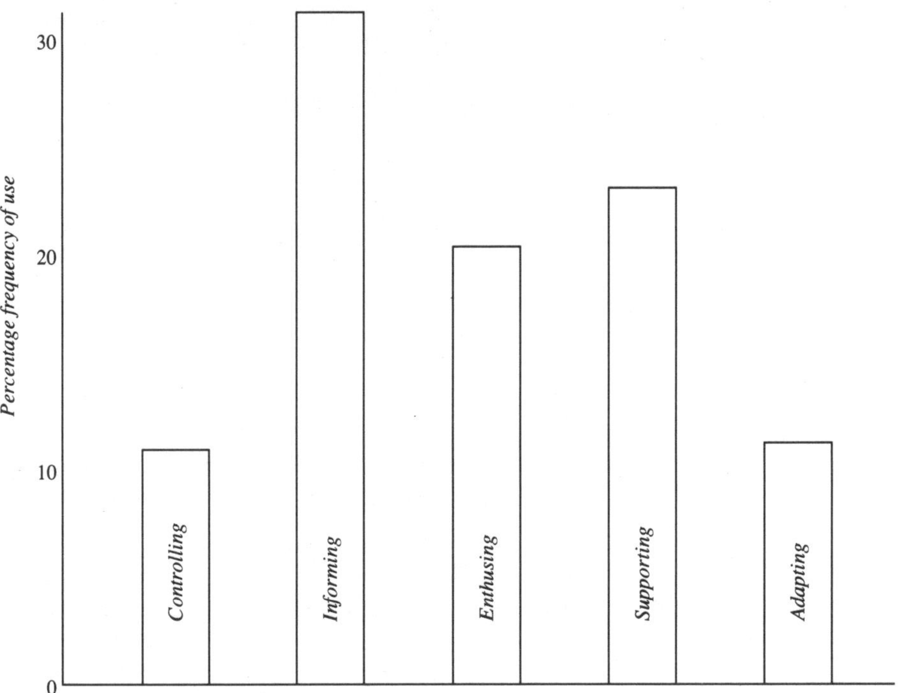

Figure 8.8 Effective trainer behaviours—frequency of use during training

used by effective trainers. Effective trainers appear to spend up to 80 per cent of training time giving and receiving information, facilitating the development of others and generating high levels of commitment and a bias towards action. Some common behaviours from each category are given below.

Informing Providing new information, explaining theories and procedures, providing back-up information, demonstrating skills, relating theory to practice, seeking information from learners, providing feedback to learners, responding to queries from learners, assessing learning.

Supporting Coaching, counselling, encouraging, re-framing, reflecting, suggesting, facilitating action planning.

Enthusing Selling benefits, displaying personal commitment, providing a dynamic delivery, managing individual resistance effectively, developing an effective group culture.

Controlling Prescribing exercises and activities, allocating time to discussion and so on, exercising effective control of dialogue and behaviour, maintaining a focus on effective learning.

Adapting Changing direction, pace, delivery as appropriate.

Conclusion

It should be clear from this analysis that the effective delivery of training, that is training which is focused primarily on informing, supporting and enthusing, will be heavily dependent on the depth and accuracy of research and preparation undertaken during the definition and design stages of the quality circle. If this research has not been effectively undertaken, that is, if training is not geared virtually 100 per cent to real needs, then resistance or apathy is likely to be considerable.

Faced with learners who are unconvinced that training is actually relevant to their real needs, many trainers resort to a control or adapt strategy in order to avoid catastrophe.

If training is to be effective, trainers must be totally convinced of the practical relevance and potential benefits that can be accrued and they must be able to substantiate this conviction with soundly researched information, practical suggestions for real applications and personal powers of persuasion. If this level of objective commitment is not present, training inevitably sinks to the 'give it a try' type of waffling and fudging that leaves learners totally unconvinced and trainers perpetually depressed.

It is obvious, therefore, that if training is to have a substantial impact on organizational effectiveness, it cannot be designed in isolation from the realities of the field of application. The generalized training course has little to offer above the opportunities afforded to share ideas, discuss theories and meet with others who may operate in similar situations. Such events are often enjoyable, relaxing and entertaining and, when thoroughly researched and effectively presented, they may result in real improvements in individual effectiveness. Their fundamental weakness lies in the fact that they are isolated from the field of application and are, therefore, limited to working with one link of a chain and, as we are all aware, strengthening one link does not result in a stronger chain, unless we happen, luckily, upon the weakest link. Given the enormous complexities that influence organizational effectiveness, in training terms this is a very long shot indeed.

9 Effective training—the organizational context

In previous chapters we have considered the factors that influence training effectiveness at the level of the individual being trained. In other words, we have examined the effectiveness of the training experience. Obviously, if we fail at this stage training will not result in the occurrence of any positive organizational changes—indeed, quite the opposite may happen. However, success at the individual level, that is a successful training experience, does not automatically guarantee that role effectiveness and, consequently, organizational effectiveness, will subsequently improve either.

An individual's ultimate role effectiveness within an organization will be a consequence of the various factors at play. A proportion of these factors are internal (that is, to do with the individual) and some are external (to do with the working environment). Role effectiveness is not just determined by the particular levels of competence that the individual has the potential to display. The working environment in which the individual is obliged to function will inevitably act as a brake or an accelerator on the maximization of whatever potential competences exist. It is clear, then, from all that has been said about quality thus far that we must see a fundamental move towards the latter situation. Organizations can no longer indulge themselves in the destructive tendencies of the former.

Training cannot, alone, maximize human potential; it can only (when it is successful) *increase* it. At the end of a successful period of training, an individual will possess an improved *potential capability*. Whether or not this potential will be translated into actual performance improvement is totally dependent on the nature of the environment in which the person must operate. This situation can be effectively described in terms of the now familiar force-field diagram, as shown in Figure 9.1. The drivers and barriers shown are not exhaustive, but they offer an indication of common situations.

It is clear from Figure 9.1 that organizational effectiveness can be improved simply by reducing all or some of the common barriers to performance listed on the right, assuming, of course, that they do, in fact, exist and also assuming that it is they that are acting as a brake to the maximization of existing human capabilities. It is highly likely that

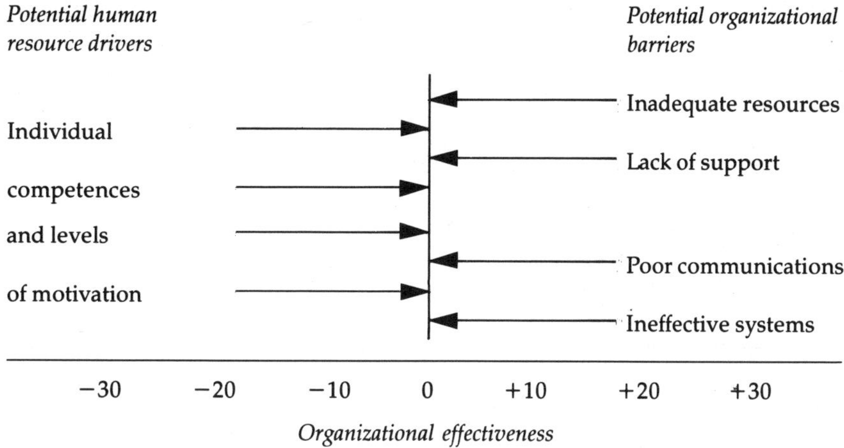

Figure 9.1 *Some factors influencing organizational effectiveness*

this situation represents the way things really are in the vast majority of organizations today. My own experiences suggest that ineffective recruitment procedures, management's lack of courage in dealing with inadequate performers and virtually nonexistent systems of communication are effectively nailing corporate feet to the floor in the race to survive. Real improvements in these three areas alone would immediately transform the effectiveness of many organizations.

Such actions are, however, not enough in themselves to guarantee long-term survival. Long-term survival means continuous improvement and this can only be achieved through a sustained investment that is aimed at increasing human resource capabilities while systematically reducing organizational barriers to the maximization of those capabilities.

Training has traditionally focused almost exclusively on the human resource potentials listed on the left of Figure 9.1 and ignored or failed to influence the common organizational barriers listed on the right. This situation cannot be allowed to continue. If training is to become part and parcel of corporate strategy and corporate financing, we must recognize the fact that training cannot be effective if it is designed and delivered in virtual isolation from the realities of the operational environment. To be truly effective, training must be completely integrated with the achievement of corporate goals. Corporate goals cannot be achieved by people alone or by systems and physical resources alone, but only through the effective integration of both. The analogy with computer software and hardware applies readily here: neither is of any use without the other and improved software will only result in improved computer performance if the existing hardware is capable of utilizing it. In terms of the attainment of organizational goals, this means that training must broaden its sphere of influence to include the right-hand side of the equation as well as the left. Training must become a catalyst for positive change in all aspects of organizational development and not limit itself to the human resource dimension only—to do this is to fight a battle we cannot win. The key to achieving this task is improved communication.

Converting human potential into improved organizational effectiveness

Organizational barriers to improved performance in the work-place

I suggested earlier that training cannot, of itself, improve organizational effectiveness because it cannot, of itself, guarantee that improved performance will occur in the work-place. The potential for improvement that effective training produces will translate into actual improvement only where no organizational barriers are present. In the overwhelming majority of cases, organizational barriers *are* present and they act as a filter of actions in much the same way as a variable light filter operates (see Figure 9.2).

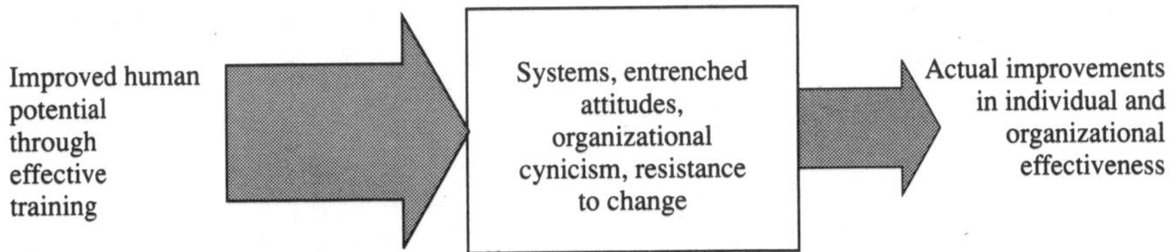

Figure 9.2 *The organizational filter*

It can be seen from Figure 9.2 that the potential generated through effective training will only be translated 100 per cent into actual improvement if the organizational filter is, to maintain the analogy with light, completely transparent. In the vast majority of cases it exerts some degree of opacity and, in the worst cases, it acts as a complete block.

Much has been written of late concerning the need to develop a 'learning culture' within organizations. This preoccupation has tended to overlook the fact that learning will occur in *all* organizations; it is an inevitable process. *All* organizations are learning organizations, but it is *what* is learned that needs to be influenced. I offer below a list of some of the things I have learned in a number of organizations:

- the appraisal system is unfair
- effort is not always recognized
- the boss has favourites
- meetings are a waste of time
- some people are coasting
- management is secretive

- management does not take training and development seriously
- if you want to get on, do not rock the boat
- there are ways to shortcut the system
- restrictive practices operate.

These and other negative factors are common contributors to the organizational filter and they operate in a number of specific ways. Again, a force-field diagram can be used to analyse the situation and identify the major influences at work. In Figure 9.3, some of the potential benefits of effective training are considered in relation to a range of potential barriers that may exist in the work situation. Again, we can see that the full potential developed through training will only be translated into actual performance improvement if the negative possibilities existing in the work situation are eliminated.

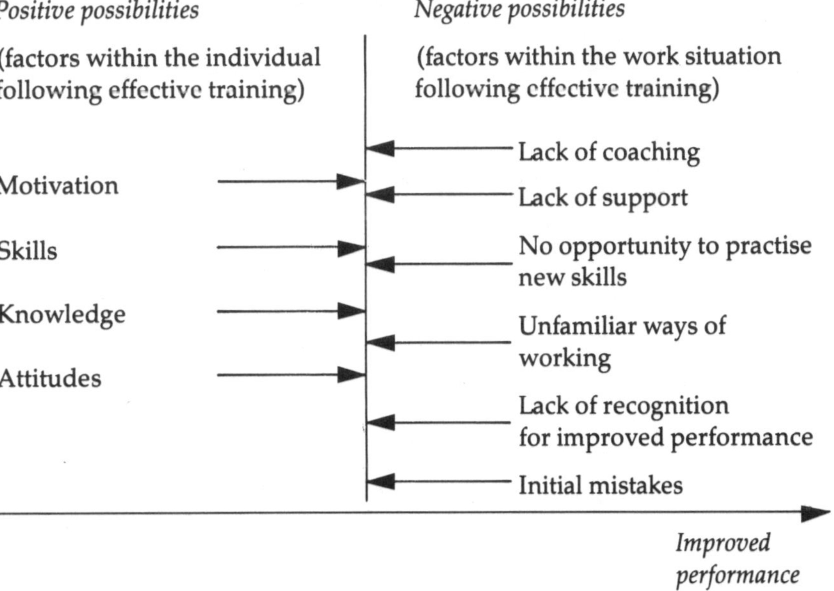

Figure 9.3 *Potential benefits and barriers in the work situation*

The immediate post-training environment is particularly important for consolidating potential improvement. Training, as we have already noted, should produce beneficial change. In the case of the individual, this means changes in the way responsibilities are carried out. If no changes are attempted, then the training process has not been effective. If the training process has been effective, individuals will attempt to carry out their work activities in ways that are not familiar to them or to carry out activities that are completely new.

These changes may be relatively minor or quite substantial. For example, they may involve minor changes in the way an assembly procedure is carried out or they may involve major changes, such as the formal appraisal responsibilities of the newly appointed supervisor or the presentation responsibilities of the newly appointed trainer. However major or minor the required changes may be, there will be a period of uncertainty and tension early on. During this period the individual may experience a sense of frustration when newly tried methods do not produce immediate benefits, but actually result in a performance or confidence *dip*. This situation can be represented graphically as shown in Figure 9.4.

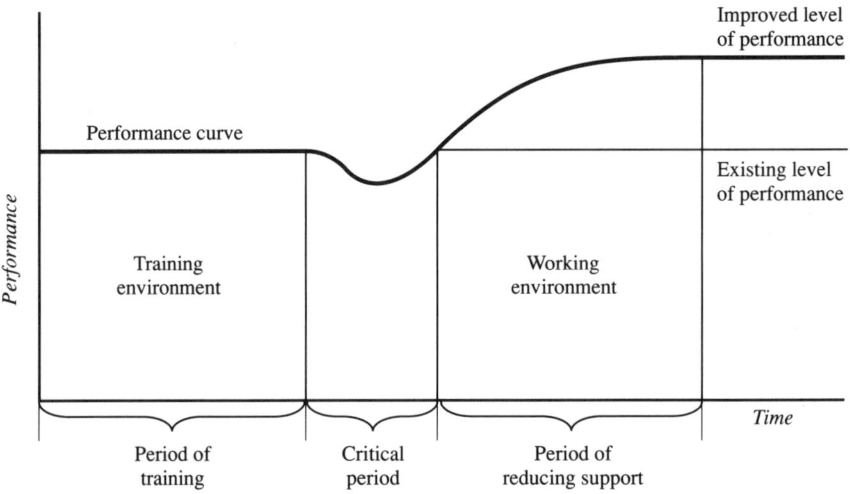

Figure 9.4 *A typical performance improvement curve*

The curve in Figure 9.4 shows that performance improvement is not generally a simple case of incremental gains and that the learning process is not completed instantly the training event finishes. In the very early stages following a period of training, performance and confidence may dip and this period is crucial. If work-place support and encouragement are lacking at this stage, the potential benefits accrued through effective training will not be translated fully into operational improvement—they may even be lost altogether. Obviously this situation will be different in different training contexts. In the case of training that is highly procedural in nature, post-training checks are commonly included to ensure that performance reaches a satisfactory standard or the individual is coached, re-trained or removed from the training programme.

This may not be the case (and usually is not) where training is aimed at process improvement. This form of training encompasses large areas of management, supervisory and trainer development. In these instances it is *rare* to find that the post-training environment is structured so as to maximize the development of the potential that has been generated through an effective training experience. In the vast majority of cases individuals are left to their own devices as far as the development of potential is concerned.

This situation may be illustrated through the common post-training experiences of managers who attend courses aimed at improving some area of management competence. The current marketing literature for management training courses include such regulars as Time Management, Stress Management, Interpersonal Skills, Assertive Management and so on. Managers attend these courses, often enjoy them and come away with some new ideas and some measure of commitment to changing the way they do things. In the overwhelming majority of instances no one else within the manager's organization has had anything substantial to do with the course, has no idea what was covered or what may be expected to result from it in terms of changes to working methods. When the course ends, therefore, the manager returns to the work situation and attempts to put some of the new ideas into practice, but what commonly happens then is that he or she finds out that in the real world things do not go as smoothly as they do in a role playing exercise and that the meticulously detailed action plan somehow seems less and less practical when it is overlayed with the realities of day-to-day management. Unless the individual now persists, unaided, and tries to adapt idealized theories into workable techniques, what commonly happens is that over a period of weeks and months everything fades into a vague blur and all that is remembered is the odd joke and one or two interesting statistics.

My own limited research indicates that this is what happens to the majority of training that is not integrated in some way with the working environment. It is completely predictable. Although psychologists do come up with some pretty dubious assertions from time to time, one truth, well known to everyone, is that learning will only occur if the learning process provides the learner with some form of reinforcement or reward. The reward may be intrinsic (a sense of growth or personal achievement, interest or the satisfaction of curiosity) or extrinsic (the attainment of a certificate, a promotion, more pay or the regard of colleagues or superiors).

During the training experience, the individual will, in all probability, have received a good deal of reinforcement for learning from trainers and fellow learners alike. In other words, the training environment will have been a rich source of extrinsic reinforcement for learning. On returning to the work environment, however, the manager commonly faces a situation that lies somewhere between studied indifference and outright cynicism. I once returned, as a newly appointed technical instructor, from a two-week intensive instructional skills course to be told by my immediate line manager, in no uncertain terms, that what I had been exposed to on the course was 'OK if you live in a dream world', but that it would be largely inappropriate there.

Reasons for the existence of these barriers

Faced with an environment that is often, at best, indifferent to learning, most normal human beings give up or at least do not reach the performance levels they are capable of reaching. Why should they? This is a serious weakness in the training cycle and it is one that we in the training profession must address with some urgency. There are a number of common reasons for the continuance of this situation.

- Many training endeavours, particularly of late, tend to focus exclusively on the individual and the development of (theoretically) context independent, generalizable, 'competences'. The underlying assumption is that these competences can be acquired in the training environment and then transferred to the working environment. This is the 'wind 'em up and let 'em go' view of training and individual effectiveness. This scenario can only work if such generalizable competences can, in fact, be identified (this is a very questionable assumption as far as management and training are concerned), that they can be trained for (that is, they can be acquired to an operational degree during the training process), that they can be accurately and effectively assessed and that they will transfer from the training environment (or the formal assessment situation) to the working environment 100 per cent.

The problem is that this general obsession with individual competence tends to reinforce the isolationist view of the role of training in bringing about effective organizational change. Of course individual competences are an important factor influencing organizational effectiveness, but they are only one part of the equation. To focus almost exclusively on the identification and accreditation of specific competences while ignoring situational variables is a recipe for mediocre results and an explosion of check-lists and checkers.

It is somewhat ironic that while the manufacturing industry is slowly waking up to the message that inspectors and checkers can actually work *against* the development of quality, the training profession seems hell bent on generating armies of them.

Along with these developments, the somewhat missionary zeal that has accompanied many of the learner-centred approaches to training has also focused attention almost exclusively on the individual rather than the individual operating within a specific context, which is the reality of the situation.

- This 'wind 'em up' philosophy leads to the assumption that training providers can, in fact, do the winding. The organization is, therefore, abjurated of all responsibility in facilitating what is required. This results in the training provider effectively becoming the sole arbiter in terms of training content. Deprived of information concerning the actual contexts in which individuals operate, training can—and too often does—become unrealistic. This process further exacerbates the division between the training provider and the organization.
- Because the training cycle—definition, design and delivery—is commonly isolated from the work environment, it is highly likely that no one other than the individual being trained has a vested interest in whether or not any particular change actually results when they return to the work-place. Generalized training cannot, by its very nature, be explicitly linked to situational needs or address spectrum problems and opportunities in anything other than a superficial manner. Training, therefore, may be seen by others within the organization, particularly line managers, as an unwelcome intrusion into work

routines—a process that exacerbates current crises (and there always *are* current crises) rather than being part of a possible solution. This commonly leads to the situation where training is viewed as something of an indulgence 'when there are all these urgent problems to deal with'.

Effective training—an integrated approach

From the preceding sections we can see that, if we are to maximize the potential benefits of training and development activities, we must extend our sphere of influence into the work environment. At present this does not occur in the majority of instances. In general terms, the major weaknesses of many training programmes are:

- training is not tied directly and clearly to the attainment of organizational goals
- training outcomes are rarely specified as business outcomes and are not stated in terms that are clearly measurable and specific to individual business situations
- the link between desired business outcomes and the contribution that training can make is not specified clearly
- training is focused on individual responsibilities and neglects the influence of organizational and group factors on the attainment of desired business outcomes
- the responsibilities and rewards associated with the achievement of desired training outcomes in the work-place are not clarified for those who influence these outcomes but who are not themselves directly involved in the training and learning process.

In other words, training is, unfortunately, often insular, vague and detached from the day-to-day realities of the operational environment. We are back to the situation, in quality terms, of not meeting the needs of our customers. In quality training terms, we are not meeting the needs of Customer 2.

This problem can only be addressed through processes of strategic planning, communication, data collection, analysis, interpretation and clarification that are a great deal more sophisticated than those that exist in the overwhelming majority of current instances. In particular, a great deal more effort is required at the definition stage of the quality training cycle than is at present expended. To be truly effective, training must address the following points:

- training must be clearly linked to the attainment of specific, work-based outcomes that can be measured and that will have a positive impact on the achievement of desired business outcomes (broadly speaking, these work-based outcomes may be related to the acquisition of role competences within a particular situation, such as training new entrants to the organization, improvements in current work practices, such as to reduce scrapped components by 20 per cent over a period of 6 months, re-training existing staff or they could be related to emerging opportunities, such as product/service diversification or the exploitation of new technology, new markets and so on, possibly training new and existing staff

- the links between the achievement of the particular outcomes and the attainment of superordinate organizational goals must be clear and specific
- the work-based competences that need to be developed in order to achieve the particular outcomes must be clear and specific
- the links between training and the achievement of these particular work-based competences must be clear and specific
- the work environment required in order to achieve the particular outcomes must be clear and specific.

Obviously this is a detailed process, but it is a necessary one. The more steps that are left out or inadequately undertaken when training decisions are made, particularly major decisions, the more we are trusting to luck rather than basing our actions on objective data. In many cases, of course, (particularly situations involving training that is highly procedural in nature) these points are self-evident, but the analysis can often indicate areas where improvements can be made.

The approach advocated above is intended to integrate the training and operating environments in order that each can maximize the potentials of the other. When desired work outcomes are specified clearly, the training professional has an objective basis on which to design effective training interventions or, indeed, to ascertain whether training is appropriate to the particular requirements that exist (training is not a universal panacea). When the post-training environment is designed specifically to reinforce learning and to consolidate the development of appropriate competences, results will follow almost inevitably. In this way training will come to be seen as an obvious necessity if organizations are to survive.

Making it happen—extending the influence of training

In previous chapters I have used the quality model, particularly with regard to the notion of internal customer–supplier networks, to analyse training weaknesses. The application of the quality model to training leads to the conclusion that many of the difficulties we experience stem from the fact that training often tends to be supplier-led or focused on one customer, the training participant, to the exclusion of others. The previous chapters have hopefully convinced you that training the individual is only *part* of the battle in helping organizations to become more effective. The challenge, therefore, is to extend the influence of the training process into the operational environment. This can only be achieved by involving the 'ghosts' (see page 91), the customers we do not train, at the definition and design stages of the quality cycle and during the post-training period when support is commonly required. In practical terms this means that:

- internal customers are an extremely valuable source of information regarding the improvements that could accrue from changes in the operating methods of their internal suppliers (this can include information that clarifies the training needs of internal suppliers and it should be included in any personal development plan aimed at improving organizational effectiveness)

- internal suppliers have a positive or negative effect on their internal customers in terms of the realization of their full potential, which is particularly true of situations in which the customer is attempting to change working practices (for example, in the period following training), and internal suppliers must be aware of likely changes *before* they occur and be committed to the facilitation of these changes.

Clearly internal customers and suppliers have a positive role to play at the definition and design stages of training and in the post-training environment. In the ideal situation the internal customer and the internal supplier should receive some tangible benefit from the success of a training intervention. There are some practical examples to further clarify this point.

Jim is a machinist who works on batch production in a medium-sized engineering factory. He has been sent on a training course to learn how to use an improved cutting tool that produces a smoother finish than that currently obtained and reduces machining time by 10 per cent.

His foreman, Clive, can see that using the new tool will help resolve many of the bottleneck difficulties that occur during rush periods. These bottlenecks give Clive a lot of problems with the assembly shop supervisors.

Dave is an assembly-line worker who has a bonus linked to productivity. Dave can see that the smoother finish on components from Jim will make assembly easier and probably reduce the number of accidental cuts that occur.

Although this fictional example is inevitably somewhat contrived, it is clear that this situation training is linked to specific business outcomes, that is, 10 per cent reduction in machining time and easier assembly. One of Jim's internal suppliers, Clive (remember, a supplier is someone who is capable of affecting an individual's work performance for better or worse and so Clive, as Jim's foreman, is certainly in a position to do this) will benefit directly from the success of the training that Jim undertakes. Jim's internal customer, Dave, is also set to benefit. It is highly likely, therefore, that Clive will support Jim during the post-training period (when production rates may dip owing to initial mistakes and unfamiliar procedures) and ensure that his potential to use the new tool is realized in the work situation. Dave, too, is likely to be patient in the anticipation of the long-term benefits.

In such an instance it is not difficult to justify investment in training (assuming that it is cost effective) because benefits to internal customers and suppliers are evident and quantifiable. Problems arise when the situation is less obvious. Consider the next, real situation.

Jill is a supervisor in an electronics company and, as such, she is responsible for a team of eight technicians. Jill has been in the post just over a year and, during her recent performance appraisal, Jill's boss suggested that she may wish to broaden her understanding of supervision and management by attending a supervisory management course run by a prestigious training organization.

Jill attends the course, enjoys it and feels that she has benefited from the experience. On her return to work, Jill's boss asks her how the course went and she replies that it was fine and that she enjoyed it. Her boss also asks her if she now feels more confident as a supervisor. Jill replies that she had not realized that there was so much to supervisory management. Nothing else happens.

This is a very different situation. Jill has been sent on a training course without a desired business outcome having been identified beforehand. The training *may* result in benefits to the organization or it may not—it is difficult to tell. Jill's boss (one of her internal suppliers) has not identified any specific benefits that will accrue to him if the training is translated into changes in Jill's work methods. He therefore has little incentive to follow up the training and no systematic approach to determine whether or not it has been of practical use. Jill may change the way she works and these changes may result in benefits to the organization. On the other hand, she may make changes that have little or no impact or even create problems that were not there before. Essentially it is up to her: if she decides to make no changes whatever then, in all probability, no one will be affected.

If in the future there is a downturn in the fortunes of the company and costs need to be cut, it is not unreasonable to expect that this sort of training will be one of the first things to go. In a situation where costs and benefits are given a long hard look, could it be justified? I sometimes use this example as a case study on trainer training courses. A common response in discussing the merits of the case is that the training will not do Jill any harm and may broaden her perspective, giving her some good ideas that she can incorporate into her work. This is true, it may. However, giving Jill three days' paid leave and a book on supervisory management may also achieve that *and* would be a lot cheaper.

If training is to be taken seriously, and by this I mean that if we are to get to a situation where cutting the training budget, even in bad times, is seen as a last resort, then we must link training to business growth and survival much more clearly than is presently the case.

Part of the difficulty to be overcome lies in the sort of situation described in the case study above. Jill's manager is well intentioned in giving her the opportunity to attend a supervisory management training course and, in all probability, some good will come of it. The question that must be asked, however, is whether or not the time and money invested could have been put to *better* use in terms of improving the effectiveness of the organization. Put another way, what specific benefits would be lost if Jill had *not* been sent on the course?

This question is difficult to answer in this case because training is not linked to the attainment of a specific business goal. It is, in effect, a gesture, a desire to 'give people training'. It is a nice gesture admittedly, but it is not part of a strategic programme of organizational development. Unless potential work place benefits are specified before training is undertaken, we are effectively hoping for the best.

Strategic training—the six-point cycle

The overall strategic process leading to training decisions should therefore include the following stages:

1 The process must be driven by clearly articulated business needs. This means that objectives must be set that specify a desired future situation. This must be clearly and quantifiably beneficial to the organization. Some typical examples are:

- to reduce scrapped components by 10 per cent over a period of four months
- to attain an average invoice processing time of three days by the end of this financial year
- to have an electronic mail system operational within ten months.

2 Once a desired future situation has been specified, a thorough analysis of all potential barriers to its achievement is undertaken. This analysis can be conducted using an Ishikawa, or fishbone approach (see page 118). Potential problems can be analysed in terms of machinery, methods, materials and manpower using this method.

3 When all potential barriers have been identified, human resource implications can be analysed in relation to:

- required changes to equipment/machinery
- required changes to working methods/systems and so on
- required changes to materials
- required changes to manpower base, for example, recruitment implications, reallocation and so on, possible changes in traditional working practices, industrial relations/personnel considerations.

4 Where appropriate, human resource implications can be translated into specific competence requirements associated with the attainment of the desired situation. These competence requirements can then be compared with existing competence levels to determine whether any gaps are present. These gaps constitute a training need.

5 When specific competence requirements have been identified, the process through which they can be achieved, that is, the learning process, is considered. This learning process may include:

- formal training courses
- secondment
- job rotation
- self-directed learning
- coaching
- shadowing
- mentoring.

6 The work-place implications of this learning process, with particular reference to the role of important internal suppliers (for example, immediate line management), must be specified clearly and communicated effectively. The personal and organizational benefits accruing from the successful attainment of these competences must be clear to all concerned.

You may protest that I am resorting to the use of competences after arguing extensively against them. This, however, is not the case. The competences identified through the above process are context specific and are geared to the achievement of a specified business outcome within a particular business situation. In other words, they are a means to an end rather than ends in themselves. The success of training will not, therefore, be measured solely in terms of whether or not these competences are achieved, but by whether or not the desired *business outcome* is achieved. In different working environments, with different cultures, different competences may be required to achieve the *same* business outcomes and different learning processes may be required in order to develop them.

The whole process, then, is totally dependent on the effectiveness of the initial stage: defining a desired business outcome. Obviously there is no sure-fire method of generating good ideas for improving the way things are done—this is where creativity comes in—but the TQ principle of continuous improvement means that the six-point cycle described above must be *continuously* applied throughout the organization—the training function included. Continuous improvement must become the norm; managing the status quo is no longer an option in an increasingly competitive and uncertain world. In general quality terms, continuous improvement can be considered in relation to:

- improving external customer satisfaction
- improving the quality of external suppliers
- improving internal supplier–customer effectiveness
- extending customer information bases
- improving internal communications
- reducing waste
- preventing special causes of variation
- reducing random causes of variation
- quantifying quality costs
- improving production methods
- improving internal systems
- improving flexibility and adaptability.

10 TQ training—meeting the challenge

The challenge of change

Charles Handy has suggested that, 'the nature of change is changing'. I believe he is right. We live in a world of increasing unpredictability and dramatic upheaval. Why has this occurred?

In order to approach an answer to this question it is necessary to appreciate that there are very different types of change possible. A French proverb asserts that, *'Plus ça change, plus c'est la même chose'* or, translated, 'The more something changes, the more it remains the same'. This at first seems a puzzling contradiction. If something changes, how can it remain the *same*? The proverb actually addresses itself to the common phenomenon whereby change occurs only at a surface level while an underlying consistency remains unaltered.

This situation arises frequently in therapeutic contexts and may be seen clearly in the actions of many individuals who, throughout their lives, experience a repeated succession of disastrous jobs or relationships. They are constantly changing employers or partners, but these changes only expose the underlying reality that, in fact, something central to the individual remains fundamentally unaltered. Paradoxically, the only way they could *really* change, would be *not* to change. This could be thought of as a *change of change* as Handy has identified.

Although seemingly esoteric, these considerations are, in fact, very relevant to an understanding of the current challenges we face. Change has indeed changed. This may be more clearly seen in terms of changes in technology from the turn of the century until approximately the middle of the 1960s.

During this period of time change was primarily *incremental*, that is, changes were refinements in the way things were done. This was essentially a general 'honing' process, similar to the refinements made to theoretical physics in the 250 years between the proclamations of Newton and the arrival of Einstein.

A more down-to-earth example of this form of change can be found in the evolution of the humble typewriter. This machine has undergone a number of refinements over the past 60 years or so, but the fundamental *purpose* of the machine remains unaltered. In theory, a person could have begun their working lives as a typist in the 1920s and have been systematically trained to cope with developments up to the current use of desktop publishing systems in the 1990s. This change has been incremental. Incremental change is the sort of change we have been used to.

Let us, however, consider a different example. Imagine that in the 1920s we had begun our working lives engaged in the manufacture of slide rules, then used to make mathematical calculations. We, too, could have been trained to deal effectively with the changes in materials, machine technology and production methods that occurred up until the mid 1960s. Then we would have faced a very different problem: the development of microelectronic technology combined with a phenomenal drop in production costs that led to the emergence of the cheap electronic calculator.

Electronic calculators are not *refinements* of slide rules; they represent a fundamentally different *type* of change. Someone with a lifetime's experience in the design and manufacture of slide rules has very little to offer the manufacturer of electronic calculators.

The changes that have occurred during the evolution of the typewriter are essentially *procedural* changes. The change that wiped out the slide rule industry was a change in the *process* of mathematical calculation.

Process changes are appearing with increasing regularity. They have two major characteristics: they are *fundamental changes* and they are *unpredictable*.

Consider the incredible political changes that have recently occurred in Eastern Europe and the USSR. Who could have accurately predicted them five years ago?

Organizations are faced with similar problems in accurately predicting the future and the most forward-looking have come to the inevitable conclusion that it simply cannot be done.

The complex interactions between developments in communications, technology, demography, work patterns, world-wide competition, environmental considerations and so on mean that precise accuracy is not a viable option in terms of predicting the future. Ten-year plans are out. Instead, organizations must develop cultures that encourage flexibility of response, a predisposition towards change, accurate perceptions of changing trends and customer demands and a willingness and desire to engage in the process of innovation and continuous development for their people, products and services. Quality cultures.

Developing quality cultures—the quality training approach

Quality cultures do not arise spontaneously, nor do they arise overnight. They require that genuine commitment exists at all levels within the organization, particularly at the top, to teamwork, individual capability and responsibility, multidimensional communications, effective systems of recognition and reward, leadership and a sense of shared vision.

Quality is not a procedure; it is a *process* and, as such, it is never finished. Quality cultures promote and sustain change. In previous chapters I have equated change with learning and, in this sense, quality cultures are truly learning cultures. It follows, therefore, that those organizational variables that significantly influence the learning process and the learning environment will be central to the development of quality cultures. These variables can be broadly considered as being *formal* and *informal.*

Formal variables include the quantity and effectiveness of training and development opportunities that exist within the organization. Informal variables include such things as management's attitude towards delegation, the ways in which power and authority are exercized, the organization's response to mistakes and the effectiveness of communications.

If we are to be successful in creating quality cultures, then both sides of the equation—formal *and* informal variables—must be considered. Quality cannot be achieved by training first-line staff and printing glossy poster exhortations if redundant management attitudes and practices remain changed in word only.

The reasons quality cultures do not exist are rooted in the history and structure of organizations. They will not be easy to change, but if they do not change they will not survive. Quality cultures will require a lot of people to do a lot of things very differently from the ways in which they have been done in the past. Some will inevitably find such changes unacceptable. They cannot be allowed to remain. Quality cultures grow painfully, slowly, but they can die in an extremely short period of time.

The role of training and development

Training and development has a central role to play in the generation and sustainability of quality cultures. Early on in the transition from conventional cultures, training and development must play an evangelical role. Trainers must be obsessed with quality and be expert in understanding and applying quality procedures. This is particularly true in terms of management and supervisory development. The maxims that apply to the first-line production worker must also apply *throughout* the organization and, above all, they must apply to the training function.

Quality training will differ significantly from traditional training. Traditionally, training has been seen as the means by which job-specific competences may be achieved. These competences in turn are specified largely in terms of sets of requirements or procedures that need to be carried out. This view of training will not be effective in the future.

Job requirements, methods of working, responsibilities and so on must be seen as being essentially *temporary*. That is, they must be seen in the context of change, as inevitably being subject to continuous change from external sources and also being the originator of continuous change themselves. Procedures remain valid only if processes remain unchanged, but this is not the nature of processes. Quality training must, therefore, be both *procedure and process* focused. This means that *every* quality training and development activity has two clear aims.

1 quality training aims to ensure that appropriate procedural, conceptual and practical skills are acquired (in plain language the what, why and how) in order that an individual may *effectively carry out a set of role requirements in a particular context*
2 quality training aims to develop a set of attitudes and values that *generate commitment to the provision of quality products and services throughout the whole organization*, that is, a commitment to continuous development.

Quality comes from the combined effects of the skills and values present in the people who work within organizations. Skills are highly differentiated throughout an organization—financial, marketing, engineering, personnel, production, training, research and so on. Values, too, are commonly subject to extreme diversification: cost reduction, cost effectiveness, technical excellence, departmental conservatism, the formal and informal organization and so forth.

Quality training, while remaining the vehicle through which appropriate skills and knowledge are acquired, is actively concerned with the development of value systems that are highly integrated throughout the organization. Central to these integrated value systems are the concepts of excellence, ownership, teamwork, commitment, flexibility and continuous improvement.

Quality trainers

The consequences of these changes will profoundly affect the training and development function and the role of trainers within and outside organizations. In future it will not be adequate to simply equip the operationally competent with the rudiments of instructional skills in order that they may, with very differing levels of adequacy, train others.

Those involved in quality training will be concerned with the complexities of the organizational and human side of their enterprise as much as (if not more than) the technical and procedural aspects. Trainers will need to understand the psychological and social processes that influence attitude formation and attitude change, they will require a framework for understanding individuals and structuring the social interactions of training in such a way as to facilitate the development of a quality-oriented culture and they will be excellent communicators and influencers.

Trainers must extend their sphere of influence into the operational environment and permeate the organizational filter. This means that the strategic role of training and development within organizations will be given a higher profile than that which exists at present.

The key to quality

The key to quality is, above all else, commitment and commitment must be clearly present in those charged with training and development responsibilities.

I have long felt that commitment is the single most important difference between truly effective and ineffective teachers and trainers. I do not believe that it is simply the case that excellent trainers are merely the product of an interaction between knowledge and highly polished presentation skills.

I have personally attended (a few) training events that remain memorable after many years and which profoundly affected my development and understanding. I do not remember them for the polished presentation skills of the trainer.

Conversely, I have attended (many) training events and seminars in which no presentational step is a hair's breadth out of place: the eye contact is there, the voice, the smile, the laser-printed overhead-projected information, in colour, the purpose-designed video—but not a lot else. The medium has sometimes overtaken the message.

I am not arguing that presentation skills have little effect on learning because they obviously do, but it is well to remember that glossy presentation is a poor substitute for effective content and genuine commitment.

The development of the procedural skills necessary for the successful delivery of training, although important, will constitute only the basic requirements in terms of quality training. The ability to identify training needs, clarify objectives, design programmes of learning and use the overhead projector, video, CBT system and whatever other aids are currently in vogue, is no guarantee that a trainer will be able to capture the interest and enthusiasm of an individual or group. However, the generation of enthusiasm, interest and commitment is a fundamental requirement of quality training and it can only be generated by people—it cannot be generated by machines.

Technology-based training has tremendous potential, but it also has limitations. It is essentially limited to the transmission of information. As I have discussed elsewhere in this book, information is an essential component influencing the effectiveness of individuals and groups, but it is not the only variable involved. Trust, and shared values constitute the human dimension of quality and they do not come from machines, they come from interactions between human beings.

Quality thrives on inspirational leadership. Quality cultures generate inspirational leadership at all levels within an organization because quality is a philosophy that transcends individual specializations, departmental boundaries and stifling hierarchies. The director of research and development can profitably talk quality with the first-line assembly worker. Quality is a unifying language that has the potential to break down the organizational and class barriers that threaten our economic future.

We are presently trapped in a vicious circle. We have a shortage of inspirational leaders, managers and trainers. I believe that this is primarily due to the effects of the organizational filter. The vast majority of organizations undervalue, underdevelop and underuse the abilities of the people they employ. This dampens spirits and leads to mediocrity, further justifying the belief that investment in people is a waste of time.

This circle must be broken and it can by using the philosophy and techniques of TQM, but it will require that inspirational leaders, trainers, managers and directors come forward to take up the challenge. TQ is, in a sense, a belief, a vision and it requires visionaries.

It is this extra dimension, the dimension of leadership, that will set quality training apart from the overwhelming majority of training that has been undertaken in the past.

This requirement raises the question of whether, in fact, it is possible, other than in a rudimentary sense, to train quality trainers and managers. Certainly we can train people to follow the basic procedures involved in these important occupations, but are these procedures really enough?

The philosophy that underpins much current trainer and management training, that is, the competence model, is taken directly from skills-based, convergent areas of application. In such areas it works extremely well. However, inspirational training and management is much more an art than a science; more a process than a procedure.

The inspirational trainer or manager is best thought of in similar terms to the inspirational writer or composer. The competence-based philosophy is more appropriate to the development of efficient spellers and piano tuners. Competences are geared to competence, but we need trainers and managers who are more than simply competent. After all, would you describe Shakespeare as a competent author or Mozart as a competent composer?

We need trainers and managers who are capable of acting as role models, leaders and guides; men and women who are able to inspire others to reach their full potential—talented trainers and managers. Of course we can no more train talent into a manager or trainer than we can train bravery into a fireman. We must identify and recruit potential, personality and attitude, then we can get on with the process of skill development and the liberation of this talent.

Quality training, therefore, cannot be achieved without cost—cost in terms of material and financial resources and cost in terms of the very high levels of human ability and effort required to achieve excellence. However, this cost must be set against the current costs of providing training that does not meet TQ requirements: customer dissatisfaction, lack of faith in the training process, ineffective development of human potential and so on. More importantly, this cost, this investment, must be considered in terms of the returns that are possible. Quality cultures liberate talent, release the creative energies that are locked in the prison of the organizational filter. I firmly believe that in the UK there are infinitely more 'prisoners' than 'free' citizens. We are, in many ways, victims of a cultural tendency to shoot ourselves repeatedly in the foot. I have used the Japanese model frequently as an example of what can be achieved when TQ principles are applied to organizations, but, although

I admire these achievements, I feel that there is a tendency to look in awe at the Japanese, to perhaps consider that they are in some way superhuman. They are not. They simply have been diligent, systematic and, above all, committed to applying the principles espoused by Deming. There is absolutely no reason—other than cultural inertia—why the same, and perhaps more, cannot be achieved in Britain. Although the British often find it difficult to itemize their strengths, it is salutary to remember that Britain can claim the awarding of 65 Nobel Prizes to Japan's 5. We have no shortage of potential; our problems lie in the appalling and systematic waste of this potential.

Training and development—quality training and development—is the only way to break the vicious circle and promulgate quality. Quality training demands considerable levels of ability and commitment from trainers. I believe that the selection, recruitment and training of trainers must therefore proceed on a very different basis from that which has, in my experience, characterized many of these processes in the past. It follows, therefore, that private-sector organizations and public-sector funding bodies must recognize the considerable benefits of a TQ approach to training and development and reflect this recognition in the care with which they select and develop their training professionals and in the resources that are made available to them. They must also accept the fact that renumeration packages are widely recognized as being an effective indicator of the esteem in which particular occupations are held and influence the career choices that talented people make. It is encouraging to note that there are instances indicative that the more forward-looking organizations are getting the message as far as training is concerned.

If we are to meet the challenge of providing a TQ approach to training, practical resource commitment is essential. As quality cultures begin to develop, our customers, both internal and external, will bring their increasing awareness, expertise and continuously ascending expectations to bear on the training and development services we provide for them. This is inevitable and it is to be welcomed. This process will either see current providers replaced by others or it will guarantee their survival. No middle option will be available.

This point brings us full circle to the basic problem discussed early on in this book: that government and senior management need to be convinced that substantial investment in training and development makes sound economic sense. We began with an analysis of the demise of the British motor cycle industry, a process that took a mere 25 years to complete. I often feel that there are far too many uncomfortable parallels to be drawn between the situation that existed in the motor cycle industry in the early 1960s and the one facing the training profession today.

However, we are now in the fortunate position of having the benefits of hindsight, an awareness of the mistakes that were made, the techniques of TQM and time, on our sides. Let us make sure we use them wisely.

Self-analysis inventory

Give each of the statements below a rating of 1–6 where:

1 = very strongly disagree
2 = strongly disagree
3 = mildly disagree
4 = mildly agree
5 = strongly agree
6 = very strongly agree

1 Teams should be structured to have clear lines of individual authority and responsibility.

2 The trainer's major role is to ensure that training is carried out in the most efficient way.
3 Organizations need to take big risks if they are to survive.
4 Training is about helping people to learn and grow.

5 The learner is the best judge of what needs to be learned.

6 When an individual is at work, personal problems should be left at the door.
7 Ultimately, training must be evaluated in terms of clearly measurable financial costs and benefits to the organization.

8 An important part of the trainer's job is to get people moving, to shake them up a bit, put a bit of new life into them.

9 Management's counselling responsibilities are as important as their financial and production responsibilities.
10 The learner is the only person who can judge whether training has been effective.
11 The most important part of an appraisal interview is to tell people what their strengths and weaknesses are.

12 Effective training should be structured so as to give people the skills to do their jobs in the shortest possible time.

13 The really good people in any organization never have tidy desks.

14 People would be more effective at work if organizations showed more care and concern for them.

---

15 End-of-course evaluation sheets are the best way of helping trainers improve their performance.

---

16 A manager's ultimate responsibility is to manage effectiveness and this means sorting out incompetent staff.
17 A thorough research of facts and information is essential if training is to be effective.
18 Most training is too long, full of waffle and boring.

---

19 The trainer is really a facilitator of learning, a guide, a helper and a friend.

---

20 If training fails, this means that the trainer has failed to meet the needs of the course participants.
21 The real reason why investment in training is so low is that managers know that a lot of it is a complete waste of time.

---

22 Computer-based training systems offer the greatest potential for achieving performance improvement.
23 Training should include humour—people learn better when they are happy.
24 The most important attribute a manager or trainer can have is the ability to support others and help them overcome their difficulties.
25 Training can only be effective if it is structured in consultation with the learning group.

---

26 If people fail to reach the standards required to do a particular job, then managers must replace them.

---

27 Training is most effective when it is based on systematic skills analysis.
28 Trainers have got to be really into their subject, really enthusiastic about it.

---

29 Teams can only be effective if people genuinely care about each other.

---

30 Trainers should aim to keep their direct input to an absolute minimum.
31 Trainers must maintain a proper professional distance between themselves and the people they train.
32 A manager's main responsibility is to organize effectively.

---

33 It is best to go into a training session with 50 per cent more than you think you can deliver.

---

34 Good trainers make sure there is enough time for course members to relax and relieve the tensions that training often builds up.
35 Every trainer's motto should be 'Negotiate, negotiate, negotiate'.

---

36 If people are being paid to do a job, then they have a moral responsibility to give their best at all times.

---

37 The most effective methods of recruiting suitable staff are based on objective psychometric and skills testing.
38 Most people do not work hard because they are bored out of their minds.
39 Learning will only happen in a warm, trusting and caring environment.

---

40 Training is effective when learners feel they have achieved what they wanted to achieve.

---

41 The best way to bring up children is to give them clear rules so that they know where they stand.
42 Appraisal systems can only be effective if subjective judgements are completely eliminated.

---

43 Too many trainers take training too seriously—it is only a job.

---

44 Appraisal interviews are really counselling interviews.
45 Critical end-of-course evaluations may be painful, but trainers must take such comments on board.
46 Some people should not be sent on training courses because they are in the wrong job and training cannot improve them.

---

47 Improved work performance is most effectively achieved through a structured sequence of graded learning experiences.

---

48 Appraisal interviews are a joke—most managers just want clones of themselves.
49 It is inevitable that personal problems will affect someone's work performance and that is why a staff welfare worker is a neccessity for all organizations.

---

50 Trainers must strive to adapt training to meet the needs of all course participants.

---

51 Managers and trainers must always lead by example in terms of effort, dedication and timekeeping.
52 Planning and preparation are the key to effective training.
53 You have got to really believe what you are saying to be a very good trainer.

---

54 Children have to be loved unconditionally—no matter what they do—if they are to grow into caring adults.

---

55 All really effective trainers probably experience deep feelings of inadequacy from time to time.

56 A lot of group training should be more about developing real skills and less concerned with simply keeping everybody happy.

---

57 Motivation at work depends mainly on the balance between the financial benefits obtained and the individual's dislike of doing the job.

---

58 People should not stay in a job more than two or three years at most—after that you start to go downhill.

59 Happy working relationships are the most important part of effective organizations.

60 In terms of training, the customer is always right.

Score sheet

Put your score for each statement against the statement number below.

1	21	41 . . . .
2	22	42 . . . .
3	23	43 . . . .
4	24	44 . . . .
5	25	45 . . . .
6	26	46 . . . .
7	27	47 . . . .
8	28	48 . . . .
9	29	49 . . . .
10	30	50 . . . .
11	31	51 . . . .
12	32	52 . . . .
13	33	53 . . . .
14	34	54 . . . .
15	35	55 . . . .
16	36	56 . . . .
17	37	57 . . . .
18	38	58 . . . .
19	39	59 . . . .
20	40	60 . . . .

Scoring schedule Put your score for each statement against the statement number below and add the columns vertically to produce five separate scores.

1	2	3	4	5 ....
6	7	8	9	10 ....
11	12	13	14	15 ....
16	17	18	19	20 ....
21	22	23	24	25 ....
26	27	28	29	30 ....
31	32	33	34	35 ....
36	37	38	39	40 ....
41	42	43	44	45 ....
46	47	48	49	50 ....
51	52	53	54	55 ....
+ 56	+ 57	+ 58	+ 59	+ 60 ....
=	=	=	=	=
Score A	Score B	Score C	Score D	Score E

In keeping with the spirit of quality, any comments on this book would be appreciated by the author. Also, if anyone wishes to know more about the applications of the principles outlined in these pages, please contact:

Human Factors Associates
Winster
21 Grove Park
Wanstead
London E11 2DN

Recommended reading

Berne, Eric, 1961, *Games People Play*, Penguin.

Crosby, Philip B., 1978, *Quality is Free*, McGraw-Hill.

Crosby, Philip B., 1985, *Quality Without Tears*, McGraw-Hill.

Dale, B.G., and Plunkett, J.J., 1990, *Managing Quality*, Random House.

Gabor, Andrea, 1990, *The Man Who Discovered Quality*, Random House.

Goldzimer, Linda, 1989, *Customer Driven*, Hutchinson Business Books.

Setsuo, Mito, 1990, *The Honda Book of Management*, Kogan Page.

Pascale, Richard T., and Athos, Anthony G., 1981, *The Art of Japanese Management*, Penguin.

Peters, Tom, 1987, *Thriving on Chaos*, Pan.

Walton, Mary, 1990, *The Deming Management Method*, Mercury.

Williams, Allan, Dobson, Paul and Walters, Mike, 1989, *Changing Culture*, Institute of Personnel Management.

Index

Further titles in the McGraw-Hill Training Series

THE BUSINESS OF TRAINING
Achieving Success in Changing World Markets
Trevor Bentley ISBN 0-07-707328-2

EVALUATING TRAINING EFFECTIVENESS
Translating Theory into Practice
Peter Bramley ISBN 0-07-707331-2

DEVELOPING EFFECTIVE TRAINING SKILLS
Tony Pont ISBN 0-07-707383-5

MAKING MANAGEMENT DEVELOPMENT WORK
Achieving Success in the Nineties
Charles Margerison ISBN 0-07-707382-7

MANAGING PERSONAL LEARNING AND CHANGE
A Trainer's Guide
Neil Clark ISBN 0-07-707344-4

HOW TO DESIGN EFFECTIVE TEXT-BASED OPEN LEARNING:
A Modular Course
Nigel Harrison ISBN 0-07-707355-X

HOW TO DESIGN EFFECTIVE COMPUTER BASED TRAINING:
A Modular Course
Nigel Harrison ISBN 0-07-707354-1

HOW TO SUCCEED IN EMPLOYEE DEVELOPMENT
Moving from Vision to Results
Ed Moorby ISBN 0-07-707459-9

USING VIDEO IN TRAINING AND EDUCATION
Ashly Pinnington ISBN 0-07-707384-3

TRANSACTIONAL ANALYSIS FOR TRAINERS
Julie Hay ISBN 0-07-707470-X